THE
LEAGUE OF KITCHENS
COOKBOOK

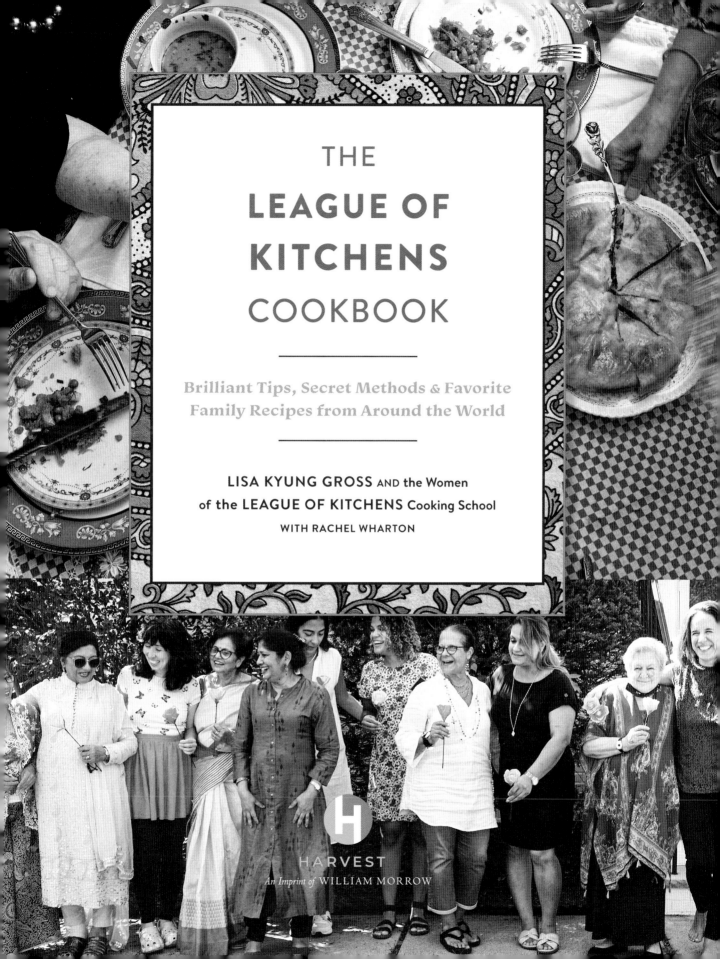

THE
LEAGUE OF
KITCHENS
COOKBOOK

Brilliant Tips, Secret Methods & Favorite
Family Recipes from Around the World

LISA KYUNG GROSS AND the Women
of the **LEAGUE OF KITCHENS** Cooking School

WITH RACHEL WHARTON

HARVEST
An Imprint of WILLIAM MORROW

To my grandmothers, Gloria Gross and Young-Ae Oh,
and all the grandmothers through the ages

CONTENTS

INTRODUCTION

People always ask me about the most important things I've learned running the League of Kitchens, the immigrant-led, home-based cooking school I started in New York City in 2014.

They want to hear how to make Despina's perfect Greek salad, with its different shapes and textures—the feta crumbled into the salad by hand, the tomatoes cut into wedges, the red onions sliced thin as paper. It's so simple, yet so amazing. They want to hear how Yamini taught me to turn up the heat under the ghee when making the tarka for dal, to really toast and sizzle the cumin seeds, curry leaves, red chile powder, asafetida, garlic, tomatoes, and green chiles. I was so scared of burning them, but if you don't crank the heat, they don't bloom, and you don't deepen their flavor. They want to hear about Nawida's Afghan eggs, semi-scrambled in her special way, with fresh tomatoes and green chiles fried in oil, served with soft bread and a whole mint leaf in every bite. It's just so good. And they want to hear how to make a guacamole that's better than any you've ever tasted, all because of the way Angie taught me to cut the avocados.

I've absorbed all this and so much more over the years that I've run the League of Kitchens, where more than a dozen women from all over the world invite people into their homes to cook and share a meal (and now, post 2020, also welcome students into their homes virtually). Yet I always say that the most important thing I've learned is not a recipe or a technique. It's that you have to cook with love.

I say that because I've thought a lot about what cooking with love really means. When you ask any of our instructors why something they make tastes so good, or what their secret really is, love is their answer—every single time. Cooking with love means cooking with care. It's cooking with intention and attention, with the wisdom that comes from experience, from mastering all those almost invisible little nuances that just make something uniquely amazing and delicious. I think you have to love eating to be a good cook, too, because you have to care about flavor and recognize what tastes good, and also what makes the people you're feeding feel good, even when it's dinner you pull together in an hour. Maybe especially when it's dinner you pull together in an hour.

That kind of love is exactly what you'll find in this book. The recipes are not fancy—they're the everyday, healthy, flavorful meals our instructors make for their families all the time. But they focus on the love—the details that are passed down from cook to cook yet rarely make it into printed recipes. At first glance, you might think that you already know how to cook a lot of the things in this book—steak tacos, eggs scrambled with tomatoes, chicken curry, a chicken cutlet. But I think you will find that we have the very, very best versions of them, because they're coming from some of the world's very best home cooks. I think of recipes as a blueprint for a new life experience. And I wanted the very best blueprints you could have.

That's why I founded the League of Kitchens—because I saw that all the detail and nuance and wisdom of recipes from other cultures were often missing from cookbooks, and even from cooking classes. I always call my instructors a culinary dream team, because they're really gifted in every part of the cooking process: shopping for ingredients, planning meals throughout the year and the change of seasons, using every bit of every ingredient to minimize waste, and whipping up outrageously delicious meals in tiny New York City kitchens with incredible ease and grace. They're also gifted hosts and excellent teachers; experts at setting a beautiful table and making you feel at home at that table; and patient with telling people what they're doing and why, over and over again.

And it's no coincidence that they're all women, even though I didn't plan it that way, at least not at first. When you're looking for people who are exceptional home cooks—and I've now interviewed hundreds of really good home cooks—you really want people who have a deep knowledge of their cuisine and culture, and the recipes and skills that are both passed down and well-earned. That tends to be women in their fifties and sixties, and it tends to be the grandmas, people who have both learned and taught. Our Ukrainian Russian instructor is our oldest instructor—she's ninety—and our Mexican instructor is our youngest. She's thirty-nine, but everyone says that she cooks like she's already a grandma—the ultimate compliment.

*   *   *

My own grandmother is the reason I started the League of Kitchens. Not because she taught me how to cook, but because she didn't. My mother, who is now a professional artist—an abstract painter—came to the United States in the early 1970s from Busan in South Korea. She was twenty-three at the time, the youngest of six, and came to the US as a nurse. Then, a few years later, she met my father, who is a fourth-generation New Yorker of Hungarian Jewish descent. My Korean grandmother, my halmoni, came over when I was born to help my parents in the D.C. suburbs of Maryland, where I grew up. She had planned to stay with us until a second child was born. My parents ended up not having a second child, but my halmoni stayed anyway,

and lived with us the whole time I was growing up—we shared a bedroom until I was nine. Our beds were pushed together, and I used to hold her hand when I was falling asleep.

My grandmother was a wonderful cook. She grew up at a time in Korea when women made everything from scratch and preserved food for winter. When my mom was growing up, my grandmother made all of their soy sauce, kimchi, doenjang (fermented soybean paste), gochugaru (dried red chile powder), and the red pepper paste called gochujang. They had an extensive vegetable garden, pigs, ducks, rabbits, and a goat—they were pretty much homesteading.

I have many memories of my halmoni making kimchi while I was growing up, sitting on newspapers on the floor of our kitchen, chopping the cabbage on a cutting board on the floor, and then mixing it in this huge pink plastic tub. I also remember her making ganjang gejang (whole raw crabs cured in a soy sauce brine). She was a very tiny woman, maybe four-foot-nine, and I can picture her taking those live crabs, grabbing them around the middle and scrubbing them with a sponge under the faucet, then putting them into this big glass jar. They would be crawling up the side, and she'd take a giant chopstick and poke them down before pouring the boiling brine on top of them. Another memory I have is that when I would come home from school and wanted some sort of snack, I would watch her take hot white rice from the rice cooker that was on in our kitchen twenty-four-seven, squeeze a small palmful in her fist into a little log shape, and then sprinkle it with salt and toasted sesame seeds. It was such a delicious, simple snack.

I have those memories, but that's mostly it, when it comes to cooking with my grandmother. Whenever I would want to really help her in the kitchen, or when I would show any kind of interest in cooking, she would say, "Oh, don't worry about cooking. You should go study. Studying is more important."

I think this is a very common experience for the children of immigrants, because our parents and our grandparents wanted us to succeed in ways in which they weren't able to. My grandmother wanted me to have the educational and professional opportunities that she didn't have, and would have loved to have had—she was unusual for a woman of her generation in that she completed high school, wrote poetry her whole life, and owned and ran several small businesses—a hair salon and a pharmacy, among others, all while raising six children. But she had dreamed of becoming a concert pianist. It was for those same reasons that she didn't teach my mother how to cook either. My mom's two older sisters learned to cook by my grandmother's

side, but by the time my mom was growing up (she was the youngest of six), my grandmother told her, "Oh, do something else. Go to school, go do what you want, don't worry about all this."

So my mother and I both studied when we were growing up, instead of learning how to cook. By the time my grandmother passed away—she was ninety-two—I was at Yale, still studying hard.

I should also say that my other grandmother inspired me, too. That's my Jewish grandmother, my father's mother. Her parents had come to New York City from Hungary in the early 1900s, and my grandmother wanted nothing to do with that part of her life—she wanted to be a super-cosmopolitan and sophisticated New Yorker, and she was. She was a very different kind of cook than my halmoni, and a very different kind of grandmother. But her kitchen also paved the way for the League of Kitchens. It was because of her that I grew up really interested in all kinds of food, across all cultures, and in the idea that dining and food could be an experience. I grew up sitting in her kitchen looking through her old copies of *Gourmet* and her cookbooks from legends like Marcella Hazan, Julia Child, and Craig Claiborne, who wrote the original *New York Times Cookbook*. My Jewish grandparents would frequently take me out to eat, and when I got older, they took me on several trips abroad to Europe and Asia, where eating was always a central focus.

When I was little, my Jewish grandmother would do this thing with me at restaurants— she would order something I knew I liked, and I would order something that I had never tried. That way, if I didn't like what I had ordered, I could switch with her. She also had a rule that I never had to finish anything if I didn't want to. And I think that both these things encouraged me to become a more adventurous eater. I remember when I was a kid, I had never had whole artichokes, and I wanted to try them, so she made them for me, and we had them on special artichoke plates, which of course she had. Another time she made osso buco from Marcella Hazan's cookbook and taught me how to eat the marrow—the most delicious part—with a tiny cocktail fork. She and my grandfather loved food, loved going out, loved to travel, and food was a source of joy and pleasure for them.

* * *

After college, I moved to New York City with my boyfriend Dan, who is now my husband and the father to our two daughters. It was 2004, we were in our early twenties, and we were falling in love with cooking and exploring food in New York City. We were having dinner parties for our friends and finding so much pleasure in food shopping and learning about new cuisines and foods and traveling to other neighborhoods and boroughs. We lived in a fifth-floor walk-up on Twenty-Eighth Street and Third Avenue, so we were always shopping at Kalustyan's, one of the most amazing food stores on the planet. We were expanding our palates and our knowledge of food, and we were both trying to teach ourselves how to make all the things our grandmothers cooked for us when we were growing up.

For me, that was mostly Korean food, but I didn't have any recipes, and neither did my mother. So I tried to teach myself from cookbooks and the internet, but nothing ever tasted as good as the way my halmoni made it. Everything was good—but there was something missing, some special touch or flavor from what I remembered from my childhood.

I had this fantasy of finding another Korean grandmother I could learn to cook from in her own kitchen. What I realized, even then, is that there are often these subtle differences in technique, or method, or maybe even picking out ingredients, that make the difference between cooking that's good and cooking that's exceptional. As much as I adore cookbooks and watching food videos online, there is something different about learning from someone who has been cooking this food for forty years, somebody who learned it from their family. Somebody who can tell you, "When it sounds like that, you do this. When it feels like this, you do that."

These are things you really need to learn from a person with experience—it's that love, that grandma genius.

At that time in my life, I had all kinds of jobs: I worked at a downtown performance space, I temped as a paralegal, I was an assistant to a choreographer, I taught high school English at a private school, and I also sort of fell into food writing for an alternative newspaper called the *New York Press*, which no longer exists (it's a long, somewhat boring, somewhat funny story of how that came about). They paid sixty bucks an article, or maybe even less, but it was just such an education, a chance to learn about the intersection between food and culture and all these other issues—it really deepened my knowledge of and interest in food in terms of how food intersects with pretty much every topic: politics, the environment, culture, family, gender issues . . . everything.

I liked everything I was doing, but I knew this wasn't my end point. I decided to move to Boston to go to a very experimental Master of Fine Arts program at the School of the Museum of Fine Arts and Tufts University. You could basically do anything you wanted in that program—and almost everything I did ended up relating to food. (My thesis project was the collaborative creation of a decentralized public urban orchard of fifty-five pairs of heirloom apple trees across seventy communities called the Boston Tree Party—many of those trees are still growing.) After graduate school, I moved back to New York City. I wanted to do something that connected to the diversity and cultural richness of the city, and that fantasy of finding a Korean grandmother came back to me. I thought, well, what if I could find not just a Korean grandmother to cook with, but amazing home cooks from all over the world living right here in New York City that I and others could cook with?

I knew immediately that I wanted the teachers to have been born outside the United States, just like my own grandmother. One of the things that would be so powerful about the experience, I felt, would be learning about cooking and food culture directly from someone who had grown up in that culture. As I thought about it more, the idea became just as much about creating opportunities for meaningful cross-cultural learning, connection, and exchange as it was about creating a really amazing eating, drinking, and culinary learning experience. Because even in New York City, which is incredibly diverse, there are not always opportunities for *meaningful* interaction between immigrants and non-immigrants or even between immigrants from different groups, especially for those of us who move here as adults. You might talk with somebody at the bodega, or at the dry cleaner, or maybe in your building lobby, but most interactions are cursory or service-based.

And I knew I wanted these incredible home cooks to teach in their homes. Throughout grad school I had been exploring the idea of home as a place of personal and societal transformation, and I knew that this cooking experience would be so much more powerful in someone's home, rather than in a neutral commercial kitchen. When you're in someone's home, even for an afternoon, you really get to know them, to recognize them fully as fellow human beings—you see their passion and their warmth, and you even sometimes meet their families. After a few hours of cooking with someone side by side in their own kitchen, or eating with them at their dining room table, maybe you even feel like an extended part of that family, too. There's a feeling of intimacy when you're a guest in someone's home. And you also get a more immersive experience of their culture—you get to see how they decorate their home, what their cooking tools are like, how they set their table, and how they serve and eat their food.

The other reason I wanted this experience to take place in the home is because home is really where you get the most astounding food in the world, and where you find the fullest expression of most cuisines. There's always this divide, if you look at culinary history, between court cooking traditions, the traditions of royalty and the aristocracy, and then the peasant cooking traditions, which are the cooking traditions of everyone else—what most people cook at home. Also, in many places around the world, there is "home cooking" and street food or festival food—restaurant culture is a relatively new thing. Even today, this idea that the apotheosis of culinary skill and cuisine in a given culture is in a restaurant is just not true—that idea is really a nineteenth-century Western European invention. In most parts of the world, the real cooking of a place is just so multilayered or

labor-intensive, or uses so many spices—or is considered too humble or plain or common—that it's just not practical for a restaurant to serve it. What you can have in a West African or Middle Eastern or Japanese person's home, the home of somebody who's a really excellent cook, is such a different caliber and experience than what you would have at most restaurants. If you're looking for a very full expression of a cuisine, you need to have it in someone's home, or learn how to make it yourself.

So, yes, you could go to some cooking school in Manhattan and be in a commercial kitchen and learn some Persian dishes from a culinary school–trained restaurant chef who's learned a few recipes from a book, but that's so different from really learning and understanding the history and the stories and the cultural context, and also the way the food is all eaten together and on what dishware, about the underlying philosophy behind Persian food, about the philosophy of utilizing different elemental qualities like "hot" and "cold" and "wet" and "dry" and how that impacts health, and about this home cook

as a person, and all of her stories connected to food, to plucking walnuts from trees or what she watched on TV or family arguments or just these really everyday human parts of life.

* * *

Initially, I assumed this was going to be another temporary public art project, more like the things I had done in graduate school. I would find a group of people to cook, pay them to do it, then move on to something else. I started a small pilot project to test my idea, working with Jeanette, who is from Lebanon, and Afsari, who is from Bangladesh, both of whom still teach with the League of Kitchens today. To create the format of our classes, I took cooking classes at five different cooking schools in New York City to evaluate the experience from the perspective of a student: What did I like best about each class? What was missing? What was the structure? What kind of materials did I get to take home? I took all those experiences and ideas, and we used them to help create what we hoped would be an ideal cooking class.

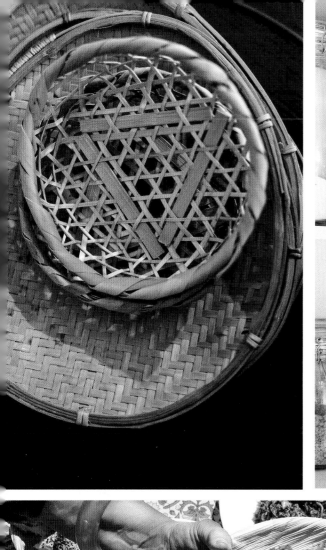

Early on, I realized that doing this as a temporary thing was silly. First off, preparing for the initial classes was a huge amount of time and work, not just for me but for the instructors. We planned menus, figured out how to structure the classes, shopped for ingredients and created shopping guides for students, bought extra sets of cooking tools for the students to use during the classes, did recipe writing and testing for a packet that students would take home, figured out what kind of training support was needed for Jeanette and for Afsari, and then provided that support, and then fine-tuned what works in home-based cooking classes and what doesn't through hands-on trial and error.

But the second thing I realized was that these classes were just incredibly special: my friends and family who took the pilot classes loved them. And the instructors loved teaching them. It started to feel like a waste to spend so much time and effort finding instructors and training them and setting everything up just to run for a brief amount of time. I started to think that maybe instead of creating a short-term project, I could make this into a business—a unique kind of recreational cooking school. And so that's what I decided to do.

The next step was to find more instructors, which, in general, is one of the hardest parts of running the League of Kitchens. That first year, we had just 6 instructors, and to find them I met with more than 150 people. Then I did close to twenty-five in-home cooking auditions. I was looking for people who'd create an experience where a student would go tell their friends, "I just had the most incredible food at the most amazing class with the most unbelievable instructor." Early on, I did a huge amount of outreach to different community groups and nonprofits and even posted on Craigslist. Word of mouth is so important, too—the people we hire are usually the people in their communities who everyone knows is one of the best cooks. Like the person at the potluck party who everyone is always excited to see what they bring. It's like, "Oh, where are the sweets that Rachana brought?" or "What did Shandra bring?"

Today the list of cuisines we offer classes for reflects the people we've met so far who are the most exceptional cooks and teachers. Sometimes people say, why not Korean, or why not Chinese? The answer is that we just haven't found those teachers yet—we always hire based on the people we find, as we find them. A perfect example is Mirta, who grew up in the foothills of the Andes in Argentina, and whose cooking is Argentinian-Italian. I was so blown away by her personality and her passion for food and culture. She did an in-home cooking audition where I tasted her homemade mayonnaise and her milanesa de pollo, which is still one of the dishes I talk about the most. I hadn't ever guessed that Argentinian-Italian cuisine would be on our list of cuisines, but I was like, okay, I guess we're going to offer it, because we have to hire this woman. We are always looking, and always open to hiring new people, and there is an endless number of cuisines we hope to add as we continue to grow. (In fact, if you think you know anyone who fits the description to join the League of Kitchens, please tell us!)

As I write this, the League of Kitchens currently employs fourteen women from fourteen different countries, all of whom are compensated for the time they spend preparing for classes, teaching classes, and cleaning up afterward (and for their work on this book). The League of Kitchens support staff and I do all the behind-the-scenes work—the marketing and promotion, the customer service, the class scheduling, the bookkeeping and payment processing, the recipe writing and testing, and the website updating—so that our instructors can focus on their classes and doing what they do best: cooking, teaching, sharing, and hosting, either online or in their homes.

Some of our instructors are formerly stay-at-home moms, some are retired professionals, some still work, some came to the United States for business, some as refugees, some have been in the United States for decades, others for just a few years. They're all special in a lot of ways: They have deep knowledge of traditional culinary techniques and methods, they're warm and gregarious hosts, they're intelligent teachers, and they make food that is beautiful, no matter how simple the dish. They're also totally comfortable hosting groups of strangers, most from other cultures, in their homes. And, of course, their food is always dream-about-it-that-night delicious. Just as special, they have also now become friends with each other—their own League of Kitchens community. They hang out with each other, take each other's classes, and wish each other Eid Mubarak, Merry Christmas, or happy birthday in our League of Kitchens WhatsApp group. And now, ten years in, we have celebrated together the weddings of many children and the births of many grandchildren.

* * *

The League of Kitchens is a project about recognizing and celebrating the contributions of immigrants to our food culture and society, but it's also a feminist project. There's no staff at the in-home workshops, it's just the instructor and her students. The instructors are given an opportunity to share and shine. They are queens of their kitchens: experts, hosts, and teachers, which shifts the conventional power dynamic between immigrants and non-immigrants. This is not a charity endeavor. They don't thank their students for paying them. The students feel truly privileged and honored to be there, to be eating

this food, to be learning from these women, and to be hearing their stories and learning about their lives.

And when you look at who cooks at home around the world, the people who cook for their families day in and day out, it's mostly women. Yes, men in many cultures cook. But most everyday cooking around the world is done by women. And the way that most culinary culture has been passed down around the world for the last ten thousand years is from mother to daughter, grandmother to granddaughter, aunties to nieces. But because this culinary knowledge has been passed down orally, in the home, between women, it's mostly been invisible and undervalued. Even with our instructors, I think it's very common for their families and communities to take their excellent cooking for granted. After our instructors do their training with us and start teaching classes, we collect student feedback and send it to them. Many of them say they print that out and read it to their children, who say, "Mom, we totally took you for granted. You really are such an amazing cook."

Even my own Korean grandmother didn't see the value in what she did in the kitchen. I have come to realize that she didn't value her own cooking skills, even though she was really good at cooking, because those skills weren't valued by her family or culture or society. They were just taken for granted, and they were expected.

I've come to see that our instructors are culinary and cultural lineage holders in their cultures and communities. That's a concept that comes out of Eastern spiritual traditions, in particular Buddhism and Hinduism, where teachings and practices are passed down orally between teacher and student. To be a lineage holder within these traditions is to hold the knowledge, the exper-

tise, the teachings, and practices of a culture. At the heart of what we're doing with the League of Kitchens, I see now, is recognizing and celebrating this incredible knowledge and expertise that our instructors have, and creating a platform through which they can share it. I feel so lucky that I get to hang out with these incredible women and to learn from them, and that my company is giving them a way to do what they love, and to be recognized and compensated for it.

I have also come to realize that in a certain way, this, the whole idea for the League of Kitchens, came out of my desire to mend a cultural loss in my own family. Which, it turns out, many people in our American culture and society have also experienced—a disconnection from ancestral knowledge, traditions, and culture, because of modernization, forced and chosen migration, and cultural assimilation. At first, the League of Kitchens was just something that I thought sounded really cool that I wanted to create and experience, but now I realize that in some ways, I was also trying to heal a kind of rupture that I had experienced in my connection to Korean culture and my Korean heritage.

There was also another way in which creating the League of Kitchens was personally healing for me. I grew up going to a Jewish day school until I was thirteen, and at that time, I was the only person with Asian heritage in the entire school. But most of my identity growing up was Jewish, because I didn't know any other Koreans besides my mom and my grandmother. And so I always felt like an outsider, to some extent, in both Jewish and Korean contexts—never fully Jewish, never fully Korean. But what I realize in retrospect is that I was always *both* an outsider and an insider. I experienced both cultures from both those perspectives, moving back and forth between them. And this experience is what gave me the ability and the skills to start and run the League of Kitchens. In that wound was a gift. Because what am I doing? I'm helping to bridge the gap between our mostly American students and our immigrant instructors, and I can see things from both perspectives. And I'm able to easily connect with people from any culture because I can relate to and understand a multitude of perspectives and experiences.

*   *   *

So often, our classes start out feeling a little awkward—a group of strangers has traveled somewhere they probably haven't been to, entered an unfamiliar apartment building, knocked on a stranger's door. They're all outsiders, at first. But our instructors are so warm, kind, and hospitable, passionate about cooking and sharing their cultures, that you can't help but let your guard down. You can't help but start to relax and start to feel comfortable. You can't help but fall in love with them. And by the time everyone leaves, everyone is hugging and exchanging phone numbers, your instructor feels like your new favorite Uzbek aunt or Nepali grandma, and some part of the world that formerly felt abstract and distant now feels personal. The world is now a little smaller, and that all came about through food and through cooking and the love it carries—and what could be cooler than that?

A Note About Our Recipes

We feel that the crux of this cookbook is the strength of the recipes, which has been the guiding principle of the League of Kitchens. We have all worked hard to make sure that these recipes

will be mind-expanding from both a flavor and technique perspective. We want to ensure every recipe is as thorough as possible, and we also hope that the headnotes at the start of each recipe will provide cultural context, humanity, and emotional connection. Each of these recipes has been painstakingly vetted and curated not just by me, but by the instructors, who have been making them for their friends and families their entire lives.

To that end, we believe that what really sets these recipes apart from those that appear in so many other cookbooks is the rich level of detail. Most cookbooks try to compress every single step into as few words as possible, often so that the recipe is shorter and appears more straightforward. We wanted to take the opposite approach and give the same experience you'd get in one of our classes. In those, you see how to take out the tiny hard point of white membrane, which never cooks down, from the top of a plum tomato. You see how to use your knuckles to press breadcrumbs onto a cutlet. These are the details that only get passed from one cook to another, and the details that we always try to make sure are passed on to our students.

To be honest, the way we write recipes might seem a little long-winded, at first. Instead of calling for ¼ cup sliced onion in the ingredients list, for example, we often prefer to tell you specifically how to slice it in the recipe's steps. Instead of telling you to add ½ cup rinsed rice to the soup, we'll instead tell you how to rinse the rice. We know from experience that small details do affect the flavor of a finished dish and can also just make putting a dish together easier on the cook. (That's why we also repeat exact amounts for ingredients in the body of the recipe, in addition to the ingredients list. We find it so helpful

to not have to continuously glance back up at the ingredients list as you cook your way through the directions!)

It may seem strange that our recipes are this precise and that detailed, because our instructors are the kind of home cooks who never measure, who cook entirely by feel and from experience. But we want you to be able to truly re-create their recipes, and to have them come out tasting as good as they would if our instructors were there cooking along with you.

And because you probably haven't spent your life cooking Nepali food, Burkinabé food, or Indonesian food (or if you have, you probably haven't spent your whole life cooking the thirteen other cuisines in this book), we're assuming that you may not always know exactly how these recipes should end up tasting. So in your first time through a recipe, we encourage you to get out your scale, your ruler, your timer, and your measuring tools, and to *follow the recipe exactly*.

After that, once you have a feel for the recipe and a sense of how it should taste, feel free to riff on these recipes to your own tastes or with the ingredients you have in your kitchen. That's what our instructors do.

THE LEAGUE OF KITCHENS PANTRY

What follows is a checklist of less-common tools, equipment, oils, spices, and other ingredients that appear in many recipes in this book, as well as substitutions, where possible. I have found that keeping most of these on hand will make cooking either easier or more delicious—often both!

Tools

Box grater: Many of our recipes call for grating things with several sizes of graters—small holes, star holes, or large holes. A box grater is very handy, as it has several sizes of grater in one tool, and it's also a little easier to hold than a handheld grater.

Citrus juicer: When juicing a significant number of lemons or limes, it helps to have a tool to do this. (Though many of our instructors can do a very impressive job with just their hands!) I like the OXO citrus juicer. It works really well and juices directly into a container that's also a measuring cup, which is handy.

Digital scale: I highly recommend using a scale to measure the ingredients in this book by weight rather than cups or counts—which really vary by region, season, or supermarket—particularly when it comes to herbs, ginger, onion, and garlic. You'll get results that are closest to what the instructors make.

Electric kettle: Many of our recipes call for adding boiling or very hot water, which is much faster and easier to do using an electric kettle.

Electric spice grinder: A must-have if you want to make your own cardamom powder or your own roasted coriander and cumin powders (pages 23 and 24), all of which will really transform so many of the recipes in this book.

Handheld mandoline and a protective glove: A mandoline is ideal for slicing vegetables paper-thin or cutting them into julienne. I was always afraid to use one until I got a protective mesh glove—a game changer. But you can also use a knife or sometimes the slicing blade on a food processor.

Mini blender: These are perfect for making small amounts of spice pastes for a curry or other dishes. (Mini blenders are also known as personal or "bullet"-style blenders.) You can make most things that call for one in a larger blender if that's all you have, but you'll either have to add a lot of water or make much bigger batches to get the mixture to puree.

Mortar and pestle: Smooth versions are great for crushing seeds or spices or making pastes with very small amounts. But you can usually use a spice grinder or a heavy bottle and a cutting board instead.

Masala dabba: A masala dabba is a South Asian spice box. It's not a necessity, but it definitely makes it easier to measure out and handle a lot of different spices when you're making South Asian food.

Nonstick cookware: There is a long-standing debate about whether to use nonstick cookware. But nearly all of our instructors rely on nonstick pots and pans to make so many of their dishes without worrying about sticking or burning—especially stews, beans, grains, and rice dishes. You can make anything in this book without one by being extra careful and using a heavy-bottomed pan. But our suggestion is to at least invest in a 12-inch (30cm) nonstick wok, which you can use for so many different types of cooking techniques in this book, not just for stir-frying. Just be sure to check the manufacturer's recommendations for cooking with nonstick pans, particularly over higher heats.

Rice cooker: An absolutely amazing tool to help make dinner quicker. Most of our instructors use one to cook perfect basic rice every time, even though many of them make different types of rice. I recommend buying one from Zojirushi.

Ruler: A lot of recipes call for ingredients to be cut into unfamiliar sizes—it's helpful to actually have a ruler with you in the kitchen, since many of these measurements may be smaller or larger than you would expect. Don't worry, you don't have to measure every single piece—just use it to gauge your first few pieces or to spot-check as you work to ensure all pieces are roughly the same size.

Oils

Coconut oil: Coconut oil is a traditional everyday cooking oil in much of Southeast Asia but is used less often in the United States because it's so much more expensive here. You could use a neutral oil in any recipe that calls for it, but it adds a wonderful, distinctive flavor.

Sunflower oils: Unrefined sunflower oil has a nuttier flavor and tastes much more like sunflower seeds, though the refined version also has a distinctive flavor of Eastern and Central Europe, where it's the primary cooking oil. Unrefined sunflower oil is harder to find, but when it's called for, it will give your food a more traditional flavor.

Mustard oil: Mustard oil is a key ingredient in many Asian cuisines. There's controversy in the United States about its toxicity and its effects on health, and as a result, it has been banned for consumption. It has been proven safe in small doses but is often sold at South Asian markets in the US labeled as massage oil—many people of South Asian heritage buy mustard oil and use it in their day-to-day cooking. (Like with coconut oil, they would use it even more except that it's expensive here.) If you can't find it, our Bangladeshi instructor Afsari says to heat 1 tablespoon of neutral oil over medium heat in a pan, add ½ teaspoon of crushed brown mustard seeds, and cook for 30 seconds, stirring continuously with a spatula. Use this oil, with the crushed mustard seeds, as a substitute for mustard oil.

Neutral oil: When neutral oil is called for, our instructors use corn oil, vegetable oil, canola oil, or refined sunflower oil. I like to use an avocado/olive oil blend or "extra light" olive oil.

Palm oil: Thick and bright orange, palm oil is used as a primary cooking oil in many parts of Africa and has a nutty flavor and aroma. It's made by pressing the bright orange fruit from a specific kind of palm tree. (They're usually called oil palms, as opposed to the date palms that produce dates.) Any African grocery will stock it, but you can find an organic version in some health food stores.

Untoasted sesame oil: Some of the recipes call for untoasted sesame oil, which is more like a neutral oil than the toasted version used to flavor dishes.

Spices and Special Ingredients

Ajwain seeds: Popular in South Asian cuisines, these are slightly bitter and very aromatic, especially when bloomed in hot oil or ghee. (Chewing a pinch can also help relieve indigestion!)

Aleppo pepper: Milder than crushed red chile flakes and with a subtle sweetness. You could use a mix of hot and sweet paprika. Marash pepper is also very similar.

Asafetida: Also known as hing, this is the ground resin of giant fennel plants. Used widely in South Asian cooking, often in place of garlic and onion, it has a pungent aroma but adds a distinctive savoriness to a dish.

Black cardamom pods: These are related to the green varieties but come from different plants. While green cardamom is floral and delicate, black cardamom gets an intense smokiness from being roasted over a fire.

Black pepper powder or finely ground black pepper: The majority of our instructors use prepared ground black pepper sold in jars instead of freshly grinding it. It's much finer and is ideal for adding to a dish as it's cooking, as it incorporates much more easily. (And when you're putting in more than a sprinkle, it's much easier to measure out.) You can substitute freshly ground if that's all you have, but it should be very, very finely ground.

Black salt: Also known as kala namak in India, this is a kiln-fired purple-pink rock salt with a little sulfur, which gives it its pungent smell. It's often used in pickle and chutney recipes.

Chiles: In most of our recipes we give a range of hot chiles. The maximum amount is what the instructors would use if they were cooking for themselves, and will typically be very, very hot.

The smallest amount is what I use for a small amount of chile flavor but very little heat—typically what I would add when serving my two children.

Cloves: Make sure the whole cloves have buds on top—those hold most of the flavor!

Curry leaves: Curry leaves are kind of like a cross between a vegetable and an herb in South Asia, because you use so many of them in a dish. You can often find fresh ones at South Asian supermarkets, or frozen or dried varieties online. If you see fresh ones, buy a lot and keep them in the freezer—they'll last for a long time.

Diamond Crystal kosher salt: Many recipes and cookbooks now use this salt as a standard because of its clean flavor and moderate level of saltiness. We've tested all the recipes in this book with Diamond Crystal kosher salt, so if you want your food to be perfectly seasoned when using our recipes, definitely use this. If you're using a different brand or a type with smaller or larger crystals, you may need to adjust the salt quantities to taste. For iodized table salt, for example, you'd usually use about half of what we recommend.

Dried mint: Seek out Mediterranean or Middle Eastern shops for the best and freshest dried mint, where you can also get a large bag for a lot less money. (Or you can grow it/buy it fresh and dry it yourself. Our Lebanese instructor Jeanette will pluck all the leaves off the stems, scatter them on a baking sheet, and let them dry in her oven with the heat off but the light on.)

Indian bay leaves: Known as tej patta, these are longer, ribbed, and have a different, more cinnamon-like flavor than European bay laurel. They're easily found online or at any South Asian grocer.

Indian flat cinnamon: Also known as Desi cinnamon or Desi shard, you can use these in South Indian dishes instead of more standard cinnamon sticks to get a more traditional flavor—they're less spicy and more floral. Usually one 2-inch (5 cm) regular cinnamon stick (about 2 g) equals one 3-inch (7.5 cm) piece of Indian flat cinnamon.

Jaggery: A raw, unprocessed cane sugar with a molasses-like flavor (and lots of minerals). You can also substitute an equal amount of any dark brown or unprocessed sugar, like panela or coconut sugar. Jaggery can be dry and hard when you take it out of the package—you can break it up with a screwdriver, or a hammer, or even a mortar and pestle. It's also much easier to handle if you take it out of the package and put it in another container a day or two beforehand to help it soften up.

Jimbu: A Himalayan dried herb from the allium—onion and garlic—family that often gives Nepalese cooking its unique flavor. In the United States, you'll most likely have to buy this online, unless you live in a city with a large Nepali population. Store in the refrigerator or the freezer, and it will last even longer.

Jêruk purut lime leaves: The lime trees in Indonesia, which are called jêruk purut, have leaves with a sweet, "limey," and floral punch that really stands out in whatever dish you're adding them to. (These are often labeled kaffir lime leaves, though kaffir is now more widely known to be a racial slur in the Arabic language. Today you'll often see the term makrut, as well.) Like curry leaves, you can sometimes find fresh ones at Asian supermarkets, or frozen or dried varieties online, but Shandra, our Indonesian instructor, actually keeps a small lime tree in a brightly lit corner of her home in New York City. Even if she doesn't get any fruit, she always has plenty of leaves!

Sumac: These dusty red berries are dried and ground and have a deep purple-red color and a lemony-tart flavor. The ground-up powder is often dusted on top of Middle Eastern and Mediterranean dishes—in a pinch, a little spritz of citrus or vinegar can provide the same hint of acidity. Sumac is increasingly easy to find at conventional supermarkets, but if not, you'll find it online or at Middle Eastern stores.

Turkish red pepper paste: This red pepper paste is usually sold in Middle Eastern markets. (It's often from Turkish brands, where it's labeled "aci biber salcasi" for the spicy version or "tatli biber salcasi" for the sweet version.) Our Lebanese instructor Jeanette often cooks with the sweet version, and it adds an incredible depth and umami, with a little bit of sweetness, to any dish. It's such a versatile ingredient that you can use to add a little more oomph to any dish that calls for tomato sauce or tomato paste—it's especially good with eggs.

Wild Greek oregano: Despina uses wild Greek oregano in all her recipes. Because it's grown in hot and dry conditions, it has a much stronger and more aromatic flavor than common oregano. You can buy it online or at Greek grocery stores.

Garlic-Ginger Paste

MAKES ABOUT 13 TABLESPOONS

This paste should be made in a small personal "bullet" blender or a spice mill that has an attachment for wet ingredients. You'll get the best results if you make sure to weigh the ginger to get ¼ pound (115 g), instead of going by size, because the water content of fresh ginger varies so widely. If you're worried about these flavors lingering in a blender you use for drinks, our Bangladeshi instructor Afsari says to slice a small potato and blend it with water to remove the spice flavors.

This paste can be stored in a glass jar in the fridge for about 2 to 3 days, or in the freezer for up to 6 months. Since most of Afsari's recipes call for 3 tablespoons of garlic-ginger paste, I freeze it in plastic bags in 3-tablespoon portions. Just let them thaw slightly on the counter before you use them.

⅛ pound (60 g) garlic (about 1 medium head or 18 medium cloves)

¼ pound (115 g) fresh ginger (usually about a 5-inch/13 cm by 2 inch/5 cm piece)

1 **Peel the garlic:** The easiest way to peel the ⅛ pound (60 g) garlic (about 1 medium head or 18 medium cloves) is to first smash the cloves with the side of a knife, which also makes them easier to puree. Set aside.

2 **Prepare the ginger:** Use a spoon or butter knife to scrape away only any very dry, rough, or damaged parts of the skin of the ¼ pound (115 g) fresh ginger, but don't peel it, as that is where all the aromatic oils and flavor are. Slice the ginger against the grain into rough ¼-inch (0.6 cm) coins, which will prevent it from getting stuck in the blender blade.

3 **Process the paste:** Put the peeled and smashed garlic, the sliced ginger, and ½ cup (120 ml)

water into a small blender or spice mill that can process wet ingredients. Pulse until everything is totally smooth and fluffy, shaking the base of the blender or mill once or twice to make sure nothing is sticking to the blades.

Roasted Cumin Powder

MAKES ABOUT ½ CUP (60 G)

Roasting and grinding your own cumin powder will give you a much better flavor in any dish you make that calls for ground cumin. You can double or triple this recipe, but you don't want to halve it—½ cup (60 g) cumin seeds is the ideal amount to toast (a smaller quantity would be more likely to burn) and to grind in a spice mill. This is a good thing to make when you're already in your kitchen doing other things, since there's quite a bit of waiting involved.

½ cup (60 g) cumin seeds

1 Heat a heavy bottomed 8-inch (20 cm) skillet, preferably not nonstick, over very low heat. Once the pan is hot, wipe out any oil or moisture that may have accumulated so that the pan is totally dry.

2 Add the ½ cup (60 g) cumin seeds in a flat layer across the bottom of the pan and let them cook on the lowest setting possible, shaking every once in a while, until they're easily broken with a fingernail or until one easily snaps between your front teeth. (You don't want them to get too dark brown.) This often takes 15 minutes or more.

Continued

3 When they're done, let them cool fully to room temperature in the pan—this also takes 15 minutes or more.

4 When the seeds have fully cooled, process them in a spice mill or coffee grinder (that you don't use for coffee) until they're fully ground into a powder but you can still feel just a little graininess between your fingers.

5 Transfer the ground cumin seeds to a plate covered with parchment paper to cool for 2 to 3 minutes. When the cumin has cooled, lift the paper and make a funnel to transfer it to a glass jar with a tight-fitting lid.

6 This will last for about a month before the flavor begins to fade.

Roasted Coriander Powder

MAKES ABOUT ½ CUP (40 G)

Just as with the roasted cumin powder above, this is so much better than any store-bought prepared ground coriander. There are a lot of little nuances that really make this the best way to prepare this spice. You can double or triple this recipe, but you don't want to halve it—½ cup (40 g) is the ideal amount to toast (a smaller quantity would be more likely to burn) and to grind in a spice mill. Like with the cumin powder, this is a good thing to make when you're already in your kitchen doing other things, since there's quite a bit of waiting involved.

½ cup (40 g) coriander seeds

1 Heat a heavy-bottomed 8-inch (20 cm) skillet, preferably not nonstick, over very low heat. Once the pan is hot, wipe out any oil or moisture that may have accumulated so that the pan is totally dry.

2 Add the ½ cup (40 g) coriander seeds in a flat layer across the bottom of the pan and let them cook on the lowest setting possible, shaking every once in a while, until they're all crunchy and aromatic. (You don't want them to brown.) This usually takes about 5 minutes. If you taste one between your molars, it should almost shatter when you bite it.

3 Let the coriander cool fully to room temperature in the pan for 30 minutes; otherwise it will become a gummy paste rather than a powder when you grind it.

4 When the seeds have fully cooled, process them in a spice mill until they become a very fine powder and you don't feel any graininess. Hold the grinder in your hands and shake the grinder gently up and down a few times while grinding so that everything gets consistently ground.

5 Transfer the coriander to a plate covered with parchment paper to cool for 2 to 3 minutes. When it's cool, lift the paper and make a funnel to transfer it to a glass jar with a tight-fitting lid.

6 This will last for about a month before the flavor begins to fade.

チキン
鶏肉

Pollo

झुरब्की

TOByK

KOTÓПOUJO

ٹکڑ

Курица

CHICKEN

ご
ゲ

कुक्कुरा

Pollo

Ayam

चिकन

Poulet

Kabob Tavahi-e Morgh

(PERSIAN CHICKEN KABOBS WITH PAN-ROASTED TOMATOES)

Instructor: Mahboubeh Abbasgholizadeh

"This version is a modern, urban version of kabob, created by women of my mother's generation who wanted to be more independent." —Mab

These kabobs are super simple and flavorful with a nice lightness. The chicken has a great way of absorbing the saffron and onion flavor, but Mab says she also makes them with ground turkey or even salmon. (You can never have too many ground meat recipes—everyone loves them, and they're affordable, fast, and easy.)

Whichever meat you're using, it's very important to try to squeeze as much water out of it and the onions as possible before you form the kabobs so they don't fall apart when you pan-fry them. One of the best parts of this dish is the way Mab cooks the tomatoes, by just salting them and pan-frying them in a skillet with the leftover drippings.

Typically, says Mab, kabobs are a celebration dish for the whole family, often cooked outside by men. This is the stovetop version women like her mother created for weeknights and for urban apartment kitchens. The kabobs, tomatoes, and basmati rice together, along with some slices of raw onion, make a great easy meal—my kids love it.

Serve with: the saffron rice on page 170, plain basmati rice, or lavash. This is also great with just a dollop of plain whole milk yogurt, stirred until smooth, served alongside. (Ideally you would take a bite of the kabob with onion, tomato, and bread or rice, and then have a bite of yogurt in between.)

¼ teaspoon (0.25 g) saffron threads
(about 1 large pinch)

2 pounds (900 g) ground chicken

1½ pounds (680 g) red onion
(about 3 medium), divided

¼ pound (115 g) fresh parsley (about 1 bunch)

¼ pound (115 g) fresh cilantro (about 1 bunch)

4 tablespoons (60 ml) olive oil, divided,
plus more as needed

1 teaspoon Diamond Crystal kosher salt,
plus extra for sprinkling

¼ teaspoon finely ground black pepper

¼ teaspoon crushed red chile flakes, or more to taste

¼ teaspoon roasted coriander powder (page 24)

¼ teaspoon ground sumac

⅛ teaspoon ground cinnamon

2 pounds (900 g) slicing tomatoes
(about 2 to 3 large)

1 large lemon, for serving

1   **Make the saffron water:** Grind the ¼ teaspoon (0.25 g) saffron threads (about 1 large pinch) with a mortar and pestle into a fine powder (you can also use the end of the handle of a wooden spoon and a small bowl). Put the ground saffron in a small glass jar or drinking glass (a 4 ounce/120 ml mason jar is perfect) and add ½ tablespoon of room-temperature water, preferably filtered. Cover the glass and set it aside in a warm (or at least not cold) place.

2   **Prepare the kabob ingredients:** Put the 2 pounds (900 g) ground chicken in a bowl and set it aside. (This is to let any excess water from the chicken collect in the bottom of the bowl.)

3   Peel the 1½ pounds (680 g) red onion (about 3 medium).

Continued

4   Grate some of the onion over the largest holes of your box grater into a medium mixing bowl until you have about 1½ cups (350 g). Use your hands to squeeze out as much of the onion liquid as you can and discard it. Set the grated onion aside.

Ideally you want rough pieces of onion, not a shredded puree. Some graters even come with horizontal, square-shaped holes for cheese or potato, which work even better.

5   Slice the remaining onion into rings about ⅛ inch (0.3 cm) thick. (This is for garnishing the kabobs.)

6   Remove the stems from the ¼ pound (115 g) fresh parsley (about 1 bunch), right up to where the leaves begin, then finely mince the leaves. Add 1 cup of the parsley to the bowl with the grated onions, and then set aside any extra for garnishing the kabobs. Remove the stems from the ¼ pound (115 g) fresh cilantro (about 1 bunch), right up to where the leaves begin, then mince it finely. Add 1 cup to the bowl with the grated onions. Set aside any extra for garnishing the kabobs.

7   To the bowl with the grated onions, parsley, and cilantro, add 2 tablespoons of the olive oil, the 1 teaspoon Diamond Crystal kosher salt, ¼ teaspoon finely ground black pepper, ¼ teaspoon crushed red chile flakes, ¼ teaspoon ground coriander, ¼ teaspoon sumac, and ⅛ teaspoon cinnamon. Mix everything together with your hands.

8   Drain and discard any water that may have accumulated in the bowl with the chicken, squeezing the chicken gently to remove as much as possible. Add the drained chicken to the bowl with the onion, herbs, and spices, then mix everything together with your hands. Add the saffron water, then add another ½ tablespoon

of room-temperature water to the glass to rinse out the rest of the saffron and add that, too. Mix everything with your hands until all parts of the chicken are visibly yellow. Set this aside.

9   Slice the 2 pounds (900 g) slicing tomatoes (about 2 to 3 large) into ½-inch (1.3 cm) rounds. (Ideally you will have at least 2 pieces of tomato per person.) Set them aside.

10 **Cook the kabobs:** Heat the remaining 2 tablespoons of olive oil in a 10-inch (25 cm) nonstick skillet over high heat until the oil is very hot, then lower the heat to medium. You can test it by dropping in a small piece of the kabob mixture—it should sizzle immediately. If not, raise the heat slightly.

11 Take ⅓ cup (about 5 tablespoons) of the kabob mixture and form it in your hands into a sausage shape that is about 5 inches (13 cm) long and ¾ inch (2 cm) wide. (If the mixture is sticky or hard to handle, wet your hands as you go.) Put the kabob in the pan, then quickly form 3 or 4 more kabobs, laying them into the pan as you go—the kabobs will be touching slightly, that's fine.

12 As the bottoms of the kabobs brown (usually after 4 to 6 minutes per side), use tongs or two forks to gently flip them to the other side. When both sides are browned and the meat is firm to the touch (or a thermometer inserted into the center reaches at least 165°F/75°C), remove them to a plate or platter. Loosely tent the plate with foil so they stay warm, or you can also set them in an oven on the lowest setting.

13 Continue to form and cook kabobs until they're done, adding more oil to the pan if necessary. When the kabobs are done, use the same pan to fry the tomatoes.

The best way to cook these kabobs is to form them and place them right in the pan as you go, so they don't flatten or break. A smaller pan is ideal for that because you can only cook a few at a time—otherwise it's easy to burn a few while you're busy forming other kabobs. But if you have help forming or frying, you can try a larger pan or two smaller ones.

14 **Cook the tomatoes:** Turn the heat under the kabob pan to medium-high. Place as many of the sliced tomatoes as will fit into the pan, sprinkle the tops lightly with salt, and let them cook until the bottoms brown and char slightly, about 3 minutes. (For any top or bottom slices, make sure the cut side is facing down.)

15 Then flip them, sprinkle salt on the other side, and let them cook for just 45 seconds more—you don't want the tomatoes to be too mushy. Remove the tomatoes to another serving plate or to the platter with the kabobs. Repeat until all the slices are fried.

16 **Serve the kabobs:** Sprinkle the reserved chopped parsley and cilantro over the tops of the kabobs and slice the 1 large lemon into thin wedges.

17 You can put the kabobs, tomatoes, and sliced onions in the middle of the table family style with bowls of rice or lavash, or put one or two kabobs on each plate with rice or bread, a few sliced onions, and at least one slice of tomato. Ideally you would take a bite of the kabob, layered with onions, tomato, and a little bread or rice; you could also roll a kabob in a piece of lavash with a slice of tomato and a few onions to make a sandwich. Serve the lemons on the side so that each diner can squeeze them over their plates.

Breaking Down a Whole Chicken

While developing recipes for this book, Nawida showed me how to break down a chicken in minutes. I used to be afraid of cutting down a chicken. Now I use this technique in every recipe that calls for bone-in chicken parts. The really eye-opening detail for me is that she uses her hands to crack and break through the joints, and then it's much easier to cut through those places.

It's a better value to buy a chicken whole, and the neck and back are often left out of commercially prepared packages. These parts don't have a ton of meat, but they do add a lot of flavor to a gravy or soup. (Nawida doesn't use the kidney, heart, or liver for soups and stews, but sometimes serves them as kabob.)

Like all of our instructors, Nawida takes the time to really clean the chicken as she's cutting it apart, removing all the skin and fat. This yields stock, broth, or gravy with better texture. All of our instructors also use a large knife or cleaver to cut the chicken into smaller parts than you'd typically find in an American supermarket—three pieces for a breast and two for a drumstick or thigh. When you expose more bone marrow, you end up with more flavor. A bonus is that smaller pieces are also easier to cook and to serve. (Just watch out for small bones and shards while you're eating—smaller pieces can split apart while cooking.)

Many of our instructors also prefer to wash chicken under running water before they cook with it to get rid of any pieces of bone or fat still clinging to the skin. The USDA recommends against this, as it can spread bacteria around your sink. If you choose to do the same, just make sure to clean your sink carefully when you're done.

One last tip: Whole chickens vary widely in size. If you end up with a chicken larger or smaller than what the recipe calls for, it'll be fine—just adjust the salt up or down by a pinch or two, as necessary.

Here's how to do it:

1. Remove any giblets, kidneys, heart, or other organs from the interior of the chicken. Save them for another use or discard them.

2. Use your hands to break or crack the joint where the drumsticks are attached, then use a large, sharp knife (or a pair of kitchen shears) to cut off the drumsticks.

3. Use your hands to crack or break the bones where the rest of the legs and thighs are attached to the breast, then use the knife to cut the thighs away. Separate the thighs.

4. Use your hands to crack or break the bones where the wings are attached to the body, then use the knife to cut each of the wings away.

5. Use your hands to crack or break the bones where the neck and backbone are attached to the breasts, and then use the knife to cut both away from the breasts. Set them aside. Then use the knife to separate the breasts.

6. You should now have two thighs, two wings, two breasts, plus the neck and backbone, which you can add to the pot, in many cases, or save for stew.

7. Remove any leftover scraps of tendon, blood, or anything else that isn't bone or meat and discard them.

8. To break down these parts into smaller pieces, put them on a cutting board. Place the knife on top of the chicken and use the pressure of your hand to cut down through the bone. If you have a sturdy pair of kitchen shears or butcher's scissors, you can also use those to cut the chicken into pieces.

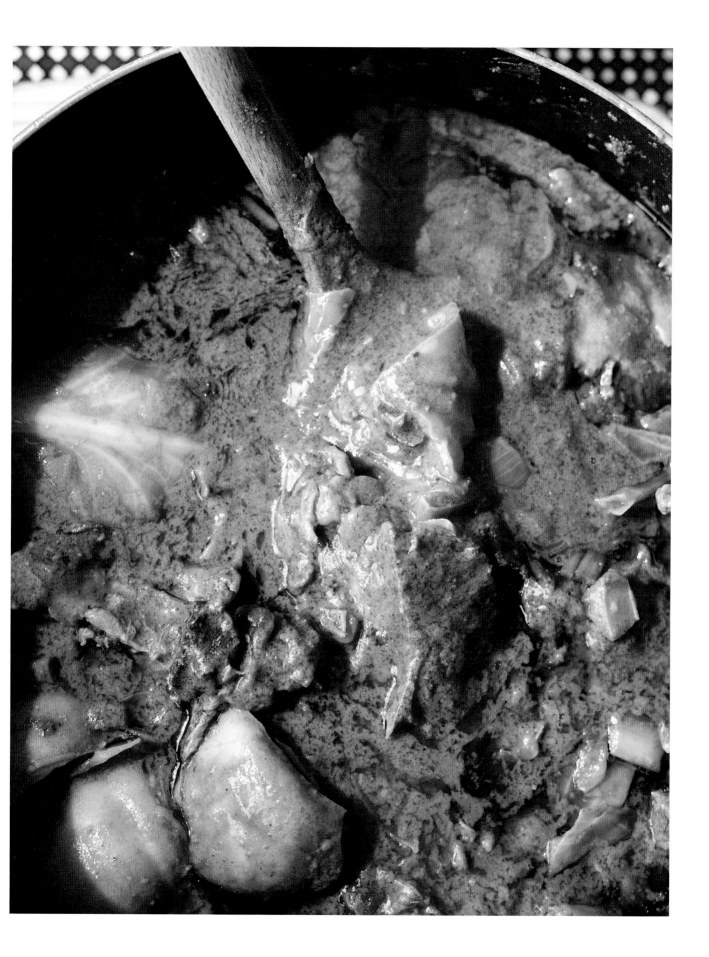

Milanesa de Pollo

(ARGENTINIAN FRIED CHICKEN CUTLETS)

Instructor: Mirta Rinaldi

"When my mom would ask, 'What do you want for dinner?' everyone would say, 'Milanesa!' Because everybody knew my mom made the best milanesa in the world." —Mirta

These are the best chicken cutlets I've ever had—super crunchy and juicy, and perfectly seasoned, with a subtle garlic flavor. And they're so good because this is one of those recipes that's just filled with brilliant tips and tricks—ones that Mirta learned from her mom, and ones she's developed herself while making thousands of milanesas over the course of her life.

The first important element is how she marinates the cutlets—she adds both grated garlic and finely chopped parsley to the egg dip—something you don't see in the restaurant version. The next important technique is how she breads the cutlets. She puts a piece of parchment paper on a baking sheet, pours out a pile of panko (using panko is something she started doing when she came to the States), and then she buries the cutlet in the breadcrumbs, lifting the edges of the parchment to gather the crumbs together around the chicken. She then uses a technique that she learned from her grandmother—she uses her knuckles to press and roll the breadcrumbs into the chicken, which results in superior crumb coverage. And last, before she fries the cutlets, she sets up a wire cooling rack on top of a baking sheet and covers half with paper towels. After she fries each cutlet, she first briefly rests it on the paper towel side to absorb excess oil, and then soon after, she moves it to the rack so that it can continue to drain without getting soggy. This results in the crispiest cutlets you'll ever have. Whenever I make these, my kids gobble them up.

Mirta always marinates a big batch of milanesas—usually using 5 pounds of chicken breasts—so that she can freeze a bunch. That way she has plenty to give to her daughter and to friends, and she always has an easy delicious dinner at the ready, anytime.

Mirta will often turn leftover cutlets into cold sandwiches on a sturdy but soft roll that is known as pan francese in Argentina, topping them with mayo, lettuce, and tomato. This is her favorite sandwich to bring on a picnic. When served hot, she says the perfect trio is milanesas, mashed potatoes (regular or sweet), and a salad.

Serve with: mashed potatoes of any kind and a simple green salad.

1½ pounds (680 g) boneless, skinless chicken
    breasts or thin cutlets

⅛ pound (60 g) fresh flat-leaf parsley
    (about ½ bunch)

¾ ounce (20 g) garlic (about 6 medium cloves)

2 large eggs

1 teaspoon Diamond Crystal kosher salt,
    plus extra for sprinkling

¼ teaspoon black pepper powder

3 to 4 cups (250 g) panko breadcrumbs

Neutral oil, for frying

3 large lemons, for serving

1   **Put the chicken breasts in the freezer:** If you didn't buy pre-sliced cutlets, put the package of 1½ pounds (680 g) boneless, skinless chicken breasts in the freezer while you prepare the marinade.

2   **Prepare the marinade:** While the chicken is in the freezer, prepare the ⅛ pound (60 g) fresh flat-leaf parsley (about ½ bunch). Cut the stems off where the leaves begin, then discard them.

Continued

Chop the parsley (you should have only leaves and tender stems), going back and forth with your knife until it's very finely minced. (You can also process it in a mini blender or food processor, if you have one.) You should end up with about ¾ cup chopped parsley leaves. Put them in a large mixing bowl.

3   Using the small holes of a box grater, grate the ¾ ounce (20 g) garlic (about 6 medium cloves) into the bowl with the parsley. (It will come out to about 1 tablespoon of grated garlic.)

4   Crack the 2 large eggs into the bowl and add the 1 teaspoon Diamond Crystal kosher salt and ¼ teaspoon black pepper powder. Use a fork to beat the eggs and mix everything together. Set the bowl aside to let the flavors meld while you prepare the chicken cutlets.

Mirta nearly always makes and cooks her cutlets right away, but you can also make the cutlets and marinate them for an hour or two in the refrigerator or even overnight.

5   **Prepare the cutlets:** If you didn't buy pre-sliced cutlets, hold one of the semi-frozen chicken breasts down with one hand on a large cutting board and use your sharpest knife in the other hand to cut it into thin cutlets about ½ inch (1.3 cm) thick. Use the pressure from your top hand to help cut the chicken evenly. You should be able to get 2 to 4 cutlets for each breast—it's okay if they're different shapes. If you cut them too thin, they can dry out too fast while you fry them, so it's better to err on the side of being too thick.

6   Once you're done, if you have any cutlets (hand-cut or store-bought) that are too thick or have thicker spots, cover them with parchment or wax paper to keep mess at a minimum, and pound them out to ½ inch (1.3 cm) thick with a meat pounder or a heavy bottle. If you end up with some very large cutlets, just cut them into smaller portions—or leave them whole to serve family-style.

7   Once you're done cutting the chicken (or if you're using pre-sliced cutlets), sprinkle a little Diamond Crystal kosher salt on each of the pieces on one side only, then put them salt-side down in the bowl with the egg mixture, one at a time. (If you salt both sides, you'll end up with too much salt.) Use a fork or spoon to gently mix all the chicken into the marinade, so every piece is covered. Set the cutlets aside to marinate while you prepare the panko breading.

8   **Prepare the breading:** Line a rimmed baking sheet with parchment or waxed paper. Line another baking sheet or a large plate or platter and set it to the side. Spread about half of the panko in a thick layer so that you are fully covering most of the middle of the baking sheet—the primary goal is to have enough panko so that when you put down each cutlet, it will be fully surrounded by the panko.

9   Lay one of the cutlets down on the baking sheet in the middle of the mound of panko. Use a fork to dab a little of the garlic and parsley from the egg marinade over the top of the cutlet—use a light touch, so it's mostly garlic and parsley and not much of the liquid. Dry your hands, if necessary, and then use your hands to scoop the panko up and over the sides and top of the cutlet, making sure to completely bury the cutlet with panko—you can also lift the sides of the parchment paper to help consolidate the breadcrumbs around the cutlet. Use your knuckles to very strongly press and pound the panko into the cutlet. Flip the cutlet over, cover it with more panko, and repeat on the other side, pressing the panko in until every piece of the cutlet is completely covered and when you hold it up the panko sticks in place. Gently shake off any excess and place the panko-covered cutlet on the baking sheet or large plate or platter.

10 Repeat this process with the remaining cutlets, adding more panko as needed. You can stack the completed cutlets on top of each other, if needed. (After they're breaded, you can separate them with parchment paper and freeze them in an airtight container or zip-top plastic bag for up to a month. Defrost them before you fry them.)

11 **Fry the cutlets:** Set a wire rack into a baking sheet and cover half of the rack with paper towels.

12 Pour neutral oil into a 12-inch (30 cm) skillet with deep sides so that it covers the bottom and is ¼ inch (0.6 cm) deep. Heat it over medium to medium-high heat until the oil shimmers. Test it with a piece of panko—bubbles should appear immediately around the edge, and the panko should float.

13 Cook the cutlets 3 or 4 at a time—or however many will fit in your pan with about ½ inch (1.3 cm) in between each cutlet. As you add the cutlets, you should see big bubbles begin to appear on the edges, and the bottoms should begin to brown quickly but not burn—adjust the heat as necessary. Flip them when you can see that they are very golden brown on the edges, after 2 to 4 minutes. If some pockets are lighter in color, turn the cutlets back over and press them a little with tongs or a spatula so the pockets cook quickly. When the cutlets are golden brown on the other side and cooked through, remove them to the paper towel lined side of the pan and let them sit for a minute or two, flipping them once so that both sides can drain excess oil. Then move them to the uncovered side of the rack. You can move them to a serving platter as new batches come out of the pan.

14 Repeat this process until all the cutlets are cooked. In between batches, use a slotted spoon to scoop out any escaped breadcrumbs into a piece of paper towel. If you have a lot of burnt crumbs, you can change the oil—this often happens after you've fried two or three batches. You may also find you need to add a little more oil between batches as well.

15 While the last of the cutlets are frying, cut the 3 large lemons lengthwise into wedges and put them on a small serving plate.

16 **Serve and eat the cutlets:** Serve the cutlets hot or at room temperature. Put the lemon wedges on the table along with the platter of fried cutlets and encourage everyone to squeeze fresh lemon juice over the top of each cutlet just before they eat them.

CHICKEN

Korma Murg

(AFGHAN CHICKEN AND POTATO STEW WITH ONION GRAVY)

Instructor: Nawida Saidhosin

"I learned this from my mother and grandmother—I have been making it as long as I can remember." —Nawida

This is a chicken curry made in the Afghan style. The ingredients seem simple, but they combine to make such a rich, flavorful dish. One great thing about Nawida's recipes is that she tends to cook over high heat, so her dishes cook very quickly. Nawida, who for ten years cooked daily for a family of thirty-five people, is just a blazingly fast cook in general: She tends to do all of the cutting and chopping right in her hands, a holdover from when she'd do the majority of her cooking in a kitchen without counters.

A pile of paper-thin onions in this dish is the secret to the flavor—they keep melting and melting, says Nawida, and eventually become the gravy. Nawida has the best method for breaking down a whole chicken, which is what she always uses to make this dish. It was game-changing for me. (For instructions, see page 32.) But you can also use a mix of bone-in chicken breasts, thighs, drumsticks, and wings—just make sure to cut them into smaller pieces through the bone. Exposing the bone marrow makes for a richer and more flavorful sauce, and the small pieces are also easier to hold and eat off the bone, since this dish is meant to be eaten with your hands. Just make sure to look out for small pieces of bone or bone shards as you eat.

Serve with: the rice with garlic and cloves on page 179, plain basmati rice, or bread, like lavash or pita, and at least one other vegetable, like the stewed Afghan okra on page 249 or the Afghan eggplant on page 269.

3 to 4 pounds (1.4 kg–1.8 kg) bone-in chicken parts, or 1 whole chicken

½ ounce (15 g) garlic (about 4 medium cloves)

1 pound (450 g) russet potatoes (about 2 medium)

1 pound (450 g) yellow onions (about 2 medium)

1 tablespoon roasted coriander powder (page 24)

1 tablespoon Diamond Crystal kosher salt

1 teaspoon black pepper powder

1 teaspoon ground turmeric

⅛ to ½ teaspoon red chile powder, to taste

½ cup (120 ml) neutral oil

1 tablespoon tomato paste

⅛ pound (60 g) fresh cilantro (about ½ bunch)

1   **Prepare the chicken:** If you're using a whole 3- to 4-pound (1.4 kg–1.8 kg) chicken, follow the instructions on page 32 to cut it apart before moving on to the next step.

2   Use your hands to remove all the skin and any pockets of yellowish fat underneath from all the chicken parts. If you see any leftover scraps of tendon, blood (or anything else that isn't bone or meat), remove them with a paring knife or scissors and discard them.

A paper towel can make it easier to grip the skin to pull it off, especially from the wings, and you can use a pair of clean kitchen scissors to cut away the fat if it doesn't easily pull away. A little leftover skin or fat is fine—just try to remove as much as possible so that the gravy ends up flavorful but not greasy.

3   Following the instructions on page 32, use a large, sharp knife (or a pair of kitchen shears) to cut the breast crosswise through the bone into three pieces about the same size. Use the same

Continued

method to cut the thighs into 2 or 3 pieces about the same size as the pieces of chicken breast, and then the wings into two pieces.

4   Go over all the parts again and discard any bits of skin, fat, tendon, or blood, then set the chicken aside.

Like many of our instructors, Nawida likes to wash the chicken pieces under running water in the sink after she cleans them. The USDA recommends against this, as it can spread bacteria around your sink or your kitchen. If you choose to rinse the pieces, just make sure to clean your sink carefully when you're done.

5   **Prepare the ingredients:** Peel the ½ ounce (15 g) garlic (about 4 medium cloves), then roughly chop it—it should not be minced. You should end up with about 1½ tablespoons.

6   Peel the 1 pound (450 g) russet potatoes (about 2 medium) and cut them into 8 pieces lengthwise. Set them aside in a small bowl filled with cold water.

7   Peel the 1 pound (450 g) yellow onions (about 2 medium), making sure to remove any outer layers that are especially tough or coarse (you want the slices to eventually melt into the sauce). Cut the onions in half from the root to the stem, trim the ends, and then slice each half into half-moons as thinly as you can from root to stem, or use a mandoline (and ideally wear a protective glove). You should end up with about 3 cups. Set the onions aside.

8   Measure out 1 tablespoon ground coriander, 1 tablespoon Diamond Crystal kosher salt, 1 teaspoon black pepper powder, 1 teaspoon ground turmeric, and ⅛ to ½ teaspoon red chile powder into a small bowl and set it by the stove.

9   **Fry the onions:** Put the ½ cup (120 ml) neutral oil in a 5-quart (4.8 L) Dutch oven or stockpot, preferably with a heavy bottom.

10 Heat the oil over medium-high heat until it begins to shimmer. Add the onions and fry them, stirring and scraping the bottom of the pot almost constantly to make sure they don't burn. They're done when they're very golden, have shrunk considerably in size, and many of the slices are beginning to brown along the edges. This will take quite a bit of time even over medium-high heat—usually 10 to 15 minutes.

11 **Add the chicken:** When the onions are soft and beginning to brown, quickly but carefully add the chicken pieces (make sure to add the neck and back, if you have it) to the pot, a piece at a time, shaking off any remaining water into the bowl as you go. The heat should still be on medium-high. Stir the chicken with a spatula for about a minute, scraping up any sticky browned bits from the bottom of the pot, until all the pieces are mixed together with the onions and begin to color on all sides. Let the chicken cook, stirring and scraping frequently, for 10 minutes. The onion will continue to reduce and melt away, becoming more like a gravy.

12 **Season the korma:** Stir in the 1½ tablespoons chopped garlic, 1 tablespoon tomato paste, and the combined spices from the small bowl. The heat should still be on medium-high. Let everything cook and sizzle, stirring frequently and scraping the bottom of the pot so nothing sticks to the bottom or burns, for 2 minutes.

13 Add ¼ cup (60 ml) water, stirring so that everything is mixed together. Cook for 1 minute.

14 **Add the potatoes:** Drain the potatoes and add them to the pot. Use your spatula or spoon to gently stir them into the pot, until they are covered with the gravy and underneath the chicken, so they cook evenly. Add another ¼ cup (60 ml) water, stirring so that everything

is mixed together. Cook for about 1 minute so that the water heats through, then turn the heat down to medium-low and cover the pot.

15 **Finish the korma:** Let the korma cook, covered, until the potatoes are just cooked through, usually 10 to 15 minutes, then turn off the heat and let it sit, covered, until you're ready to serve it. (The chicken should be fully cooked through by this point as well; if you're using a thermometer, it should read at least 165°F/75°C when inserted near a bone.)

16 Prepare the ⅛ pound (60 g) fresh cilantro (about ½ bunch). Cut the stems off where the leaves begin, then discard them. Finely chop the cilantro (you should have only leaves and tender stems). You should have about ½ cup.

17 **Serve the korma:** Serve the korma hot (you can gently reheat it if necessary), sprinkling the cilantro over the stew just before you serve it. You can serve this family style in a serving bowl on the table or individually—just put at least one piece of chicken and potato on each plate with some of the gravy, usually alongside (not on top of) a serving of rice or bread.

Nawida Saidhosin

Born in Kabul, Afghanistan, Nawida grew up watching her mother and grandmother cook for the family, which included four sisters, a brother, and her father, a general in the Afghan army. After she got married, she moved to Pakistan to live with her mother-in-law's family, where she was responsible for cooking three elaborate meals a day for a household of thirty-five people—plus the four or five guests who were typically present at any meal. After briefly living in Russia with her husband, she came to the United States with her son Bahram in 2010, when he was just five years old. Nawida is now remarried to an Indian man (she loves to cook Indian food, too), and they have two young children—Sanam and Abram. There is nothing in the world more important to Nawida than her children's education—but she also loves the independence and freedom she has found in the United States. She recently trained to become a barber and is hoping to open her own shop.

How did you learn to cook? From my mother and grandmother. They were excellent cooks. I learned all the Afghan traditional foods from them. When I was small, as soon as I would get home from school, I would go to the kitchen to watch them and help. Then when I was thirteen, I started taking on the responsibility of cooking for the whole family. I never got bad feedback from my family. And when guests came to eat, they would say, "Oh, Nawida made this? Are you serious?" It was so exciting.

What do you think made your mother and grandmother's food so good? The secret is that they made everything very fresh—when it was the season of eggplant or okra or tomatoes, we had that. When it was winter, we didn't eat those things. They were also very focused on their work—and their skills, passed on from one generation to the next, were very good from longtime experience. Like many Afghan families even now, I also try my best to never use canned stuff or ingredients that are not fresh. Sometimes I go to three stores to get the ingredients I want. When I was small, we grew so many things in our garden—we grew potatoes, tomatoes, cilantro, dill. In the morning when you came out, the smell made you crazy—you just wanted to pick and eat everything right away. I love taking my kids to a pick-your-own farm in New Jersey. They get so excited. I want them to feel what it's like to pick and eat really fresh, delicious food.

What do you enjoy about cooking? When I have stress, what makes me happy is to go to the kitchen to make something. Besides Afghan food, I cook Persian and Russian and Indian dishes. And then because I love to cook, when I start cooking, I forget what was making me unhappy. Also, food cooked at home brings love between the family. Before we got married, my husband ate at restaurants most of the time. After we got married, he said, "Nawida, I just want to eat at restaurants when I have no choice. The rest of the time I want to eat in the house." I also enjoy cooking for my friends and neighbors. Sometimes they drop in when they smell cooking coming from my apartment!

How is food traditionally served and eaten in Afghanistan? Everyone sits on the floor around a dastarkhaan—a kind of tablecloth or thin rug that's put on the floor, and you put plates of food on top. If it's a party, two people will usually share a plate or tray because in Afghanistan, there are so many people at every event, it's hard to have that many plates. Everyone eats with their hands. My mother always wanted us to take the fork and the spoon, and my father would say, "Why don't you let them use their hands? It's more delicious." You're going to get the real taste of the food with the hands.

What do you make when you want to cook something yummy just for yourself? I like the tomato eggs (page 107), very spicy. And if it's lunchtime, I love to make eggplant burani bonjon (page 269). If I'm alone, I make it with just one eggplant. It takes ten to twelve minutes to make just a little plate. It's very easy, and it's very super delicious.

What is your advice to someone who is just learning how to cook? Sometimes when I'm tired and I make something, my husband says, "Nawida, you did not put love there today." I say, "No, it's delicious." And then he says, "No, Nawida, it's good. But you did not put your love inside. You need a little bit of love there." So you need to put love in your food, that's one thing. My other advice to a new cook is also to decide on a dish, get all the ingredients together, follow the recipe step by step, and then try to stay focused on the dish you are preparing.

What do you like about teaching for the League of Kitchens? I like teaching people from different age groups and different cultural backgrounds, both in person and online. But personally, I really love the in-person classes. I get to interact with the students one-on-one when they're cooking with me in my home, and we prepare and then enjoy the dishes together. It makes me happy to teach and share, and I especially love to share my culture with my students, and also to get ideas from them and to hear about experiences from their countries, their cultures. On the TV, the only thing they show about Afghanistan is the war and all the bad things. But if you're inside the culture, it's so much love. It's so much respect. Family, parents with kids, it's different. They're very good people, very beautiful people, with good hearts. I am really proud of Afghanistan. I love my country, and I love sharing about it. I cannot express how much I love the League of Kitchens.

Nawida Saidhosin.

نویده سید حسین

Sauce Pâte D'Arachide

(BURKINABÉ PEANUT BUTTER STEW WITH CHICKEN AND VEGETABLES)

Instructor: Yipin Benon

"My kids love the sauce from this dish—you just put it on rice and ohhh, they enjoy it." —Yipin

Yipin's mother taught her this rich peanut butter stew served over white rice—it's really a sauce that families cook in Burkina Faso in many ways, and it's also a staple in other parts of West Africa. Yipin says this is a great dish that you can make a lot of to serve a large family or group. She also says that she never does it the same way twice, though it always has softened peppers, onion, garlic, and tomatoes, which are the foundation of much of Burkinabé cooking. This recipe is the basic, everyday approach. When she's making it for a special occasion, she will sometimes add smoked fish or nuts and all of the vegetables, but you can just add one or two—I like to add all of them because the vegetables are so delicious cooked in the peanut butter sauce, and that way, you have a full one-pot meal. (Yipin jokes that in her family, she's the only one who eats the vegetables.)

Yipin also always adds one whole Scotch bonnet chile near the end, for the "beautiful perfume," as she puts it, that it adds to the stew. You want to make sure the pepper is not damaged or broken, or else it will make this dish too spicy. Anyone who wants some chile heat can cut off a piece for their bowl. You could also serve a hot sauce made from Scotch bonnets on the side. (If you can't find Scotch bonnets, which are sometimes labeled Jamaican hot peppers, you could use a habanero.) Yipin usually adds a Goya Sazón seasoning packet and chicken bouillon—if you don't have them or don't want to use them, you can add the noted additional salt amounts—it's still a super savory and satisfying dish without the added seasonings.

When Yipin buys the chicken for this dish, she usually gets a whole one from a "live chicken" poultry market that will slaughter and clean a small chicken that's about 2½ pounds (1.2 kg) to order—you don't need a huge 4- or 5-pound chicken for this dish, since

the chicken's main role is to add flavor, not to be the center of the dish, and you also want the pieces to fit in a single layer in the pot while you fry them. If you can find a whole chicken that small, you can use that, following the instructions on page 32 for how to cut it into smaller pieces, but you can also just use a mix of bone-in chicken breasts, thighs, drumsticks, and wings. Just make sure to cut them into smaller pieces—you really want them no larger than 4 inches (10 cm) wide. As with many of the other chicken stews and soups in this book, exposing more bone marrow by cutting the chicken pieces through the bone makes for a richer, more deeply flavored dish.

For this recipe, Yipin likes to use organic peanut butter that has no added sugar or fat—she says it tastes closest to what she would get at home in Burkina Faso by grinding the peanuts herself. Like many of the cuisines in this book, Burkinabé cuisine is traditionally eaten with your hand, and Yipin and her husband will tell you that it's much more delicious that way. Scoop a big spoonful of sauce pâte d'arachide onto a pile of fluffy white rice, and enjoy.

For the sauce pâte d'arachide

2⅓ to 3 pounds (1.2 kg–1.4 kg) bone-in chicken parts, or 1 whole chicken

5 teaspoons Diamond Crystal kosher salt, divided (plus 4½ more teaspoons, if you're not using the Sazón and bouillon powder)

1 Goya Sazón seasoning packet, any flavor, such as cilantro and tomato, optional

1 tablespoon garlic powder

⅓ cup (80 ml) neutral oil

Continued

¾ ounce (20 g) garlic (about 6 medium cloves)

⅓ pound (150 g) bell pepper, any color (about ½ large)

½ pound (225 g) red onion (about 1 medium)

1 pound (450 g) plum tomatoes (about 4 medium)

⅓ pound (150 g) scallions (about 5 medium)

⅓ cup (80 ml) tomato paste

1 cup (240 ml) organic creamy peanut butter (with no added sugar or fat)

5 small bay leaves

1 whole Scotch bonnet chile, optional

1 teaspoon chicken bouillon powder, optional

Cooked white rice (either parboiled or jasmine)

For the vegetables

¼ pound (115 g) fresh okra (about 10 to 12 pods)

¾ pound (340 g) eggplant (1 small Italian eggplant, or 5 to 6 tiny eggplants)

13 ounces (370 g) green cabbage (½ small cabbage)

1   **Prepare the chicken:** If you're using a whole 2½- to 3-pound (1.2 kg–1.4 kg) chicken, follow the steps on page 32 to cut it apart before moving on to the next step.

2   Following the instructions on page 32, use a large, sharp knife or cleaver (or a pair of kitchen shears) to cut the breast crosswise through the bone into three pieces about the same size. Use the same method to cut the thighs into two or three pieces about the same size as the pieces of chicken breast, the legs into two pieces, and then the wings into two pieces.

3   Trim any excess skin. Use your hands to remove any pockets of yellowish fat underneath the skin. A little leftover fat is fine—just try to remove as much as possible so the gravy ends up flavorful but not greasy.

Like many of our instructors, Yipin likes to wash the chicken pieces under running water in the sink after she cleans them. The USDA recommends against this, as it can spread bacteria around your sink or your kitchen. If you choose to rinse the pieces, just make sure to clean your sink carefully when you are done.

4   Put the pieces skin-side down in a large (8-quart/7.5 L) nonstick pot. (You want the chicken in as close to one layer as possible.)

5   Sprinkle the chicken pieces with 1 teaspoon of the Diamond Crystal kosher salt. Cover the pan, leaving the lid slightly ajar unless there is a hole for the steam. Turn the heat to medium and cook the chicken pieces, covered, for 10 minutes, or until they begin to turn a little golden and fry in their own fat.

6   Sprinkle the 1 Goya Sazón seasoning packet, if using, and 1 tablespoon garlic powder over the chicken and stir it in so that it covers the chicken. (If not using the Sazón, add 1 teaspoon of Diamond Crystal kosher salt.) Cook, stirring occasionally, for about 1 minute, then add the ⅓ cup (80 ml) neutral oil and mix everything together.

7   Fry the chicken pieces, stirring occasionally, until they're very brown on all sides, about 10 minutes. Remove the chicken from the pan to a bowl, cover the bowl with a plate or foil, and set it aside.

8   **While the chicken is cooking, prepare the rest of the ingredients:** Fill a large saucepan with 10 cups (2.4 L) of water and bring it to a boil. (This is for cooking the cabbage.)

9   Peel the ¾ ounce (20 g) garlic (about 6 medium cloves). Grate the garlic over the fine holes of a grater. You should have about 1 tablespoon. Set it aside.

10 Remove the membrane and seeds from the ⅓ pound (150 g) bell pepper (about ½ large). Cut it into ⅓-inch (1 cm) dice. You should have about 1 cup. Add it to the bowl with the garlic.

11 Peel the ½ pound (225 g) red onion (about 1 medium) and cut it into ½-inch (1.3 cm) dice. You should have about 1½ cups. Add it to the bowl with the garlic and peppers.

12 Cut the 1 pound (450 g) plum tomatoes (about 4 medium) into ½-inch (1.3 cm) dice. You should have about 3 cups. Set them aside in a separate bowl.

13 Trim the root end of the ⅓ pound (150 g) scallions (about 5 medium). Cut the white parts into ⅓-inch (1 cm) rings and the greens into ½-inch (1.3 cm) pieces, but keep them together. You should have about 2 cups. Set them aside in a separate bowl.

14 Trim just the top and tail from the ¼ pound (115 g) fresh okra (about 10 to 12 pods), but leave the pods whole. Set them aside in a separate bowl.

15 Cut the ¾ pound (340 g) eggplant (1 small Italian eggplant or 5 to 6 tiny eggplants) into quarters lengthwise, trimming any pieces of the stem that are damaged or dry. Then cut each quarter into thirds, or leave them whole if you're using tiny eggplants. Set it aside in a separate bowl.

16 Take the 13 ounces (370 g) green cabbage (½ small cabbage), core it, and cut it into quarters. To the pot of boiling water, add 2 tablespoons of the remaining Diamond Crystal kosher salt. Add the cabbage and let it boil for 3 minutes. Remove to a separate bowl.

17 **Cook the sauce pâte d'arachide:** Once the chicken is fried and you have taken it out of the pot, stir in the garlic, onion, and peppers—the heat should still be on medium. Cook for about 5 minutes, until the onions lighten in color and soften. Then stir in the tomatoes and 2 more teaspoons of Diamond Crystal kosher salt. Cover the pot, leaving the lid slightly ajar, and cook for 10 minutes, stirring every few minutes.

18 Stir in the ⅓ cup (80 ml) tablespoon tomato paste and the 1 cup (240 ml) peanut butter. Stir constantly at this point or it will stick. Cook, still over medium heat, stirring continuously, until the reddish oil pools around the edges and the center is thick, creamy, and brown, about 2 minutes. (If you're not using a nonstick pot, pay close attention to prevent sticking and scorching.)

19 Pour any liquid that has gathered in the bowl with the chicken into a measuring cup and add enough water to make 5 cups (1.2 L), then add that to the pot. Stir in the 5 small bay leaves and the eggplant chunks, raise the heat to medium-high, and bring the pot to a strong simmer.

20 Add the sliced scallions, lower the heat to medium-low, and cover the pot, leaving the lid slightly ajar if it doesn't have a hole for steam. Cook, stirring frequently, until the oil appears around the edges of the pot and the texture is thick but still soupy, about 30 minutes. Then add the fried chicken pieces and any more liquid that has accumulated in the bowl. Cook for 10 more minutes, uncovered, stirring occasionally.

21 Add the okra and the blanched cabbage to the pot, give it a stir, and then put the 1 whole Scotch bonnet chile, if using, right in the center of the pot, letting it float on top (don't stir it in). Cook, uncovered, stirring occasionally, until the okra is cooked through, about 15 minutes. Add the 1 teaspoon powdered chicken bouillon, if using, and if not, add the remaining 3½ teaspoons of Diamond Crystal kosher salt, and cook for 5 more minutes, stirring every once in a while. Taste for salt.

22 **Serve and eat the sauce pâte d'arachide:** Serve the sauce pâte d'arachide hot or warm over hot white rice, with a little of the Scotch bonnet chile, if desired.

Kotopoulo Me Patates Sto Fourno

(GREEK ROASTED CHICKEN AND POTATOES WITH LEMON AND OREGANO)

Instructor: Despina Economou

"When I was growing up, we didn't have ovens in our homes, so we would take a pan of potatoes and chicken to the bakery to roast—it was just so delicious." —Despina

When Despina was growing up in Greece, this was always considered a Sunday dish, partly because you saved meat for the weekends, and partly because everyone in town had to do their roasting in the ovens at the local bakery. By 10 o'clock in the morning on Sundays, the bakery would have fifty dishes lined up for roasting, says Despina—so many that the bakers would have to take Polaroid photos to keep track of which was whose. Made in your own kitchen, these simply dressed bone-in chicken thighs are perfect for anytime—they're so simple but so homey and satisfying. Despina always uses the best-quality wild oregano and extra-virgin olive oil—both always Greek. If you can do the same, it will really make this extra delicious.

 Serve with: the Greek salad on page 236 or the boiled greens on page 271.

3 pounds (1.4 kg) skin-on, bone-in chicken thighs (6 to 9)

1½ pounds (680 g) russet potatoes (about 2 large)

½ ounce (15 g) garlic (about 4 medium cloves)

¼ cup (60 ml) fresh lemon juice (from about 2 to 3 lemons)

6 tablespoons extra-virgin olive oil

1 tablespoon Diamond Crystal kosher salt

1½ teaspoons dried oregano (preferably Greek wild oregano)

½ teaspoon freshly ground black pepper

1 **Prepare the ingredients:** Take the 3 pounds (1.4 kg) bone-in chicken thighs (6 to 9) out of the refrigerator and let them sit for 30 minutes at room temperature before you move on to the next step.

2 Preheat the oven to 375°F (190°C) and position one rack in the middle of the oven.

3 Peel the 1½ pounds (680 g) russet potatoes (about 2 large) and remove any black spots with the tip of a paring knife. Cut the potatoes lengthwise into four wedges. If you have large potatoes (longer than 3 inches/7.6 cm), cut the wedges in half so you end up with 8 shorter pieces. Put the potato wedges in a very large mixing bowl.

4 Put the chicken thighs on top of the potatoes in the mixing bowl and set them aside.

5 **Make the sauce:** Use a garlic press to press the ½ ounce (15 g) garlic (about 4 medium cloves) into a small mixing bowl. (If you don't have a garlic press, you can grate the garlic on the small holes of a box grater or a Microplane.) It will come out to about 1 tablespoon of garlic.

6 Squeeze the ¼ cup (60 ml) fresh lemon juice (from about 2 to 3 lemons) and add it to the garlic. Add the 6 tablespoons extra-virgin olive oil, 1 tablespoon Diamond Crystal kosher salt, 1½ teaspoons dried oregano, and ½ teaspoon freshly ground black pepper. Use a fork to whisk everything together.

7 Pour the sauce over the chicken and potatoes and mix everything together well with your hands.

8 **Bake the chicken and potatoes:** Put the seasoned chicken and potatoes in a 9- by 13-inch (23 cm by 33 cm) baking dish. Use a

spoon or your hands to spread out the chicken and potatoes, making sure the potatoes are scattered evenly throughout—some may even be slightly under or over the chicken thighs; that's fine. (The goal is that the chicken and potatoes will be close together in the dish but not too piled up.) Add ½ cup (120 ml) water to the baking dish, drizzling it in along the sides so it doesn't wash the seasoning off the chicken.

9   Tightly cover the dish with heavy-duty foil (or use two layers).

10 Roast the chicken and potatoes on the middle rack of the oven for 40 minutes, then remove the foil from the dish. (There may be a lot of liquid at this point; that's fine.) Continue roasting for another 20 minutes, or until the chicken is browned and the potatoes are soft. If you're using a thermometer, it should read at least 165°F (75°C) when inserted into a thigh near the bone.

11 **Serve and eat the chicken and potatoes:** Serve the dish hot, making sure each person gets at least one thigh and several potatoes.

Pollo a la Sal con Camotes Asados

(ARGENTINIAN WHOLE CHICKEN COOKED ON A BED OF SALT WITH BAKED SWEET POTATOES)

Instructor: Mirta Rinaldi

"It's a wonderful recipe—you don't do any work!" —Mirta

There are a zillion ways to make roast chicken. I've made it many different ways myself, and this is definitely the most foolproof recipe I've tried. Every time, the chicken comes out moist and juicy with crisp golden skin—and it's fast, too, with no fussing as it cooks. Mirta learned this recipe from her cousin, who's an airline pilot. Whenever he would have a stopover in New York and stay over at her home, he would make it for her. It feels a little unsettling to pour that much salt onto a baking sheet, but don't worry, it doesn't make the chicken salty. What it does is absorb all the moisture that gets released as the chicken cooks, helping to create the crispy skin and juicy interior. Plus, because you put a sheet of parchment paper down first, cleanup is super easy. Mirta carves the chicken shortly after it comes out of the oven, instead of letting it rest for a long time. She does it right on a deep serving platter, so all those delicious juices are captured. Then she takes a pinch of the salt that cooked with the chicken and uses that to season the collected juices on the platter.

Mirta always bakes some whole sweet potatoes alongside—a fast, easy way to make this into a full meal. She typically wraps one sweet potato per person individually with foil and puts them on another rack while the chicken roasts, as they take exactly the same amount of time to cook. (If she's making more than four, she'll put them, unwrapped, on a separate parchment-lined baking sheet.) Then she splits each baked sweet potato open and seasons it with salt, freshly ground black pepper, and extra-virgin olive oil.

Note that it's important to use granule-style garlic powder rather than the soft, powdery variety (often they will both be labeled "garlic powder"). The powder kind will clump and burn on the chicken skin. The oregano is a very Mendozan touch. If you end up with a chicken that's smaller or larger in size than what we call for here, just watch the roasting time. A general rule of thumb is 15 minutes per pound at this temperature—even the largest chicken is usually fully done by about 1 hour and 20 minutes.

Serve with: a green salad.

One 4- to 5-pound (1.8–2.3 kg) whole chicken
Kitchen twine
4 cups (548 g) Diamond Crystal kosher salt
1 teaspoon granulated garlic powder
1 tablespoon dried oregano
4 medium whole sweet potatoes, optional

1 **Bring the chicken to room temperature:** About 30 minutes before you want to make this dish, take the 4- to 5-pound (1.8–2.3 kg) whole chicken out of the refrigerator.

2 **Preheat the oven:** Preheat the oven to 400°F (200°C). Make sure one of your racks is at the bottom of the oven and that the other racks are moved high enough so that there is room above it to place the chicken.

3 **Prepare the chicken:** After the chicken has rested for 30 minutes, use a clean pair of scissors to remove any pockets of extra yellow fat in or near the cavity. Be careful not to break the skin itself—a little fat left on is better than broken skin.

Continued

CHICKEN

4 Tie the legs together with kitchen twine—wrap it first around one leg, then over and around the other leg, bringing them together. (This will keep the chicken from drying out.)

5 Put the chicken on a plate and pat it dry with paper towels, then set it aside while you prepare the salt.

6 Place a sheet of parchment paper on a baking sheet. Spread the 4 cups (548 g) Diamond Crystal kosher salt in the center of the baking sheet in an oval shape. The salt should be around 1 inch (2.5 cm) thick and wide enough that it extends beyond the chicken by at least 1 inch (2.5 cm) when you set it down. Set the baking sheet aside.

7 Sprinkle the 1 teaspoon granulated garlic powder all over the chicken, then sprinkle the 1 tablespoon dried oregano all over the chicken, crushing it between your fingers as you do.

8 **Cook the chicken:** Put the chicken, breast-side up, on top of the salt bed on the baking sheet. Do your best to tuck the tips of the wings under the body of the bird, so the tips don't burn.

9 Wash your hands, then put the baking sheet with the chicken in the oven on the bottom rack. If you're making the sweet potatoes, wrap them in foil and put them on the rack around the chicken (or on the one above it.) Set a timer for 1 hour.

10 Let the chicken roast for 1 hour and then check it for doneness—if you're using a thermometer, it should read at least 165°F (75°C) inserted into the innermost part of the thigh. (A 4-pound/1.8 kg chicken should be done in 1 hour to an hour and 15 minutes, and a 5-pound/2.26 kg chicken in about 1 hour and 15 to 20 minutes.) The skin should be very crispy and golden by this point, as well.

11 The sweet potatoes are done when they're easily pierced with a knife or fork. Remove them to a serving plate.

12 **Finish the chicken:** When the chicken is done, immediately remove it from the baking sheet with two spatulas to a large serving platter deep enough to catch any juices. You will want to brush off most of the salt if any is sticking to the bottom, but a few crystals are fine. Take a small pinch of salt from the baking sheet and sprinkle it around the chicken so that it will season the juices that get released when you cut into it.

13 **Serve and eat the chicken:** Carve and serve the chicken right away, making sure to give each person some of the crispy skin and a sweet potato, if using. Spoon some of the collected juices on top of the meat.

Murgir Mangsho

SERVES 4 TO 6

(BANGLADESHI CHICKEN AND POTATO CURRY)

Instructor: Afsari Jahan

"This is my son's favorite recipe. When he was little, he would cry if I didn't make it!" —Afsari

You can find tons of recipes for chicken curries—curry is really just the name for a South Asian/Southeast Asian dish served with a gravy or sauce—but this is the one Afsari makes for her family on weeknights. It might seem complicated at first, in that you have to grind some spices and puree the ginger and garlic together into a paste, but if you get those together in advance (see page 23), this is very easy to cook, and so delicious and fragrant. One thing I love about many of Afsari's curries is how she uses onions cut in two ways. Half of the onion is finely diced in a food processor so that it melts into the sauce, and the other is sliced and fried in the oil along with the spices.

I also love Afsari's extra step of sprinkling fresh roasted ground cumin (page 23) at the end, in addition to using it earlier in the dish. It brings out all the different aspects of this wonderful spice, with deeper notes from the cumin that cooks with the curry, and a little bit of brightness from adding it at the end. Like nearly all of our instructors, she uses bone-in chicken parts cut into smaller pieces so that even more bone marrow is exposed, which adds more flavor and nutrients to the gravy. As with Nawida's chicken curry on page 53, this dish is usually eaten with the hands, and the small pieces of chicken on the bone are also easier to handle (just keep an eye out for any small bone shards that may have split off during cooking).

Afsari usually just buys a whole chicken, then cleans it and cuts it into the parts she wants to use for this curry. (For instructions, see Breaking Down a Whole Chicken, page 32.) She buys freshly butchered young chickens from a halal butcher, and her chickens are often only about three pounds, smaller than a typical grocery-store chicken. So, I usually just buy three pounds of parts, as that is what this recipe calls for. Use a mix of bone-in chicken breasts, thighs, drumsticks, or wings.

Serve with: rice, preferably basmati, and/or roti (page 173), and any vegetable side you like. You can also pair it with slices of cucumber and onion, or a simple chopped salad with cucumbers, tomatoes, red onion, cilantro, and finely chopped green chiles, dressed with salt and lemon juice to taste.

5 whole black peppercorns
4 green cardamom pods
4 whole cloves
1 Indian bay leaf (page 21) or 2 bay laurel leaves
1 2-inch (5 cm) cinnamon stick (about 2 g)
3 tablespoons garlic-ginger paste (page 23)
¾ pound (340 g) yellow onion (about 1 large)
⅓ pound (150 g) plum tomato (about 1 large)
¾ pound (340 g) russet potato (about 1 large)
1 teaspoon ground turmeric
⅛ to 1 teaspoon red chile powder, to taste
2 teaspoons roasted coriander powder (page 24)
2 teaspoons roasted cumin powder (page 23), divided
3 to 3½ pounds (1.5–1.6 kg) bone-in chicken pieces, such as breasts, thighs, or legs
½ cup (120 ml) neutral oil
1 tablespoon Diamond Crystal kosher salt
1 lemon or lime, cut into thin wedges, for serving

1   **Ready your ingredients:** Put the 5 whole black peppercorns, 4 green cardamom pods, 4 whole cloves, 1 Indian bay leaf or 2 bay laurel leaves,

Continued

53   CHICKEN

and the 2-inch (5 cm) cinnamon stick (about 2 g), preferably Indian flat cinnamon, together in a small bowl and set it aside. This is your whole garam masala.

2   If you haven't already, prepare the 3 tablespoons garlic-ginger paste (page 23), 2 teaspoons roasted coriander powder (page 24), and 2 teaspoons roasted cumin powder (page 23).

3   Peel the ¾ pound (340 g) yellow onion (about 1 large), trim the ends, and cut it in half from root to stem. Slice 1 onion half as thinly as you can, from root to stem. You'll have about 1 cup of sliced onions. Set this aside.

4   Roughly chop the remaining onion and put it in a food processor. Pulse it, scraping down the sides from time to time, until you have a chunky puree, not a fine paste. If you don't have a food processor, you can grate the onion on the large holes of a box grater. You will have about 1 cup of onion puree. Set the pureed onions aside.

Don't use a blender to puree the onions. It will turn them into a fine paste, which is not what you want.

5   Cut the ⅓ pound (150 g) plum tomatoes (about 1 large) into quarters and remove the white membrane near the stem end (it won't soften as it cooks). Cut the quarters into a ¼-inch (0.6 cm) dice and set it aside. You should have about ¾ cup of chopped tomatoes.

6   Peel the ¾ pound (340 g) russet potato (about 1 large) and remove any eyes or dark spots. Cut the potato into four pieces lengthwise, so you end up with four long wedges, then cut the quarters in half. Put them in a mixing bowl and cover them with tap water, then set them aside.

7   Measure out 1 teaspoon ground turmeric, ⅛ to 1 teaspoon red chile powder, 2 teaspoons roasted coriander powder, and 1 teaspoon roasted cumin powder into a small bowl and set it by the stove.

8   **Prepare the chicken:** If you're using a whole chicken, follow the steps on page 32 to cut the chicken apart before moving on to the next step.

9   Use your hands to remove all the skin and any pockets of yellowish fat underneath from all the chicken parts. If you see any leftover scraps of tendon or blood (or anything else that isn't bone or meat), remove them with a paring knife or scissors and discard them.

A paper towel can make it easier to grip the skin to pull it off, and you can use a pair of clean kitchen scissors to cut away the fat if it doesn't easily pull away. A little leftover skin or fat is fine—just try to remove as much as possible so that the gravy ends up flavorful but not greasy.

10 Cut the 3 pounds (1.5 kg) skinless, bone-in chicken parts into two or three smaller pieces around 2½ to 3 inches (6 to 8 cm) wide. (See page 32 for tips on how to do this—for large supermarket chicken breasts, for example, Afsari cuts them into three pieces.)

11 **Cook the curry:** Heat the ½ cup (120 ml) neutral oil in a 12-inch (30 cm) frying pan or skillet with deep sides over medium-high heat. When the oil is very hot and begins to shimmer, add the sliced onions carefully, so they don't splatter. Fry them until they've shriveled up and are lightly browned on the edges, stirring and tossing them around frequently. This usually takes 4 to 10 minutes, depending on the pan.

Afsari's trick to tell if the oil is hot enough is to add one slice of onion: If it floats immediately instead of sinking to the bottom, the oil is ready.

12 When the onions are browned, lower the heat to medium and stir in the whole garam masala until coated in the oil. Stir in the chopped or grated onion and the 1 tablespoon Diamond

Continued

Crystal kosher salt. Cook, stirring, for another 30 seconds or so.

13 Stir in the 3 tablespoons garlic-ginger paste and cook over medium heat, stirring occasionally, until you begin to see oily bubbles around the edges of the pan, 1 to 2 minutes.

14 Stir in ¼ cup (60 ml) tap water, then stir in the mixed spices. Cook over medium heat, stirring occasionally, until you begin to see oily bubbles around the edges of the pan, 1 to 2 minutes.

15 Stir in the diced tomato, and then add the chicken pieces. Stir them in until all the pieces are coated in the sauce.

16 Drain the potatoes and add them to the pot, stirring to make sure they're covered in the sauce. Let the chicken and potatoes cook, uncovered, at a simmer over medium-low heat for about 20 minutes, until the sauce has thickened and you begin to see oily bubbles around the edges of the pan. Stir occasionally to make sure nothing is sticking to the bottom—if it is, your heat is too high.

17 Add 1 cup (240 ml) tap water and cover the pot.

18 Cook, covered, over medium-low heat until the potatoes are tender and the chicken is cooked through, 20 to 30 minutes. To test the potatoes and the chicken for doneness, gently slide a sharp knife into the thickest piece—if it goes through easily, they're done. (If you're using a thermometer, it should read at least 165°F/75°C when inserted near a bone.)

19 Remove the lid, stir in the remaining 1 teaspoon roasted cumin powder, and let everything cook for 2 minutes more. Then turn off the heat and cover the pot until you're ready to serve.

20 **Serve and eat the curry:** Serve the curry hot, warm, or at room temperature on individual plates or bowls, usually with basmati rice or roti and a lemon or lime wedge on the side. (The citrus should be squeezed over the entire plate, including the rice.) You can also serve it family-style in the middle of the table.

Yipin Benon

Yipin was born in the small town of Silly in Burkina Faso in West Africa, though she grew up throughout the country. Her father, a teacher, would move to a new town every few years to work at a different school, bringing Yipin and her seven brothers and sisters with him. They were her friends, so she never felt alone even at a new school—they would walk to and from classes every day as a crew, always there for each other. Yipin always helped with the cooking when she was growing up. As a very young girl, she learned the art of making a cooking fire—carefully building a stand out of rocks to hold the pot and gathering sticks, dried leaves, and other kindling to ensure the larger cooking logs would catch fire. When she was seven, she was assigned her own dish: tô. These cornmeal-based dough balls are a staple of Burkinabé cuisine, and with the guidance of her mother and older sisters, Yipin soon became a master at making the perfect tô.

In 2010, Yipin moved to New York City, where she went on to get a master's degree and become an accountant. She also became well-known in her community for the delicious West African food that she would make and sell, and she loves to teach her West African friends in New York how to re-create the food from their home countries with ingredients in the United States. Today, she lives with her husband and three young children in the Bronx.

What do you think is special about West African and Burkinabé cuisine? The taste of West African food is really unique. Our food has a lot of different flavors and ingredients in every recipe so that when you try it, you want to eat it again soon! The goal when we cook this food is that once you start eating, it will be hard to stop, because it's so good.

What do you enjoy about cooking? I enjoy when I cook and when I see people enjoy my cooking. And myself, I enjoy eating. I love eating. That's why I cook what I like to eat. When I see something that I like, I learn, I practice, and I make it. And generally, whenever I try, I succeed. And anytime I cook something very rare, from my country, that you cannot find in America, I'll text the people I know and they will come. They'll be so glad to come and get the food. And they say, "You always make me feel like I'm still home." I feel happy making other people happy.

What do you think is the secret to being a good cook? If you cook with love, your food will taste good. My kids say, "Mom, your food is good. What did you put in there?" I say, "I put a lot of love in it." Do everything you are doing with love and you will see you'll succeed, because when you learn something that you don't love, you won't be able to reproduce it and get the taste you're looking for. Also, you need to love food yourself! You need to like to eat.

Do you have any favorite home remedies from the kitchen? When anyone in my family has a cold, I make pepper soup. I cook chicken or lamb in water with Jamaican hot peppers, tomato, and onion. After everything is cooked, I take out the peppers, onion, and tomato and blend them in the blender, and then put them back in. You drink this, you'll start sweating, everything comes out, and you are free. Also, we boil water with bay leaves, and then you cover your head with a blanket and you inhale the steam—that helps when you are coughing or congested.

How do you plan out your cooking every week? Really, I go by what I want to eat. I generally ask my family, "What do you want? Honey, what do you want to eat today?" But they usually want me to decide. Every weekend I cook for the week. I cook two different foods, and I get my chopped beef sandwich ready (page 68), which is for the kids' breakfast. I cook more on Saturdays. It's the day that everybody's home—my husband, my kids, we are all home. I want to make it happy and sweet.

Yipin Benon

ビーフ

牛肉

Carne

গরুর মাংস

Мол гӯшти

Moεγάρι

بقر

Говедина

BEEF

گوشت گاو

گاؤ

गाई को मासु

Bife

Sapi

बिफ

Bœuf

Tacos de Bistec con Salsa Roja, Salsa Verde y Guacamole

(MEXICAN RIB EYE STEAK TACOS WITH RED SALSA, GREEN SALSA, AND GUACAMOLE)

Instructor: Angelica Vargas

"The sound of your knife chopping the meat is nearly as important to the enjoyment of this dish as the flavor."
—Angie

Angie's steak tacos are the best you'll ever taste. She uses boneless rib eye steaks, which are more expensive but come edged with delicious fat, which is really the secret ingredient. She cuts the steaks thin, cooks them until the fat crisps and sizzles, then loudly chops it all together, just like taqueros do at the taco shop. Then she gently reheats the meat with its juices before folding it into warm fresh corn tortillas. This might seem like the exact opposite of what you've been taught to do with steak to avoid overcooking it, but the goal here is not medium-rare. Instead, you want everything cooked through, with the edges and fat a little bit crispy.

Raised in the state of Monterrey in northern Mexico, Angie grew up watching her mom and aunts grill steak in the outdoor kitchen on her grandparents' ranch, a tradition she's adapted to New York City. In nice weather, Angie buys 20 pounds of steaks and heads to the park to grill for family and friends, because she knows there will be leftovers to freeze for tacos when the urge hits at a later point. She also always freezes the raw meat slightly before cutting it into thinner steaks, to make it easier to cut. (You can scale this recipe up or down as needed, says Angie. A good rule of thumb is ½ to 1 pound of steak per person.)

Angie also always tells her students that good meat, good tortillas, and a good salsa make the best taco. That's why I strongly recommend you make at least one of Angie's very simple salsas to go with these, or her own extra-special version of guacamole—recipes for all follow—if not also her corn tortillas on page 165. If you make everything, this meal will blow your socks off

(and it's what my older daughter Sylvie often requests for her special birthday meal). The salsas elevate these steak tacos to another level, but they're also great to have in your fridge to put on just about anything. Both salsas are so easy to make and their flavors are perfectly balanced. But if you don't have much time, these tacos are still very, very good topped with chopped white onion, cilantro, and a squeeze of lime.

Serve with: any (or all) of Angie's condiments on pages 65–66, her habanero and lime pickled onions on page 118, and thinly sliced radishes and cucumbers, sprinkled with lime juice and salt. You can also serve these with the red rice on page 176 and black beans on page 144.

2 to 3 pounds (1–1.4 kg) boneless rib eye steaks
Diamond Crystal kosher salt
Freshly ground black pepper
¾ pound (340 g) white onion (about 1 medium)
¼ pound (115 g) fresh cilantro (about 1 bunch)
1 cucumber, optional
5 radishes, optional
2 or 3 limes
Warm corn tortillas (page 165)
Salsa Roja (recipe follows)
Salsa Verde (recipe follows)
Guacamole (recipe follows)

1   **Briefly freeze the steaks:** About 30 to 40 minutes before you want to make the tacos,

Continued

put the 2 to 3 pounds (1–1.4 kg) boneless rib eye steaks in the freezer.

2   If you're making the salsa and/or the guacamole, this is a good time to make them.

3   **Prepare the steaks:** By 40 minutes, the steaks should have stiffened considerably but will not be fully frozen. Put them on a cutting board, place one hand flat on top of a piece of steak, then use a sharp knife in your other hand to slowly cut each steak in half horizontally, so you end up with two thin steaks. Repeat this process with the rest of the pieces of steak: The goal is to make all the pieces even in thickness so they cook at the same time. If you mess up a bit, it's fine—the steaks will be chopped up once they're cooked.

You can also use a pair of kitchen scissors to cut the steaks—poke a hole in the side with the tips, then snip along the edge and up through the steak. I learned this trick from Angie, and it works great.

4   Sprinkle the steaks with Diamond Crystal kosher salt and freshly ground black pepper on both sides and set them aside.

5   Turn on your exhaust fan, if you have one, and open a window in or near your kitchen.

6   Heat a grill pan or griddle (preferably with ridges) or a large heavy-bottomed skillet (not nonstick) over medium-high heat until it's very hot, 10 to 15 minutes. (You can also use two smaller suitable pans to cook the meat at the same time, if you need to.) When the pan is ready, you won't be able to hold your hand 4 inches (10 cm) above it for more than 10 seconds.

7   Put a medium saucepan or pot with a lid near the stove—this is where you'll put your steaks after they're cooked.

8   **Prepare the accompaniments:** While you're waiting for the griddle to heat, peel the ¾ pound (340 g) white onion (about 1 medium). Cut it into pieces about ⅓ inch (1 cm) wide. Put it in a small serving bowl and set it aside. Trim all but the tender stems from the ¼ pound (115 g) fresh cilantro (about 1 bunch) and finely mince it. Put it in a small serving bowl and set it aside. Slice the cucumber and radishes, if using. Put them on a small serving plate and set aside. Cut the 2 or 3 limes into wedges, put them on a small serving plate, and set it aside.

9   **Cook the steaks:** When the pan is ready, put the steaks (as many as will fit) on the pan and use a spatula or tongs to press them down so that they are flat against the bottom of the pan, so they cook evenly. Take a pair of kitchen scissors and cut any tendons, fat, or other connective tissues that are keeping the steaks from lying flat. When the steaks are browned on the bottom—this can take anywhere from 2 to 4 minutes—flip them. Once they're flipped, again take a pair of kitchen scissors and cut any tendons, fat, or other connective tissues that are keeping the steaks from lying flat.

10 Cook the steaks for another 3 to 6 minutes, just until they are browned on all sides, the fat is crispy on the edges, and there is no longer any visible blood. Use your tongs and scissors to flip or snip or swirl the steaks as they cook—you don't have to be gentle, you can move them around to make sure they are cooking evenly and getting brown on the fatty edges. As the pieces of steak are done, put them and any browned bits into the medium saucepan or pot with a lid. Cover the pan or pot and let the steak rest for at least 10 minutes, or while you prepare the tortillas. This step ensures you end up with all the juices from the meat and keeps the steak warm and easier to reheat.

11 **Prepare the tortillas:** Either make the corn tortillas on page 165, or heat premade ones on both sides on a hot griddle or heavy-bottomed

pan over medium-high heat until they're slightly charred in spots. Stack them in a clean cotton kitchen towel and keep them covered until you're ready to serve the tacos.

12. **Finish the steak:** Remove the steak pieces from the pot with tongs, shaking off any juices. Place them on a clean cutting board and use your largest knife or a cleaver to roughly cut them first into strips lengthwise and then crosswise into rough squares—these pieces don't have to be perfectly even. Then use your largest knife to go back and forth over the slices, breaking them down until the fat is distributed throughout and the pieces are chopped and blended together, almost minced or diced. Add the chopped steak back to your pot and mix it together with any juices that might have collected at the bottom. Gently rewarm the steak over medium-low heat just until hot.

13. **Serve and eat the tacos:** Put the steak, warm tortillas, chopped onion, minced cilantro, lime wedges, and sliced radishes and cucumbers, if serving, out on the table so that each person can make their own tacos. Encourage everyone to layer some hot steak on the warm tortilla, to sprinkle the top with onion and cilantro (and with salsa and guacamole, if using), to give it a squeeze of lime, and to eat immediately. Eat the radishes and cucumbers between bites of taco.

Salsa Roja

(RED TOMATO SALSA)

MAKES ABOUT 1 CUP (240 ML)

Use half to one jalapeño for moderate heat, two for a fairly hot salsa, and three for a salsa that's very hot. You can also remove some or all of the seeds and membrane. Note that the salsa will taste spicier when hot and less spicy once it cools.

½ pound (225 g) plum tomatoes (about 2 medium)
1 to 3 jalapeño chiles
2 teaspoons Diamond Crystal kosher salt

1. Put the ½ pound (225 g) plum tomatoes (about 2 medium) and the 1 to 3 jalapeño chiles in a medium saucepan. Fill the pot halfway with water. Bring the pot to a boil over high heat and boil until the tomato skins crack and the chiles turn dusty green in color, 10 to 15 minutes. Turn off the heat, drain the water, and let everything cool until it's no longer hot. (If you have a high-speed blender, you don't have to wait—you can move ahead to the next step.)

2. Remove the stems from the jalapeños (and the seeds and membrane, if desired). If you want to use ½ jalapeño, cut it in half. Put the stemmed jalapeños, the boiled tomatoes, and 2 teaspoons Diamond Crystal kosher salt in a blender and puree on medium-high speed until the mixture is smooth. Serve the salsa warm or room temperature.

Continued

Salsa Verde

(GREEN TOMATILLO SALSA)

MAKES ABOUT 2 CUPS (475 ML)

Use half to one jalapeño for a little bit of heat, two for a fairly hot salsa, and three for a salsa that's very hot. The dried chiles add more flavor but also a lot more spice. You can also remove some or all of the seeds and membrane. Note that the salsa will taste spicier when hot and less spicy once it cools.

½ pound (225 g) tomatillos (5 to 6 medium)

1 to 3 jalapeño chiles

1 to 3 dried arbol chiles, pequin chiles, or morita chiles, optional

⅛ pound (60 g) fresh cilantro (about ½ bunch)

¼ ounce (7 g) garlic (about 2 medium cloves)

⅛ pound (60 g) white onion (about ¼ medium)

2 teaspoons Diamond Crystal kosher salt

1   Remove the husks from the ½ pound (225 g) tomatillos (5 to 6 medium) and rinse them under running water. Put the husked tomatillos in a medium saucepan with the 1 to 3 jalapeño chiles and 1 to 3 dried chiles (if using). Fill the pot halfway with water. Bring the pot to a boil over high heat and boil until the tomatillos are soft, their skins crack, and the jalapeños turn dusty green in color, about 15 minutes. Turn off the heat, drain off the water, and let everything cool completely. (If you have a high-speed blender, you don't have to wait, and you can move ahead to the next step.)

2   Remove the stems from the jalapeños (and the seeds and membrane from all the chiles, if desired) and put them in a blender. (If you want to use ½ jalapeño, cut it in half and add only half.) Remove the stems from the ⅛ pound (60 g) fresh cilantro (about ½ bunch) up to where the leaves begin and add the cilantro to the blender.

3   Peel the ¼ ounce (7 g) garlic (about 2 medium cloves) and the ⅛ pound (60 g) white onion (about ¼ medium). Put them with the boiled tomatillos and 2 teaspoons Diamond Crystal kosher salt in the blender and add 2 tablespoons of water. Puree everything on medium-high speed until the mixture is mostly smooth. Serve the salsa warm or room temperature.

Guacamole

MAKES ABOUT 3 CUPS (700 ML)

There are a million recipes for guacamole, but Angie's guacamole is really special. First off, she uses grape tomatoes and removes the seeds. This step might sound fussy, but it really is part of what makes this guacamole so good, as it keeps it from becoming watery. Second, the proportions of her ingredients are perfect. And third, the way she cuts the avocado results in a very pleasing mixture of whole pieces and mashed pieces. Whenever I make it, my kids can't get enough. I also like how Angie takes a chef's knife, whacks it into the pit, twists the knife, and then removes the pit—I recommend trying it, but be very careful taking the pit off the knife!

½ to 3 jalapeño chiles

⅓ pound (150 g) white onion (about ½ medium)

⅛ pound (60 g) fresh cilantro (about ½ bunch)

5 ounces (140 g) grape tomatoes (about 16)

2 ripe Hass avocados

1 teaspoon Diamond Crystal kosher salt, or more to taste

1 tablespoon fresh lime juice (from ½ to 1 lime), or more to taste

1 Remove the stem from the ½ to 3 jalapeño chiles, remove the membrane and seeds, if desired, then cut them into ⅛-inch (0.3 cm) dice. Transfer the jalapeños to a medium mixing bowl. Peel the ⅓ pound (150 g) white onion (about ½ medium) and cut it into ⅛-inch (0.3 cm) dice. You'll have about 1 heaping cup. Add it to the mixing bowl. Remove the stems from the ⅛ pound (60 g) fresh cilantro (about ½ bunch) up to where the leaves begin, then finely mince it. You'll get about a packed ½ cup. Add it to the mixing bowl. Halve the 5 ounces (140 g) grape tomatoes (about 16), remove and discard the seeds, then cut them into ⅛-inch (0.3 cm) dice. You'll get about ¾ cup. Add them to the mixing bowl.

2 Halve the 2 avocados and remove and discard the pits. Use a small paring knife to thinly slice the flesh lengthwise, in lines about ⅛ inch (0.3 cm) apart, then do the same crosswise, being careful the knife doesn't go through the skin. (You're making a cross-hatch.) Scoop out the flesh with a large metal or wooden spoon directly into the mixing bowl. Add the 1 teaspoon Diamond Crystal kosher salt and 1 tablespoon fresh lime juice (from ½ to 1 lime) to the bowl.

3 Use 2 large spoons to mix everything together, like tossing a salad, while gently mashing the avocado into the rest of the chopped vegetables—the goal is that some of the guacamole is crushed, while some is still in chunky pieces. Taste for salt and lime juice and add more if desired. Serve immediately.

Sandwiches de Viande Hachee

SERVES 4 TO 6

(BURKINABÉ CHOPPED MEAT SANDWICHES)

Instructor: Yipin Benon

"I used to always buy these from a shop, but then I taught myself to make it at home, so I wouldn't have to buy any premade stuff for my family." —Yipin

This popular West African sandwich is like a cousin to the banh mi. Also from a former French colony, it uses a warm baguette, smeared with mayo and hot sauce, to hold a filling of savory meat and crunchy, juicy vegetables—the contrast of flavors and textures is fabulous. Yipin's family often eats these sandwiches for breakfast, or she packs them up for lunches for herself and her kids. My kids love these sandwiches, too. Yipin will usually make a big batch of the meat and then use it for breakfast or lunch for about three days. The beef and vegetables are cooked for what might seem like a long time, but it results in meat that's filled with umami and a depth of flavor even if you choose not to use the Sazón, which Yipin likes to add for extra oomph—the beef will be browned and crispy and the vegetables will be totally melted into the meat. It's really important to use a nonstick pot for this recipe, otherwise you'll scorch the meat instead of getting it to the perfectly brown, crisped-up state that makes it so good.

For the chopped beef

1½ pounds (680 g) ground beef (20% fat)

½ pound (225 g) red onion (about 1 medium)

⅓ pound (150 g) red bell pepper (about ½ large)

⅓ pound (150 g) yellow bell pepper (about ½ large)

¾ ounce (20 g) garlic (about 6 medium cloves)

½ pound (225 g) plum tomatoes (about 2 medium)

2 Goya Sazón seasoning packets, any flavor, such as cilantro and tomato, optional

1 teaspoon Diamond Crystal kosher salt (or 2 teaspoons, if not using the Sazón)

½ cup (120 ml) neutral oil

For the sandwiches

½ pound (225 g) cucumber (about ½ large)

⅓ pound (150 g) yellow onion (about 1 small)

½ head iceberg lettuce

Soft French bread or 4 to 6 long sandwich rolls

Mayonnaise

Hot sauce, optional

1   **Start cooking the beef:** Put the 1½ pounds (680 g) ground beef in a medium (3-quart/2.8 L) nonstick saucepan, add 1½ cups (350 ml) tap water, and set over medium-high heat. Use a long wooden spoon to break up the meat into the water as it cooks, making sure the bottom doesn't burn. Cover the pot, leaving the lid slightly ajar if it doesn't have a hole for steam, and cook, stirring occasionally, for 10 minutes. Then lower the heat to medium and cook for 10 more minutes, stirring occasionally.

2   **Prepare the vegetables:** While the beef simmers, peel the ½ pound (225 g) red onion (about 1 medium). Cut it into ⅓-inch (1 cm) dice. You should have about 1½ cups. Set it aside.

3   Remove the stem and membrane from the ⅓ pound (150 g) red bell pepper (about ½ large) and ⅓ pound (150 g) yellow bell pepper (about ½ large). Cut them into ⅓-inch (1 cm) dice. You should have about 2 cups. Set aside in a separate bowl.

Continued

4 Peel the ¾ ounce (20 g) garlic (about 6 medium cloves) and grate it over the fine holes of a box grater. You should have about 1 tablespoon. Set aside in a separate bowl.

5 Cut the ½ pound (225 g) plum tomatoes (about 2 medium) into ½-inch (1.3 cm) dice. You should have about 1⅓ cups. Set aside in a separate bowl.

6 **Add the vegetables to the meat:** After the meat has simmered for 20 minutes, stir in the chopped red onion and let it cook for 1 minute, just until it softens slightly, then stir in the chopped red and yellow peppers. Cover the pot, leaving the lid slightly ajar if it doesn't have a hole for steam, raise the heat to medium-high, and cook for 5 minutes, then stir in the grated garlic and the 2 Goya Sazón seasoning packets, if using.

7 Cover the pot, leaving the lid slightly ajar if it doesn't have a hole for steam, and continue to cook for 5 minutes, then stir in the chopped tomatoes and the 1 teaspoon Diamond Crystal kosher salt (or 2 teaspoons if you're not using the Sazón). Keep the heat at medium-high so that the pot cooks at a strong simmer, and cook, uncovered and stirring occasionally, until you don't see any liquid bubbles in the pot. This usually takes at least 20 minutes, but the time will vary depending on your vegetables and your beef—it may take longer. Stir the pot every 5 minutes or so.

8 Once all the water is gone from the pot, add ½ cup (120 ml) neutral oil, mix it in, and when you hear it sizzle, turn the heat to very low. Cook for another 30 minutes, uncovered, stirring every 5 to 10 minutes. Keep the beef warm until you're ready to serve it. (If you want to make this in advance, it lasts for 2 to 3 days in the fridge but doesn't freeze well.)

9 **Prepare the bread and toppings:** Peel the ½ pound (225 g) cucumber (about ½ large),

scrape out the seeds, and cut it into ¼-inch (0.6 cm) dice. Put it in a small bowl.

10 Peel the ⅓ pound (150 g) yellow onion (about 1 small) and cut it into ¼-inch (0.6 cm) dice. Put it in a separate bowl and set it aside.

11 Cut the ½ head iceberg lettuce into shreds about ⅓ inch (1 cm) wide.

12 Warm the soft French bread or 4 to 6 long sandwich rolls.

13 **Make the sandwiches:** If you're using French bread, cut it into 4 to 6 pieces. Slice the bread open about three-quarters of the way through, like a hot dog bun or hoagie roll. Spread some mayo on the bread. Spoon in some warm beef. Use your hands to sprinkle a little cucumber and onion across the top of the beef as desired, and then a little of the lettuce. Add hot sauce, as desired. Serve while still warm. (You can also wrap these up and take them for lunch or a picnic and eat them at room temperature.)

Entraña a la Parrilla con Chimichurri

(ARGENTINIAN SKIRT STEAK WITH CHIMICHURRI)

Instructor: Mirta Rinaldi

"Chimichurri is the perfect sauce to complement almost anything, especially meat." —Mirta

Food in Argentina is all about meat. And the centerpiece of Argentinian food culture is asado—barbecue. Every household has a parilla—an outside wood-fired grill often surrounded by brick—and every party and gathering centers around the parilla. This method of cooking skirt steak on the stovetop is fast and delicious, but this dish is really about Mirta's chimichurri. I think Mirta makes the best chimichurri in the world, and I like to eat it on pretty much anything.

Mirta will tell you that true Argentinian chimichurri never uses cilantro, only parsley. It's typical to use red wine vinegar, but Mirta likes to make hers with balsamic vinegar, which is a little sweeter and stronger. Her version also has more of a kick than most, thanks to the red chile flakes. Chimichurri comes together very quickly, but Mirta says it really is best left to sit overnight, as all the ingredients meld. As she says, "It's good today, but better tomorrow." The color will fade a little, but the flavor will improve. If you want to make it in advance, it keeps in the refrigerator for about 3 weeks and 6 months in the freezer. She always has some leftover chimichurri in the refrigerator, to marinate thick slices of cauliflower or whole portobello mushrooms, or to add to grilled provolone cheese, a famous Argentinian appetizer.

As for the steak itself, in Argentina the outside cut of skirt steak (there is also an inside cut) is a traditional cut for the grill—it always comes with some of the fat and the membrane attached so that it grills up very crispy. If you're lucky enough to live near a South American butcher, they will likely sell this cut or prepare it for you this way. (Mirta buys hers from a fabulous Argentinian butcher shop in Queens called El Gauchito, where she's been going for forty years!) Otherwise, most good stand-alone butchers might also be able to provide it for you if you ask in advance. But any type of skirt steak you buy will still taste fantastic, especially with the chimichurri.

Serve with: a green salad.

For the steak

2 pounds (900 g) skirt steak

Diamond Crystal kosher salt

For the chimichurri

¼ pound (115 g) fresh parsley (about 1 bunch)

¾ ounce (20 g) garlic (about 6 medium cloves)

2 tablespoons balsamic vinegar

½ to 1 tablespoon crushed red chile flakes, to taste

1 tablespoon dried oregano

1 teaspoon sweet paprika

1 teaspoon Diamond Crystal kosher salt

1 teaspoon black pepper powder

1 cup (240 ml) extra-virgin olive oil

1   **Prepare the steak:** At least 30 minutes or up to an hour before you want to cook the steak, take the 2 pounds (900 g) skirt steak out of the refrigerator.

2   **Make the chimichurri:** Make sure the ¼ pound (115 g) fresh parsley (about 1 bunch) is well-washed and dried. Pick the leaves until you have

Continued

about 2 packed cups (50 g). Peel the ¾ ounce (20 g) garlic (about 6 medium cloves).

3   Put the parsley leaves and garlic in a food processor. Process until everything is finely chopped but not a paste. You'll end up with about 1 cup of finely chopped parsley and garlic.

4   Transfer the parsley and garlic to a 2-cup (475 ml) jar with a lid and add the 2 tablespoons balsamic vinegar, ½ to 1 tablespoon crushed red chile flakes, 1 tablespoon dried oregano, 1 teaspoon sweet paprika, 1 teaspoon Diamond Crystal kosher salt, 1 teaspoon black pepper powder, and 1 cup (240 ml) extra-virgin olive oil.

5   Screw on the lid and shake the jar until everything is well incorporated. You will have about 1½ cups. Set the chimichurri aside to meld while you cook the steak. (If you made this in advance, set it out to come to room temperature when you take out the steaks.)

6   **Cook the steak:** Turn on your exhaust fan, if you have one, and open a window in or near your kitchen.

7   Heat a grill pan (preferably with ridges) or large heavy-bottomed skillet (not nonstick) over medium-high heat until it's very hot, 10 to 15 minutes. When the pan is ready, you won't be able to hold your hand 4 inches (10 cm) above it for more than 10 seconds.

8   If your skirt steak came with the membrane, score it with the tip of a knife in a few places across the steaks to prevent the meat from curling up during cooking. (You may also need to cut your steak into pieces to more easily fit in the pan.)

9   Dry the steaks with a paper towel. Generously sprinkle the steak all over with the 1 teaspoon Diamond Crystal kosher salt, rubbing it into the meat. Lay the steaks on the pan (membrane-

side down, if they have a membrane) and don't move them until the bottom is well-browned, after 5 to 12 minutes, depending on how wide and thick your steak is. (If they have a membrane, it will also get crispy.) Flip the steak and cook just until medium rare, or the internal temperature is between 135 and 140°F (60°C), usually 2 to 3 minutes without the membrane or 3 to 4 with the membrane.

10 Remove the steak to a cutting board and let it rest for at least 5 minutes, or until you're ready to serve them.

11 Transfer the chimichurri to a serving bowl.

12 **Serve and eat the steaks:** Serve the steaks hot or warm. Slice the steaks into pieces about 1½ inches (3.8 cm) wide and serve it right from the cutting board with the bowl of chimichurri on the side.

G'elak Kabob

(UZBEK BEEF AND RICE MEATBALLS IN BROTH WITH BAY LEAVES AND POTATOES)

Instructor: Damira Inatullaeva

"This recipe I got from my mom—she was a doctor and she didn't have a lot of time to cook. When she came from the hospital in the evening, this was a very good option to cook fast." —Damira

Like her mother, Damira was a doctor before she retired, and this is what they made on busy weeknights when they had very little time to cook. (Damira's mother was a well-known allergist in Samarkand who saved many people's lives, and she continued to work as a doctor in private practice until she was seventy-nine.)

The potatoes and onions sit underneath the meat, absorbing all the rich flavor as the meatballs cook. The bay leaves are what give this dish such a special taste, and there's one small spoonful of tomato sauce, which kind of melts away and just adds some umami to the broth. Damira often serves this broth separately on the side, like consommé, topped with a little cilantro. I like to spoon the broth over the meatballs and potatoes. This dish is also very good with bread—Damira usually serves it with a kind of Uzbek non that's a circular, soft white bread with a patterned indentation in the center. Damira also notes that because this dish is so mildly seasoned and easy to chew, it's also perfect for people of any age.

This is technically an Uzbek adaptation of a Soviet-era recipe, from when that region was a part of the Soviet Union. Our Ukrainian Russian instructor Larisa has a similar recipe she calls "hedgehog" meatballs—because the grains of rice stick out of the meatballs once they cook through. This recipe calls for Turkish baldo rice, which is creamy and starchy like arborio or carnaroli, either of which make a great substitute.

Serve with: the tomato onion salad on page 231 or the radish salad on page 218—plus any kind of warm bread.

1½ pounds (680 g) ground beef (15% fat)

1 pound (450 g) yellow onions (about 2 medium), divided

⅓ cup (70 g) baldo, arborio, or carnaroli rice

1 tablespoon roasted coriander powder (page 24)

1 tablespoon plus 1 teaspoon Diamond Crystal kosher salt, divided

1 large egg

1½ pounds (680 g) red potatoes (about 4 large)

3 tablespoons neutral oil

1 tablespoon plain tomato sauce or pureed tomatoes

5 small bay laurel leaves

⅛ pound (60 g) fresh cilantro (about ½ bunch)

Freshly ground black pepper

1   **Prepare the ingredients:** Put the 1½ pounds (680 g) ground beef (15% fat) in a large mixing bowl. Peel the 1 pound (450 g) yellow onions (about 2 medium). Cut them in half. Set just one half aside, to use for the broth, then cut the rest into rough chunks. Puree the chunks until smooth in a food processor or blender. You should have about 1¼ cups of pureed onion. Add it to the bowl with the ground beef and set aside.

2   Put the ⅓ cup (70 g) baldo, arborio, or carnaroli rice in a small mixing bowl and fill up the bowl with tap water in the sink. Pour it off and repeat this process two more times (you don't need to stir it), then drain off as much of the water as you can and add the rice to the bowl with the meat.

Continued

3 Add the 1 tablespoon roasted coriander powder (page 24), 1 tablespoon of the Diamond Crystal kosher salt, and 1 large egg to the bowl with the meat.

4 Mix everything with your hands very thoroughly, for about 2 minutes. The meat will get lighter and creamier. Set the bowl aside.

5 Peel the 1½ pounds (680 g) red potatoes (about 4 large) and cut them lengthwise into ½-inch (1.3 cm) slices. Put them into a bowl of water to prevent them from browning and set it aside.

6 Take the reserved ½ yellow onion and cut it into ¼-inch (0.6 cm) slices from root to stem. Set them aside.

7 **Cook the kabob:** Add 3 tablespoons of neutral oil to a 12-inch (30 cm) saute pan or skillet with deep sides and turn the heat to high. Add the onion (you don't have to let the oil preheat) and fry it, stirring constantly, for about 1 minute. Then stir in the 1 tablespoon plain tomato sauce or pureed tomatoes and reduce the heat to low.

8 Drain the potato slices, shaking off any excess water, and lay them flat in the pan on top of the onion. They should cover most of the pan. (If you're using a slightly smaller pan, it's okay if they overlap a bit.) Sprinkle the tops of the potatoes with 1 teaspoon Diamond Crystal kosher salt.

9 Use your hands to form ⅓-cup (80 ml) portions of the meat mixture into large round meatballs about 2 inches (5 cm) wide and place them right on top of the potatoes as you form them. Leave a little bit of space between the meatballs, so they aren't touching. (You will end up with about 12 meatballs.)

10 Pour 1¾ cups (415 ml) room-temperature water into the pan, adding it along the edge, not the center of the pan. You want the water to just cover the potatoes and barely touch the meatballs, so you may need a little more or a little less, depending on the shape of your pan. Scatter the 5 small bay laurel leaves around the pan.

11 Raise the heat slightly so that the liquid just begins to simmer. Then lower the heat to medium-low or low so that the pot stays at a low simmer, cover the pan, and let it simmer for 35 to 40 minutes, until the rice in the meatballs is fully cooked—it will begin to poke out of the meatballs, so you can just pull out a piece to try it. Turn off the heat and keep the dish covered on the stove to stay warm until you're ready to serve it.

12 Trim most of the tough stem ends from the ⅛ pound (60 g) fresh cilantro (about ½ bunch). Finely chop the leaves and tender stems and set them aside.

13 **Serve and eat the kabob:** Serve the meatballs and potatoes on individual plates or on one large platter, topped with a sprinkle of finely chopped cilantro and freshly ground black pepper to taste. If there is any broth at the bottom of the pot, you can serve it separately in a small bowl topped with a little cilantro, or just drizzle it over the top of your meatballs and potatoes.

Picadillo de Carne Molida

(MEXICAN GROUND BEEF AND POTATOES)

Instructor: Angelica Vargas

"My mom made this my whole life." —Angie

When Angie was growing up, her mother would sometimes roll her homemade flour tortillas around picadillo to make little tacos, and then give them to Angie and her sister to sell at recess. They would steam as they traveled to school and get even more delicious, says Angie—and they would always sell out.

That is really the best way to serve picadillo as a taco—no other toppings at all, just the richly seasoned ground meat and potatoes wrapped inside a warm flour tortilla. In fact, even though Angie often serves her picadillo with avocado and Mexican cheeses, she usually doesn't combine them in a taco—she makes separate tacos by either crushing the avocado into the tortilla or doing the same with a piece of cheese, and then she eats this alongside bites of picadillo. This contrast of the meat with the avocado or cheese tacos makes for such a yummy meal.

Angie uses either queso blanco or queso fresco, two fresh, mild Mexican cheeses. Both are increasingly easy to find in supermarkets, but you could substitute halloumi or mozzarella for the blanco and a very mild feta for the fresco, which is a little drier and crumblier.

Angie typically makes her salsa for the picadillo very spicy, often with piquin chiles, which are small, very hot dried bright red chiles common to northern Mexico and the Southwestern United States. You can either use those or arbol chiles, which are larger and easier to find (but also hot!). Use the smaller amount if you want very little heat, or, if you're making this for kids, you may want to leave out the chiles from the sauce altogether—it's still very good.

Serve with: the black beans on page 144, the Mexican tomato rice on page 176, and either the corn tortillas on page 165 or warm flour tortillas. When Angie makes the rice specifically for picadillo, she makes sure to add at least one if not all of the vegetables, to round out the meal. She also likes to top the rice with sliced bananas when serving it with picadillo. The sweet banana is a nice balance to the spiciness of the picadillo. (Timing-wise, Angie likes to start the beans first, then the rice, then the picadillo.) With avocado on the side and sliced Mexican cheeses, this is also a very satisfying meal for a gathering.

½ to 2 jalapeño chiles

1 pound (450 g) plum tomatoes (about 4 medium)

1 to 4 arbol chiles or 1 to 8 piquin chiles, optional

3 teaspoons Diamond Crystal kosher salt, divided

¾ pound (340 g) russet potatoes (about 1 large)

½ ounce (15 g) garlic (about 4 medium cloves)

3 tablespoons neutral oil

1 pound (450 g) ground beef (20% fat)

1 ripe avocado, optional

Queso fresco or queso blanco, optional

Flour or corn tortillas (page 165)

1 **Prepare the sauce:** Stem the 1 to 2 jalapeño chiles (if you only want to use half, you'll cut one in half after it cooks). Put them in a 5-quart (4.8 L) Dutch oven or saucepan with the 1 pound (450 g) plum tomatoes (about 4 medium) and the 1 to 4 arbol chiles or 1 to 8 piquin chiles, if using. Cover everything with at least 2 inches (5 cm) of tap water.

Continued

2   Put the pot over high heat and bring it to a boil. Give everything a quick stir, then lower the heat so that the pot cooks at a strong simmer—you will have lots of bubbles, but it won't boil over. Let it simmer for 10 to 15 minutes, until the tomatoes and chiles are soft and the jalapeños turn an army green. (The tomato skin will also begin to peel away.)

3   Remove the tomatoes and chiles from the pot to a blender using a slotted spoon and let them cool. If you want to use only ½ jalapeño, put only half in the blender. (If you have a high-speed blender, you don't need to let them cool—you can move on to the next step immediately.) Add 1½ teaspoons of the Diamond Crystal kosher salt and ¾ cup (175 ml) tap water. Blend everything on high for about 1 minute, until the tomatoes and chiles are fully smooth, fluffy, and lighter in color.

Angie will also sometimes substitute 1 large or 2 medium tomatillos for 1 of the plum tomatoes, if she has them on hand. They have a bright, sour flavor and add just a little more acidity to the dish.

4   Set aside 2½ cups (600 ml) of this sauce for the picadillo. Set aside the rest of the sauce in a small serving bowl to serve with the picadillo as extra salsa. (It will likely be very spicy from the chiles if you taste it while it's still warm, but their intensity will fade a bit as it cools.)

5   **Prepare the rest of the ingredients:** Peel the ¾ pound (340 g) russet potatoes (about 1 large) and cut them into ½-inch (1.3 cm) cubes. You should end up with about 2 cups.

6   Smash the ½ ounce (15 g) garlic (about 4 medium cloves) with the flat side of a chef's knife so that they break apart. Then peel the cloves and cut them in half lengthwise. Set the garlic aside in another small bowl.

7   **Cook the picadillo:** Heat the 3 tablespoons neutral oil in a 12-inch (30 cm) nonstick skillet over medium-high heat until it begins to shimmer. Add the 1 pound (450 g) ground beef (20% fat), stirring it and breaking it up with a spatula or wooden spoon.

8   Once the meat is completely broken up and evenly distributed, stir in the remaining 1½ teaspoons Diamond Crystal kosher salt and the garlic halves. Cook, stirring occasionally, until the beef just begins to brown. (It does not need to be fully cooked through everywhere, just browned in spots.)

9   Stir in the potatoes and cook, stirring frequently, for 1 minute. Reduce the heat to the lowest setting and let the beef and potatoes cook, stirring occasionally to make sure they are cooking evenly, for 10 to 15 minutes, until the potatoes are just al dente—no longer raw, but not yet fully soft.

10 Add the reserved 2½ cups (600 ml) salsa to the pan with the beef and potatoes and raise the heat to medium-high to bring it to a boil. Reduce the heat to medium-low so that the liquid is cooking at a simmer. Cover the pan and cook, stirring occasionally, until the potatoes are cooked through, usually 10 to 15 minutes more. Turn off the heat and keep the picadillo warm until you're ready to serve it.

11 **Prepare the sides:** Taste the leftover salsa for salt just before you're ready to serve the picadillo and put it out on the table.

12 Cut the 1 ripe avocado into wedges, if using, and put them out on a serving platter. The easiest way to do this is to cut the wedges with the peel still on and serve them that way—then each person either peels off the avocado from the skin when they're ready to eat it or uses

a spoon or knife to cut pieces directly off the skin.

13 Cut the queso fresco or queso blanco into slices about ½ inch (1.3 cm) thick, if using, and put them on the serving platter next to the avocado. Warm or reheat the flour or corn tortillas (page 165), if you haven't done so already.

Both corn tortillas (page 165) and flour tortillas are very common in northern Mexico, and you could serve either kind with the picadillo—or even both. Just make sure they're fresh and warm.

14 **Serve and eat the picadillo:** You can serve the picadillo in one of two ways. You could serve it at the center of a plate, paired with tortillas, wedges of ripe avocado or sliced cheeses, the leftover salsa, and any sides. Each diner can make their own tacos or just tear off a piece of tortilla and use it to scoop up a little picadillo.

You can also serve the picadillo premade into tacos by putting just a few spoonfuls of picadillo into each tortilla and then tucking the tacos into a basket or serving dish covered with a clean kitchen towel to keep them warm. You serve the avocado and cheese on the side with extra tortillas.

Keema Curry

(BANGLADESHI GROUND BEEF AND POTATO CURRY)

Instructor: Afsari Jahan

"We always add extra garlic, because it's good for your health and it adds extra flavor." —Afsari

Afsari's food is so layered with flavors, in part because she nearly always incorporates her fresh garlic-ginger paste and freshly roasted and ground spices (page 23) in addition to whole garam masala. (Garam masala basically means spice blend, and it can be whole or ground.) This dish makes me think of a South Asian sloppy Joe, especially when scooping it up with the roti on page 173 (because it has potatoes, Afsari doesn't typically serve this with rice). It's even better when you add a little ghee and honey or jaggery (page 22) to the bread, in between bites of curry. Honey, jaggery, and ghee are always on the traditional Bangladeshi table, and with keema curry in particular, this little sweet contrast really rounds out the flavor experience so that it's sweet, salty, savory (and spicy, if you choose) all at once. I also like to eat the leftover meat reheated on a brioche bun—just like a sloppy Joe.

A few notes on the cooking process: Mixing in the water prevents the ground beef from getting clumpy—the extra water will evaporate as the curry cooks. This step also helps to bring the meat to room temperature, so it cooks more quickly. If you really want to speed up the process, you can cut the potatoes into smaller pieces, too. As with all of Afsari's food, she really likes it spicy—if you want just a hint of chile flavor, use the smaller amount.

Serve with: the roti on page 173 (or flour tortillas) and a simple salad of tomato, cucumber, onion, cilantro, and chopped green chilis with a squeeze of lemon and a sprinkle of salt. If you don't have much time, you can just put out thick slices of peeled cucumber and sweet white onion sprinkled with lemon juice, with a few whole fresh green chiles on the side for those who want more heat.

6 whole cloves

2 2-inch (5 cm) cinnamon sticks (about 3 g)

1 Indian bay leaf (page 21), or 2 bay laurel leaves

6 green cardamom pods

1 pound (450 g) yellow onions (about 2 medium)

1½ ounces (45 g) garlic (about 12 medium cloves)

3 tablespoons garlic-ginger paste (page 23)

¾ pound (340 g) plum tomatoes (about 3 medium)

1½ pounds (680 kg) ground beef (15% fat)

¼ cup (60 ml) whole milk yogurt

¾ pound (340 g) russet potatoes (about 1 large)

1 to 5 green bird's-eye chiles

20 (10 g) extra-large mint leaves

4 teaspoons Diamond Crystal kosher salt

2 teaspoons roasted coriander powder (page 24)

1 teaspoon roasted cumin powder (page 23)

1 teaspoon ground turmeric

¼ to 1½ teaspoons chile powder

½ cup (120 ml) neutral oil

Roti (page 173), or warmed flour tortillas, for serving

Ghee and honey or jaggery (page 22), for serving, optional

1   **Prepare the ingredients:** Put the 6 whole cloves, 2 2-inch (5 cm) cinnamon sticks (about 3 g), ideally Indian flat cinnamon, 1 Indian bay leaf (page 21) or 2 bay laurel leaves, and 6 green cardamom pods together in a small bowl and set it aside. This is your whole garam masala.

Continued

2 Peel the 1 pound (450 g) yellow onions (about 2 medium). Cut the onions in half from root to stem, trimming the ends. Slice the halves, from root to stem, as thinly as you can, almost so you can see through the slices. You should end up with about 3 cups. Set the onions aside.

3 Peel the 1½ ounces (45 g) garlic (about 12 medium cloves). Slice each clove as thinly as you can. (You should end up with about ¼ cup.) Set aside in a separate bowl from the onions.

4 Prepare the 3 tablespoons garlic-ginger paste (page 23) if you haven't already.

5 Roughly chop the ¾ pound (340 g) tomatoes, removing the small white triangle near the stem, which will not soften as it cooks. Put the tomatoes in a food processor or blender, add ½ cup (120 ml) water, and puree until well blended. (You should end up with about 1¾ cups.)

6 Put the 1½ pounds (680 g) ground beef (15% fat) in a bowl and chop it up with a wooden spatula. Add 1½ cups (355 ml) room-temperature water about ½ cup (120 ml) at a time, continuing to chop and mix as you add each ½ cup (120 ml) until the mixture becomes very smooth, fluffy, and loose.

7 Put the ¼ cup (60 ml) whole milk yogurt in a bowl and beat it with a whisk until very smooth. It should be the consistency of a sauce and pourable—if it's too thick, add 1 to 2 tablespoons of tap water.

8 Peel the ¾ pound (340 g) potatoes (about 1 large), making sure to remove any eyes or dark spots. Cut it into quarters lengthwise, then into rough 1-inch (2.5 cm) chunks. (You should end up with about 2 cups.) Put the potatoes in a bowl, cover them with cold tap water, and set them aside.

9 Remove the tough or broken ends of the stems from the 1 to 5 green bird's-eye chiles, making sure not to break the pods open. If you want your keema to have some heat, make a small slit in the top of some or all the chile pods with the tip of a knife. If you want just the flavor of the chiles, but no heat, snip off just the very point of the chile, to expose some of the flesh but none of the seeds or membrane.

10 Finely mince the 20 (10 g) mint leaves. You should end up with about 1½ packed tablespoons.

11 Measure 4 teaspoons Diamond Crystal kosher salt, 2 teaspoons roasted coriander powder (page 24), 1 teaspoon roasted cumin powder (page 23), 1 teaspoon ground turmeric, and ¼ to 1½ teaspoons red chile powder into a small bowl and set it aside.

12 **Cook the curry:** Heat the ½ cup (120 ml) neutral oil in a wide (12-inch/30 cm) frying pan or skillet with deep sides over medium-high heat. When the oil is very hot and begins to shimmer, add the onions carefully so they don't splatter, stir them into the oil, then fry them until they have shriveled up and are browned on edges, stirring and tossing frequently. This usually takes at least 10 minutes.

Afsari's trick to tell if the oil is hot enough is to add 1 slice of onion: If it floats immediately instead of sinking to the bottom, the oil is ready.

13 When the onions are brown, add the whole garam masala and the sliced garlic. Lower the heat to medium and cook, stirring frequently, until the garlic is soft but not browned, about 1 minute.

14 Add the 3 tablespoons garlic-ginger paste and the tomato puree. Stir until everything is mixed together, then stir in the reserved combined spices. Stir everything together well.

15 Give the beef and water mixture a stir to make sure it's well incorporated. Then, still working over medium heat, sprinkle a little of the ground beef and water mixture over the top of the browned onions and spices, then mix it into the sauce. Continue, a little at a time, until all the meat mixture has been incorporated into the sauce.

16 Raise the heat to medium-high and cook, stirring very frequently, for 10 to 15 minutes, until most of the tomato liquid has reduced, the sauce is very thick and dark, and you begin to see oily bubbles around the edges of the pan.

17 Add the ¼ cup (60 ml) whole milk yogurt, stirring frequently, and cook for another 3 to 5 minutes, until most of the water has cooked away.

18 Drain the chopped potatoes and stir them into the pot. Stir in 1 cup (240 ml) tap water, then lower the heat to medium. Sprinkle the 1 to 5 whole bird's-eye chiles, slit or trimmed as desired, just on the top of the curry.

19 Cover the pot and let everything cook over low heat for 5 minutes, then stir in the finely minced mint leaves until fully mixed in.

20 Cook over low heat, covered, until the potatoes are fully soft and tender and most of the water on the top of the pot has been absorbed by the potatoes and the oil has begun to bubble to the top, 15 to 20 minutes.

21 **To serve and eat the keema curry:** Serve the curry hot or warm on individual plates with fresh roti or warmed flour tortillas. Set out some ghee and honey or jaggery, if using, for spreading on the bread to eat between bites of curry. You can also use the roti to scoop up the curry.

Shandra Woworuntu

Shandra grew up in Banyuwangi in East Java, where her family owned a food production company, a peanut factory, a bakery, and a restaurant. When she was five, Shandra's grandmother set up a child-sized stove—with a real flame—and taught her how to cook eggs. Soon Shandra was helping to cook for her grandmother's employees. Shandra stayed in the city of Jakarta after college, to become a financial banking analyst and money market trader. But after violent demonstrations against the government erupted in 1998, Shandra became a fierce anti-violence and labor rights activist, work she pursues to this day.

Shandra, who has lived in New York City since 2001, has also worked in restaurants and managed her own catering company, and currently teaches culinary skills to survivors of human trafficking through a nonprofit she founded. She also travels the world as an anti-trafficking leader and activist. She now lives in Queens with her family.

What makes Indonesian cuisine special? Indonesian cuisine has many flavors and spices. A word for this is nano nano—"flavor the bowl." We use many different flavors—spicy, sour, sweet, salty—all mixed from about seventeen thousand islands with different dialects, demographics, cultures, and types of food. Our food is very colorful. Yellow is my favorite color, so I cook with lots of turmeric. I love combining flavors from different provinces like Bali and Java. I learned to cook from my grandma, my mom, my aunts, and my neighbors, so I learned recipes from many different regions of Indonesia. Here and globally, people only know Bali, but there's so much more!

Do you have a cooking philosophy? Food is a celebration. It's important to have peace and kindness while preparing it. You have to put love, you have to put positive energy into the food. Cooking, eating together, and having conversation is the time to bring people together. I call my dining table a dining table for peace, because we never fight during meals.

How do you plan out your cooking for the week? My job requires me to travel a lot, but when I'm in NYC, I plan out my cooking every two or three days. Planning menus is exciting—I love to pick and choose what I will cook. Usually, I will see first what I have in my fridge because I don't want to waste food. We are multicultural in my family—my husband is Puerto Rican American—so sometimes I blend Puerto Rican and Indonesian food. We enjoy many different types of food—Indonesian, Spanish, and also Italian, and American, all in our kitchen. But I always cook Indonesian food for me and for my son.

What are some of your favorite home remedies from the kitchen? My home remedies are simple: turmeric, ginger, honey, lemon—all combined they can heal any sickness. One thing for sore throat is cloves. Put about five to ten cloves in a teacup filled with hot water, and then drink the water.

What do you cook when you're alone and you want to make something tasty? I make a tuna omelet, and I eat it with rice. That's the best. I saute a lot of chopped chiles and add the tuna from a can. Then I add two eggs and make an omelet. Sometimes I put some ketchup with mayonnaise on top. This is so good. Or I just make an easy vegetable saute. I take whatever vegetables are in my fridge—usually cabbage and carrots—and I saute them with garlic, shallots, chopped fresh chiles, and a dash of white pepper. Sometimes I put eggs, sometimes not. And I eat that with rice.

What do you grow in your garden? I grow cucumbers, chiles, lettuce, tomatoes, eggplants, and herbs. One unusual thing I grow is lemongrass. I love pounding lemongrass leaves and putting them in water—it's so refreshing. I also have a jêruk purut, a lime tree, that I keep outside during the summer and put under a skylight the rest of the year. I love that tree so much, and everybody helps me take care of it. I just pick a few leaves whenever I need them. Happiness is when we harvest limes! I feel so much joy and satisfaction when I cook something I grew in my garden.

What do you like about teaching for the League of Kitchens? Food has to be shared with other people. That's how you share your culture. It makes me feel so proud that in my classes I can talk about my family recipes and share my family's stories. It makes me smile that my students will help to keep the recipes alive.

What do you feel you've learned from being a part of the League of Kitchens with women from all over the world? It inspires me. The instructors of the League of Kitchens are resilient, and they have a passion to share their food, their culture, their stories. Every time I talk about the League of Kitchens, I say it's like "share your culture, share your food, and share your smile."

Shandra Woworuntu

シーフド
魚、

Mariscos

সামুদ্রিক খাবার

θαλασσινά

مأكولات بحرية

Морепродукты

غذای دریایی

SEAFOOD

غذای دریایی .

समुन्द के जिव

Mariscos

Makanan Laut

समुद्री भोजन

Fruits de mer

Ceviche de Camaron

(MEXICAN SHRIMP CEVICHE)

Instructor: Angelica Vargas

"This disappears so fast!" —Angie

This ceviche is basically a super-refreshing shrimp and vegetable salad that comes together quickly—it's a perfect light summer dinner. The lime juice "cooks" the shrimp, and if you don't let it sit too long, the shrimp tastes bright and fresh.

Angie's grandparents had a ranch in Mexico with a huge outdoor cooking area, surrounded by many cactus and fruit trees, including a pomegranate tree. So her mom always added pomegranate seeds to her ceviche. If you don't use them, this will still be fantastic, but the crisp, juicy seeds are a really nice touch—they add a bit of sweetness to the sour, spicy, and salty. You can often find pomegranates already seeded, which reduces the amount of work.

Two other things really set this shrimp ceviche apart: Angie carefully cleans the shrimp—she goes through them one by one, removing any veins or anything she wouldn't want to eat raw. She is also extra careful not to over-squeeze the limes; if you're overzealous about getting every last little bit of juice from the limes, you'll end up with bitter notes from the peel. That's why this dish calls for so many limes—you want only the sweetest juice from each. Occasionally, Angie will even add a little soy sauce and toasted sesame oil to make an Asian-fusion-style ceviche, a trick she learned from a restaurant where she worked.

There are two ways to serve this ceviche, each of which makes for a totally different eating experience. You can serve it on top of tostadas—store-bought or homemade (recipe follows)—spreading sour cream on them first, topping them first with sliced avocado, and then adding the ceviche. Serving the ceviche this way is ideal if you don't want too much heat from the chiles in the marinade. Or you can serve the ceviche still in its lime and chile marinade, giving everyone a small bowl with a spoon. Serve something crunchy on the side, like tostadas, tortilla chips, saltine crackers, or butter crackers like Ritz—those are Angie's favorite.

Angie likes everything spicy, so she uses two of each chile, but you can use ½ to 1 of each if you want just some flavor of the chiles—just remember that habaneros are significantly hotter than jalapeños, and that you can always add more heat at the end if it's not spicy enough. Depending on who she's serving, Angie will sometimes cut the habanero into long, thin strips, so she can remove them before eating—that way she ends up with some of their floral, citrus flavor but not so much heat. When she's making it for herself, she'll cut the chiles into half-circles or rings.

Serve with: any of Angie's dishes, as an appetizer, including the Mexican ground beef and potatoes on page 78 or the steak tacos on page 63. For a main meal, just make a lot and serve it on tostadas with all the toppings.

1 pound (450 g) cleaned and deveined shrimp with tails removed (medium or large)

1 cup (240 ml) fresh lime juice (from about 6 to 10 fresh limes)

3½ teaspoons Diamond Crystal kosher salt

⅓ pound (150 g) red onion (about 1 small)

½ pound (225 g) plum tomatoes (about 2 medium)

¾ pound (340 g) cucumbers (3 to 4 small or 1 medium)

½ to 2 jalapeño chiles

½ to 2 habanero chiles

Continued

¼ pound (115 g) fresh cilantro (about 1 bunch)

1 large handful fresh pomegranate seeds (from about 1 large pomegranate), optional

1 cup (240 ml) sour cream, for serving

1 ripe avocado, for serving

Tostadas (recipe follows), tortilla chips, butter crackers, or soda or saltine crackers, for serving

1 **Prepare the shrimp:** Carefully go over the 1 pound (450 g) cleaned and deveined shrimp (medium or large) and use a small paring knife to trim away any remaining bits of vein, digestive tract, or anything else unappetizing. Go one by one, making sure you clean every shrimp. Rinse them off again.

2 Cut the cleaned shrimp into ½-inch (1.3 cm) pieces and place them in a large mixing bowl.

3 Prepare the 1 cup (240 ml) fresh lime juice (from about 6 to 10 fresh limes), if you haven't already. Pour the lime juice over the shrimp. Add the 3½ teaspoons Diamond Crystal kosher salt, then stir everything gently together so that the salt is mixed in and the shrimp is covered in the lime juice. Set the bowl aside while you prepare the rest of the ingredients.

4 **Make the ceviche:** Peel the ⅓ pound (150 g) red onion (about 1 small) and roughly chop it into ⅓-inch (1 cm) pieces. You should have about 1 cup. Add the onion to the bowl with the shrimp, gently mixing it in so that it's submerged in the lime juice. (The shrimp may already be turning a little bit pink.)

5 Cut the ½ pound (225 g) plum tomatoes (about 2 medium) into quarters. Remove and discard the seeds and pulp with your fingers, then cut the tomato into ⅓-inch (1 cm) dice. You should have about 1 cup. Gently stir it into the bowl with the shrimp.

6 Trim the ends of the ¾ pound (340 g) cucumbers (3 to 4 small or 1 medium) and cut them in half lengthwise. Scrape out the seeds with a spoon (you do not have to remove the seeds if you're using Persian cucumbers). Cut the cucumber into ⅓-inch (1 cm) dice. You should have about 1½ cups. Gently stir it into the bowl with the shrimp.

7 Stem the ½ to 2 jalapeño chiles. Cut them in half lengthwise and remove the membrane and seeds, then cut them into ¼-inch (0.6 cm) dice. Gently stir the chiles into the bowl with the shrimp.

8 Stem the ½ to 2 habanero chiles, then cut them in half lengthwise and remove the membrane and seeds. Cut them into half circles or even long thin strips, if you want to remove them before you serve the ceviche. Gently stir them into the bowl with the shrimp.

9 Remove and discard the stems from ¼ pound (115 g) fresh cilantro (about 1 bunch) so that you have only the leaves and very tender stems. Finely chop the cilantro. You should have about 1 cup. (If you have any extra, you can use it for garnishing the dish.) Gently stir it into the bowl with the shrimp.

10 Prepare the 1 large handful fresh pomegranate seeds (from about 1 pomegranate), if using. Gently stir them into the bowl with the shrimp.

If you're using a fresh whole pomegranate, roll it on the counter to loosen the seeds first, then cut it in half along the equator. If you hold it over a bowl with the cut side in your hand and then rap the rind with a wooden spoon, most of the seeds will easily pop out through your fingers into the bowl.

11 Set the ceviche aside to marinate while you finish the dish—ideally for at least 10 minutes and up to about 1 hour, or when the shrimp have "cooked" to your liking. (You can still eat the ceviche after it sits for a longer period, but the shrimp will toughen.)

12 **Finish the dish:** If you're serving the ceviche on homemade tostadas (recipe follows), this is a good time to prepare them.

13 Put 1 cup (240 ml) sour cream into a bowl and whisk it until smooth. Set it aside.

14 Just before you're ready to serve the ceviche, cut the 1 ripe avocado in half, then into slices about ⅛ inch (0.3 cm) thick. Set them aside.

Angie has many genius ways of slicing avocados, having had them straight from her grandparents' yard when she was growing up. To cut them into pristine slices, she cuts the avocado in half lengthwise with the peel still intact and removes the pit by carefully smacking the knife blade into the pit so it sticks to the knife and then rotating and pulling the knife to remove the pit (be very careful removing the pit from the blade). Then she uses a dinner knife to cut a slice near one edge, pushing and lifting it out with the knife onto her tostada or wherever she wants to place the slice.

15 Remove the habanero chile strips from the ceviche if you don't want it to be too spicy. (Conversely, if the ceviche is still not spicy enough for your taste, you can add more diced chiles or even a little hot sauce.)

16 **To serve the ceviche:** To serve the ceviche on top of tostadas, spread a little of the sour cream across the tostada. Use a slotted spoon to scoop up some of the ceviche, leaving most of the marinade in the bowl, and layer it on top of the sour cream, then top it with 3 or 4 thin slices of avocado.

To serve the ceviche with its marinade, give everyone a small bowl of ceviche in marinade with a spoon. Layer the top of each bowl with a few slices of avocado. Put the tostadas, tortilla chips, or crackers on the table, along with the whisked sour cream. (Generally, Angie only puts the sour cream on top of the tostadas or crackers before topping them with ceviche—she

doesn't mix the sour cream into the bowl of ceviche itself.)

Homemade Tostadas

MAKES 8 TOSTADAS

Packaged tostadas, which are essentially flash-fried whole corn tortillas, are increasingly easy to find, but tostadas are not hard or time-consuming to fry yourself. You can serve these with the shrimp ceviche or spread them with some pureed black beans (page 144) and top them with shredded iceberg lettuce, crumbled queso fresco, salsa roja (page 65), sour cream, and sliced avocado.

⅓ cup (80 ml) neutral oil, plus more as needed

8 corn tortillas

Line a plate with paper towels. Heat the ⅓ cup (80 ml) neutral oil in a 12-inch (30 cm) skillet over medium-high heat. When it begins to shimmer, add 1 tortilla and use a metal spatula to press it down while it cooks so that it stays flat and is submerged in the oil. Flip it every 10 seconds or so, keeping it submerged in the oil with the spatula the whole time. Fry until it's just golden brown on both sides (closer in color to honey than mahogany), then remove it to the paper towel–lined plate. The whole process should take about 1 minute per tortilla. Repeat until all of the tortillas are fried, adding more oil if necessary. Serve hot or at room temperature. These will last up to a week in a zip-top plastic bag—wait until they have fully cooled to place them in the bag.

Psito Psari

SERVES 4 TO 6

(GREEK OVEN-BAKED FISH WITH LEMON-OREGANO DRESSING)

Instructor: Despina Economou

"When I was growing up, fish was like a primary food, it was so cheap and so fresh." —Despina

Cooking whole fish can feel intimidating, but this method is easy and delicious. The real genius tip here is the way Despina roasts the fish on a wire cooling rack to re-create the flavor of the grilled whole fish she grew up eating. (She puts a foil-covered baking sheet under the rack to catch any drips.) Despina says that she used to have whole fish prepared like this three times a week growing up, the fish often bought straight from the boats coming back from the Mediterranean Sea just after sunrise. Her family would stuff them with lemon slices, garlic, and herbs to get rid of any fishy smell, she says, and then put them on the grill. The lemon, olive oil, and oregano sauce that you spoon onto the fish after it's cooked is called latholemono, and it's the perfect zesty accompaniment. My older daughter, Sylvie, usually doesn't like fish because it's "too fishy," but she will happily eat this. In Greece, they often use branzino, which is lavraki in Greek. It's generally fairly easy to find, but you can also substitute whole porgy or red snapper, or any whole fish with a mild white flesh. Try to find Greek "wild oregano" if you can—it has a stronger, more potent flavor.

   Serve with: the boiled greens on page 271 or the Greek salad on page 236.

¼ cup (60 ml) extra-virgin olive oil, plus extra for greasing and drizzling

2 pounds (900 g) cleaned, deboned branzino, whole porgy, or red snapper (about 1 large or 2 small fish)

¼ ounce (7 g) garlic (about 2 medium cloves)

2 4-inch (10 cm) stems fresh thyme

3 large lemons

1 teaspoon Diamond Crystal kosher salt, plus extra for sprinkling

¼ teaspoon freshly ground black pepper, plus extra for sprinkling

½ teaspoon dried Greek oregano

Bread, for serving

1   **Prepare the oven:** Make sure the wire cooling rack you'll be using to roast the fish is clean, then grease it with extra-virgin olive oil. (Pour a small amount on a paper towel, then rub the tines of the rack so that it's well-greased.) Line a large baking sheet with a piece of foil and set the greased cooling rack into it. Put the baking sheet with the rack in the middle setting of the oven, and preheat the oven to 400°F (200°C).

2   **Prepare the ingredients:** Rinse the 2 pounds (900 g) cleaned, deboned whole branzino, porgy, or red snapper (about 1 large or 2 small fish) in the sink and pat it dry inside and out with paper towels. Set the cleaned and dried fish on a large plate.

3   Peel the ¼ ounce (7 g) garlic (about 2 medium cloves) and cut it in half lengthwise, then crosswise into ¼-inch (0.6 cm) thick slices.

4   Wash the two 4-inch (10 cm) stems of fresh thyme, if you haven't already.

5   Wash 1 of the large lemons. Cut it in half around the equator. Cut a ½-inch (1.3 cm) thick slice from one of the halves, then cut the slice in half so you have 2 half-moons of lemon. (These will go into the fish as it bakes.)

6   **Cook the fish:** Lightly sprinkle the inside and outside of the fish with Diamond Crystal kosher salt and freshly ground black pepper. Then place the garlic slices, the sprigs of fresh thyme, and

The LEAGUE OF KITCHENS Cookbook   94

the 2 half-moons of lemon inside the cavity of the fish, making sure they are evenly spaced (or separated between the two smaller fish, if that's what you're using).

7   Drizzle ½ teaspoon extra-virgin olive oil on just one side of the fish, then use your fingers to rub the oil in so that one side of the fish is fully greased. Drizzle on a little more, if needed. Place the whole fish, olive oil side up, directly on the greased rack set into the baking sheet in the oven.

8   Bake the fish for 25 to 30 minutes, until it lifts off easily from the wire cooling rack with a spatula.

9   **Make the latholemono, or dressing:** While the fish bakes, prepare the dressing. Squeeze the juice from the 2 remaining lemons into a small mixing bowl until you have ⅓ cup (80 ml). Add the ¼ cup (60 ml) extra-virgin

olive oil, 1 teaspoon Diamond Crystal kosher salt, ¼ teaspoon freshly ground black pepper, and ½ teaspoon dried oregano. Stir everything together with a fork and taste for salt. Set it aside.

10 **Finish the dish:** Toast the bread. Slice the remaining lemon halves into wedges and put them on a small serving plate.

11 As soon as the fish is ready, use two large spatulas to lift it out of the oven and onto a serving plate. Remove the lemon slices, thyme springs, and garlic wedges from the inside cavity with a knife and fork and discard them. (If your fish has a backbone, you can use your fingers to pull it out.)

12 **Serve and eat the fish:** Drizzle some of the sauce over the fish and serve immediately, with the extra latholemono, the lemon wedges, and toasted bread on the side.

Dadar Jagung

MAKES ABOUT 12 TO 14 3-INCH (7.5 CM) FRITTERS

(INDONESIAN CORN FRITTERS WITH SHRIMP)

Instructor: **Shandra Woworuntu**

"I learned to make these with my grandma while I was still in elementary school in Jawa Timur. I would always immediately take one when they were done, and run away with it from the kitchen, because they were so good."
—Shandra

Eaten with your hands, these fresh corn fritters with garlic, shallot, and scallions are really fun for dinner, and you can make them with or without shrimp—each way is equally delicious. You leave half of the corn kernels whole and grate the other half, which gives you both texture from the corn kernels and extra sweetness from the juice. With shrimp, they're obviously more substantial and end up a little denser, too. Without the shrimp, they fry up a little crispier and lighter, which is ideal if you're serving them as an appetizer with a spread of other food.

No matter which you choose, the lime leaves from the jêruk purut, a variety of lime tree that grows in Indonesia, are crucial. Shandra grows her own (page 22), but I order them dried off the internet and then rehydrate them for about ten minutes before I add them to the batter—they work great. Shandra says you can make this dish without lime leaves and it's still wonderful, which is true, but that little punch of flavor and aroma is what really makes these so special.

When Shandra eats these, she holds a fritter in one hand and a green bird's-eye chile in the other, and she takes a bite of chile with each bite of fritter. I was a little scared to try that, but now that's my favorite way to eat them. The crunch, heat, and freshness of the chile is a perfect complement to the rich and sweet flavor of the fritter.

Because you can serve them at room temperature, these make for a great weeknight meal, even though they take a little bit of time to prepare. You can make them an hour or two in advance and serve them when you're ready to eat.

Serve with: jasmine rice, the green beans and egg on page 123, or a simple side salad.

- 2 large or 3 medium fresh or dried jêruk purut lime leaves
- ¾ ounce (20 g) garlic (about 6 medium cloves)
- ⅛ pound (60 g) shallot (about 1 medium)
- 1 ounce (30 g) scallion (about 1 small)
- 1 fresh medium-spicy red chile, such as Korean (sometimes called fresh cayenne), red serrano, or Fresno (about ½ ounce/15 g), optional
- ¾ pound (340 g) shucked corn on the cob (from about 2 large ears)
- 2 large eggs
- ½ cup plus 2 tablespoons (75 g) all-purpose flour
- 3 tablespoons rice flour (or use all-purpose flour)
- 1¼ teaspoons Diamond Crystal kosher salt
- 1 teaspoon white sugar
- ¼ teaspoon finely ground white pepper
- ½ pound (225 g) peeled medium (26–30 count) shrimp, cleaned and deveined with tails removed
- 1 to 2 cups (240 to 480 ml) neutral oil or coconut oil, for frying
- Whole red and/or green bird's-eye chiles, optional

1 **Prepare the aromatics:** If using dried jêruk purut lime leaves, put the 2 large or 3 medium lime leaves in a bowl of tap water to rehydrate and set them aside.

Continued

2   Peel the ¾ ounce (20 g) garlic (about 6 medium cloves) and the ⅛ pound (60 g) shallot (about 1 medium). Slice them both as thinly as you can, then finely mince them together on a cutting board. You should have about ½ cup. Put the mixture in a small mixing bowl.

3   Trim the ends of the 1 ounce (30 g) scallion (about 1 small) and then slice it into pieces about ⅓ inch (1 cm) wide. You should end up with about ⅓ cup of scallions. Add them to the mixing bowl.

4   Slice the 2 large or 3 small fresh or rehydrated dried lime leaves into fine slivers about the width of the tines of a fork (or cut them with kitchen scissors) and add them to the mixing bowl.

5   Cut the 1 fresh medium-spicy red chile (about ½ ounce/15 g) in half lengthwise, if using, then remove the stem end and the seeds. Slice the chile crosswise as thinly as you can. You should end up with about a tablespoon of slivered chiles. (If you want just a little flavor and color from the chiles but not much heat, use half.) Add them to the mixing bowl.

6   **Prepare the corn:** Use a large, sharp knife to shave the kernels off 1 shucked corn on the cob. Hold it in your hand in a large mixing bowl and use the knife to cut along the side so the kernels go into the bowl. Then grate the other ear into the same bowl using the large holes on a box grater. (If you have a protective glove, it's good to wear it.) Grate the cob both lengthwise and crosswise, to get every bit of the sweet juice. You can also grate the cob you shaved with the knife, too. You should have about 1½ cups of corn.

7   **Make the batter:** Break the 2 eggs into the bowl with the corn and stir them into the corn. Then add the ½ cup plus 2 tablespoons (75 g) all-purpose flour, 3 tablespoons rice flour (or more all-purpose flour), 1¼ teaspoons Diamond

Crystal kosher salt, 1 teaspoon white sugar, and ¼ teaspoon finely ground white pepper. Use a large spoon or spatula to mix everything together well.

8   Add the garlic, shallot, scallion, lime leaf, and chile mixture to the bowl, again stirring until everything is mixed together. Gently stir the ½ pound (225 g) peeled shrimp into the batter, if using. Set the batter aside just while you prepare to fry the fritters.

If you can only find large or extra-large shrimp, it's better to cut them in half lengthwise first—like butterflied shrimp, but cut through all the way. Shandra also sometimes keeps the shrimp out of the batter and then gently presses one or two shrimp on top of each fritter as she adds them to the pan, so they look even prettier. This is also a nice technique if you want to make some with and some without shrimp.

9   **Fry the fritters:** Prepare a plate lined with paper towels. To fry the fritters, add 1 cup (240 ml) neutral oil or coconut oil to a 10- to 12-inch (25 to 30 cm) skillet, preferably nonstick. Turn the heat to high and let the oil heat until it begins to really bubble, then lower the heat to medium.

10 Test one fritter by adding a scant ¼ cup (50 ml) of batter to the pan. The fritters should end up about 3 inches (7.6 cm) wide, and ideally each should have at least one shrimp. Adjust the heat up or down so you see small bubbles around the edges of the fritter but the edges don't burn. When the oil is at the right temperature, fry 2 to 4 of the fritters at a time, using a scant ¼ cup (50 ml) of batter for each one, adjusting the heat and removing any stray bits as necessary. (The fewer you cook at a time, the easier it is to move them around and flip them.) Add more oil to the pan, as needed.

11 When the fritters are golden brown on the edges and bottom (usually after about 1½ minutes), use two spatulas to flip them over and let them cook for another minute or two, until the other side is golden brown. As the fritters are done, remove them from the pan with two spatulas, shaking off any excess oil, and put them on the plate lined with paper towels.

If your batter gets too watery (the vegetables will often release water as they sit), the fritters will cook more slowly, soak up more oil, and won't be as light and fluffy. Try mixing in a tablespoon or two of all-purpose flour.

12 **Serve and eat the fritters:** You can serve these fritters hot off the skillet, warm, or at room temperature—but always eat them with your hands. Serve them with plenty of whole red and/ or green chiles, taking a bite of chile in between bites of fritter, if you'd like.

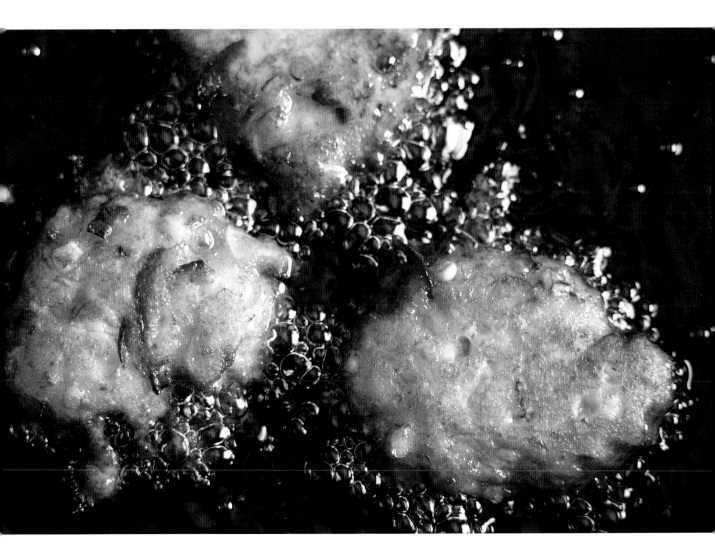

Mahi

(AFGHAN OVEN-BAKED FISH WITH QUICK PICKLED RED CABBAGE AND ONIONS)

Instructor: **Nawida Saidhosin**

"We don't have many kinds of fish in Afghanistan. We really have just one fish that we call fish! Most of the time we eat it whole, with bread fresh from the tandoor oven." —Nawida

In Afghanistan, says Nawida, fish is a rare treat that is nearly always served whole and simply prepared, because the focus should be on the fish itself. This recipe is exactly that—it's roasted just until the skin is crispy, and simply seasoned with an easy marinade of fresh garlic, lemon juice, coriander, black pepper powder, red chile powder, and turmeric. This style of fish is typically served with a lot of fresh lavash or another hot bread, and slices of red cabbage and sweet onion quickly pickled in white vinegar and water. The pickles don't even need any salt—the vinegar marinade gives them plenty of flavor.

When you serve this, the key is to eat it all with your hands—you put each bite of fish into a piece of lavash, then top it with some onion and some cabbage. Then you give it a squeeze of lemon, fold it up, and eat it almost like a sandwich.

This is already a very fast dish, but to save time, Nawida just cuts a half moon from the side of a very large whole cabbage, so she doesn't have to remove the core. You could also just core and slice a smaller cabbage if that's what you have. And if for some reason you can't find branzino, just look for another smaller whole mild fish that doesn't have many small bones.

Serve with: any kind of potatoes (in Afghanistan this dish is often served with french fries), and for dessert, the Afghan custard on page 299.

For the fish

- 1 ounce (30 g) garlic (about 8 medium cloves)
- 3 tablespoons fresh lemon juice (from 1 to 2 lemons)
- 1 tablespoon neutral or olive oil, plus extra for greasing
- 1 tablespoon roasted coriander powder (page 299)
- 1 tablespoon Diamond Crystal kosher salt
- 1 teaspoon black pepper powder
- 1 teaspoon ground turmeric
- ¼ to 1 teaspoon red chile powder, to taste
- 2 to 3 pounds (900 g–1.5 kg) cleaned whole branzino (2 medium or 1 large)
- 1 large lemon, thinly sliced, for serving
- 1 large lime, thinly sliced, for serving
- Lavash, pita, or another flatbread, for serving

For the quick pickles

- ¾ pound (340 g) red cabbage (about ¼ large red cabbage)
- 1½ cups (355 ml) white vinegar
- ¾ pound (340 g) white onion (about 1 medium)

1. **Preheat the oven:** Preheat the oven to 400°F (200°C) with a rack in the middle of the oven.

2. **Prepare the seasoning paste:** Peel the 1 ounce (30 g) garlic (about 8 medium cloves), then grate them on the star-shaped or small holes of a grater into a small, nonreactive mixing bowl. You should end up with about 1½ tablespoons. Add the 3 tablespoons fresh lemon juice (from 1 to 2 lemons), then the 1 tablespoon oil, 1 tablespoon ground roasted coriander, 1 tablespoon Diamond Crystal kosher salt, 1 teaspoon black pepper powder, 1 teaspoon

Continued

turmeric, and ¼ to 1 teaspoon red chile powder. Use a spoon to mix everything together well.

3   **Clean and season the fish:** Use a pair of kitchen scissors to trim any spiky edges off the fins of the fish, if your fish still has them. Then clean the fish inside and out under running water in the sink.

Nawida always takes extra time to make sure the fish is perfectly cleaned and prepared, the same way she does when prepping the chicken for her korma murg on page 249. Just a little more work yields a fish that's easier to eat, with a brighter, cleaner flavor.

4   Place the cleaned fish on a cutting board, then make several deep, crosswise cuts on both sides through the skin of the fish's belly about 2 inches (5 cm) apart. The cuts should be deep but not go all the way through the fish, and they should go most of the width of the fish (see the photo on page 103).

5   Use your knife to extend the existing cut along the belly all the way from the gills down to the base of the tail. (This is so you can more easily rub the insides with the marinade.)

6   Put the prepared fish in a glass casserole dish, then use your hands to rub the seasoning paste all over the fish and into every cut and crevice, including inside the belly. Set it aside to marinate while you prepare the quick pickles.

The fish only needs to marinate for 5 to 15 minutes to be flavorful, says Nawida, and letting it sit while you make the cabbage and onions is the perfect amount of time.

7   **Prepare the quick pickle:** Remove any hard white core from the ¾ pound (340 g) red cabbage (about ¼ large red cabbage), if needed, and discard it. Slice the cabbage as thinly as you can into ribbons and put them in a large,

nonreactive mixing bowl. You should have about 4 cups.

8   In a large measuring cup, stir together the 1½ cups (355 ml) white vinegar with 1½ cups (355 ml) water.

9   Pour 2 cups (475 ml) of the vinegar-water mixture into the cabbage and press or mix it together so that all of the cabbage gets touched by the liquid. Set the cabbage aside to soften, tossing it from time to time while you bake the fish.

10 Peel the ¾ pound (340 g) white onion (about 1 medium) and slice it as thinly as possible into rings. Separate the rings and put them in a medium nonreactive mixing bowl, then add the rest of the vinegar-water mixture and mix it so that all of the onions get touched by the liquid. Set the onion aside to soften, tossing from time to time while you bake the fish.

11 **Bake the fish:** Place the casserole dish with the fish on the middle rack of the oven, bake for 12 minutes, then use two spatulas to flip it to the other side. (It will stick a bit—don't worry, that's normal.) Bake for 10 to 15 minutes more, until it's totally browned and sizzling, the edges are crispy, and the seasoning paste is beginning to blacken on the bottom of the pan.

12 **To serve and eat the fish:** Remove the fish from the oven to a large serving platter. Using a slotted spoon and shaking off any excess liquid, mound some of the cabbage along one edge of the platter around the fish. Along the other edge, make a mound of onions on one side, shaking off any excess liquid, and put the lemon and lime slices in a bowl on the side. (You can discard the leftover liquid, or use it in another recipe, if you like.)

13 Serve the platter in the middle of the table, with plenty of lavash or pita and any extra cabbage and onions in bowls on the table.

エッグ
玉子

HUEVOS

চিড়

Тухум

Avjá

بیضة

Ούγα

EGGS

تخم مرغ

नैं

अण्डा

Huevos

Telur

ਅੰਡੇ

Œufs

Tukhum Banjanrumi

SERVES 4 TO 6

(AFGHAN EGGS WITH TOMATOES, CHILES, GARLIC, AND MINT)

Instructor: Nawida Saidhosin

"This is everywhere in Afghanistan. Everybody knows tukhum banjanrumi, and everybody likes tomatoes and eggs."
—Nawida

Nawida's son and husband request this dish for breakfast a few times per week, though it's also a perfect easy dinner. With the eggs gently cooked in fresh tomatoes, it has a shakshuka-like vibe but tastes very different because of the way Nawida makes it. First, the tomatoes are fried in very hot oil, which both flavors the oil and turns it a wonderful golden orange, one of the pleasures of this dish. Second, the tomatoes, jalapeños, and garlic are cut just a little bit larger than you think they would be, which helps them maintain both flavor and texture—they don't disintegrate as they cook.

Third, Nawida usually doesn't really scramble the eggs in the sauce, but gently separates the whites and yolks so both cook through to a perfect medium, and you get soft, creamy bites of both in every spoonful. It's such an incredible combination of flavors, made with just a handful of common ingredients that most of us keep in our fridge.

Tukhum banjanrumi is always served with a pile of fresh mint—you really need one leaf per bite—and lavash or squares of fresh Afghan non made in long, soft sheets and topped with sesame seeds. And when it's served for breakfast, it's also nearly always eaten in combination with sweet cardamom green tea (page 109), a pairing I have found to be really a crucial component of what makes this dish so beloved. Nawida likes to use five whole large jalapeños when she makes this dish—ideally, you drink some sweetened cardamom tea in between bites to temper the heat. If you really don't want much heat, use the smaller amount, and make sure to remove the seeds and the membrane.

Serve with: the cardamom tea on page 109, and the tea should be very sweet—that's part of the magic combination with the hot chiles and tomatoes.

7 large eggs

2½ pounds (1 kg) tomatoes on the vine (7 to 8 medium)

1 to 5 jalapeño chiles, to taste

1 ounce (30 g) garlic (about 8 medium cloves)

1 ounce (30 g) fresh mint (about ½ bunch)

½ cup (240 ml) olive oil, neutral oil, or ghee

2 teaspoons Diamond Crystal kosher salt

Pinch black pepper powder

Fresh, soft (or gently warmed) bread, preferably Afghan non, lavash, or pita, cut into serving-size rectangles or half-moons

1   **Prepare the ingredients:** Take the 7 large eggs out of the refrigerator so you have them ready to add to the pot.

2   Cut the 2½ pounds (1 kg) tomatoes on the vine (7 to 8 medium) into quarters and then into chunks about 1 inch (2.5 cm) wide, discarding the stems and the small white triangle at the stem, which won't ever cook down. (You should end up with about 6 cups chopped tomatoes.)

3   Cut the 1 to 5 jalapeño chiles into pieces about ¼ inch (0.6 cm) wide, or about the size of a dried chickpea.

Continued

4   Peel the 1 ounce (30 g) garlic (about 8 medium cloves) and chop it into pieces about ¼ inch (0.6 cm) wide. (Do not mince it.) You should end up with about 3 tablespoons chopped garlic.

5   Pick the largest leaves from the 1 ounce (30 g) fresh mint (about ½ bunch) until you have about 1 loosely packed cup.

6   **Make the sauce:** Heat the ½ cup (240 ml) olive oil, neutral oil, or ghee in a 12-inch (30 cm) nonstick wok, skillet, or frying pan over medium to medium-high heat until it begins to shimmer.

If your pan is too shallow, you'll get too much spatter, but if it's deep like a stockpot, the eggs tend to stick to the bottom. A nonstick wok is ideal for this dish. And though it might seem like a lot of oil, it's critical to the flavor and texture of the dish—you want to almost deep-fry the tomatoes in hot oil, not saute them. If you're wary of consuming too much oil, says Nawida, just ladle most of it off at the end from the top of the pot before you serve it and save it for another use.

7   Test the oil by adding a piece of tomato to the pan—it should immediately begin to sizzle. If not, let it warm a little longer, or adjust your heat. Add the tomatoes and stir them until they're evenly coated with oil.

8   Let the tomatoes cook and soften over medium-high heat for 15 to 20 minutes, stirring occasionally, until most of the liquid has evaporated and the mixture has thickened and is a deep reddish-orange color. Tilt the pan every once in a while, if you're not using a wok, to let the tomatoes fry a bit. When the tomatoes are ready, the bubbles will become larger and slower, and the oil will begin rising and pooling at the top of the pot.

9   Add the jalapeños, garlic, and 2 teaspoons Diamond Crystal kosher salt to the pan, then

cook for an additional 3 minutes, stirring frequently.

10 **Cook the eggs:** Turn the heat down to medium, then gently but quickly crack the eggs one at time in a ring around the edge of the pan just like the numbers on a clock. You want each egg yolk to remain intact and sit atop the sauce. Once all the eggs are in the pan, turn the heat to medium-low. Cover the pan, but every time you see the whites begin to set, gently jiggle the sauce to distribute it around the whites to help them cook. (If you don't have a see-through lid, just jiggle once every minute or two.)

11 When the whites are all just set (usually after 5 or 6 minutes), use a spoon or spatula to break up the whites and then gently break up and stir the yolks. You want them to cook separately and stay separate. Once the yolks just begin to cook through—usually after another 4 to 5 minutes—remove the cover and turn off the heat. Sprinkle the tops of the eggs with a pinch of black pepper powder.

You can really make the eggs to your liking—you can leave the yolks fully runny, or leave some whole. Nawida often makes them in many ways in one pot, because everyone in her family likes their eggs cooked a different way.

12 **Serve the tukhum banjanrumi:** Give each diner some bread, some eggs with their sauce, and some mint leaves, or place them all on platters family style on the table. Encourage diners to eat with their hands: Use a piece of bread to scoop a bite of eggs and tomatoes, and add fresh mint leaves as needed so that you have some in every bite.

Chai Sabz

(GREEN CARDAMOM TEA)

Steep 1 tablespoon loose-leaf green tea, preferably Ahmad brand, with ½ tablespoon ground cardamom (see page 305) in 5 cups (1.2 L) of water just off the boil for 20 minutes. No need to strain—just let the leaves settle to the bottom and gently pour the tea into a cup. You can also add sugar to taste. In Afghanistan, it's generally only sweetened when you're serving it with breakfast. Nawida likes to make the tea in an insulated coffee pitcher or a push-button insulated coffee carafe so that the tea stays hot, and she can drink it throughout the day.

Zarchoba with Thukahm

(AFGHAN EGGS FRIED IN GHEE WITH GARLIC AND TURMERIC)

Instructor: Nawida Saidhosin

"Grandmas, they all know this recipe, but the young ones, they don't know." —Nawida

This is probably the recipe in this book that I make the most often. I always have the ingredients on hand, and it's just about as easy as frying an egg, but so much more interesting and satisfying—and the red-orange color is gorgeous.

In the part of the world where Nawida is from, it's very common to add just a pinch of turmeric to eggs. The flavor blooms and softens as it sizzles in the ghee, losing its bitterness. Likewise, frying the garlic in the ghee until it's lightly golden and then removing it lends a subtle garlic perfume; neither the turmeric nor the garlic is overpowering in any way.

This recipe is the way Nawida makes these eggs for her family—she takes the garlic chips out before she serves it. (The chips are also delicious—either to eat right there or with the eggs.) When she makes it for herself, she often makes this fast dish even faster: She just roughly chops the garlic and fries it in the pan at the same time she's cooking the eggs, making sure it doesn't burn, then serves the eggs with the chopped garlic. Sometimes she makes them over-easy, and sometimes she does them sunny-side up, but both ways she'll spoon the hot turmeric-garlic ghee onto the eggs as they cook.

Nawida also says this dish is considered very warming in her culture—as in it's good in the winter and especially good for children as a cold-weather breakfast. My kids also love it and often request it. This recipe is for two eggs, but you can multiply it as needed—just use a larger pan to cook the eggs.

½ ounce (15 g) garlic (about 4 medium cloves)
2 tablespoons ghee
⅛ teaspoon turmeric
2 large eggs
Diamond Crystal kosher salt, for sprinkling
Warm or soft bread, like lavash or pita, for serving

1   **Prepare the garlic:** Peel the ½ ounce (15 g) garlic (about 4 medium cloves) and cut the cloves into slices about $\frac{1}{16}$ inch (0.2 cm) thick—thin but not paper thin.

2   **Fry the garlic:** Heat the 2 tablespoons ghee in an 8-inch (20 cm) nonstick skillet over medium to medium-low heat so that the oil begins to shimmer. (Low may even be high enough to keep the oil very hot in a skillet this small.)

3   Add the garlic and fry it, stirring constantly, until it's lightly golden and begins to crisp, about 4 minutes. Watch carefully to make sure it doesn't burn, lowering the heat as necessary. Turn off the heat and remove the garlic with a slotted spoon. Stir in the ⅛ teaspoon turmeric.

4   **Fry the eggs:** Put the pan with the turmeric-garlic oil over medium-low heat. When the oil is hot and begins to shimmer, crack the 2 large eggs into the pan. The eggs should immediately puff and redden around the edges. Use a spatula or spoon to flip some of the hot oil on the top of the eggs as they cook, then gently flip them after about 30 seconds, or when they are beginning to brown on the bottom but the yolk is still raw on

The LEAGUE OF KITCHENS Cookbook   110

top. (If the yolks break, it's fine—many cooks break them up on purpose to cook all the yolk.)

5   Cook the eggs for about 30 seconds more, again using the spatula to flip some of the hot oil onto the top of the eggs.

6   If you want still-runny yolks, let them cook for just 20 seconds more—they will be reddish-brown on all sides but still not fully cooked all the way through. You can press the yolks a little with your fingertip to tell their doneness, too. (If your eggs didn't immediately puff, your pan wasn't hot enough, and the whites might take a little longer to cook.)

7   You can also use the spatula to break up some or all of the yolk a little at this point, or just let them cook a little longer until the yolk has hardened to your liking.

8   **Serve and eat the eggs:** When all the eggs are done, remove them to a plate or bowl, pour the hot ghee from the pan over the top, and serve them hot or warm with a little bowl of salt for sprinkling and warm or soft bread, like lavash or pita.

Tahu Telor

(INDONESIAN OMELET WITH TOFU, SCALLIONS, BEAN SPROUTS, AND PEANUT SAUCE)

Instructor: Shandra Woworuntu

"If you cook eggs with coconut oil, the taste is so, so good and the aroma makes it even more delicious." —Shandra

This Indonesian tofu and scallion omelet looks and feels so fancy—it's loaded with flavors and textures—but it's actually easy to make. If you break it, you can just put it back together on the plate, because it's covered with crunchy blanched bean sprouts. On top is a required drizzle of kecap manis–a sweetened soy sauce with a flavor similar to molasses. (If you don't live near a Southeast Asian grocery store, it's exceedingly easy to make from scratch following the recipe on page 115.) Cooking this omelet in coconut oil is not required, but it really makes this dish taste extra special.

Shandra says there are actually two ways to cook this omelet—the big family-sized omelet we have here, or smaller individual omelets. Either way, if you're making it for a party, definitely make the fried shallots (page 116). For a weeknight, they're a little time-consuming, and it's still equally good without them. But you could make them in advance, as well as the kecap manis, sambal rawit, and even the peanut sauce—then all you need for this dish is eggs, tofu, scallions, and bean sprouts.

When Shandra is serving this to anyone who doesn't like chiles, she leaves the chile out of the bumbu kacang, or peanut sauce, and just makes a quick Indonesian hot sauce called sambal rawit (page 116) to serve on the side. You can streamline tahu telor even more for picky eaters—when Shandra was small, her mother would make this for her as a plain egg omelet topped only with the bumbu kacang and kecap manis.

Serve with: Jasmine rice (or Indonesian rice cakes, if you can find them) and freshly sliced cucumbers.

For the bumbu kacang (peanut sauce)

2½ tablespoons coconut oil or neutral oil, divided

½ cup (85 g) skin-on shelled raw peanuts or peeled unsalted roasted peanuts

¾ ounce (20 g) garlic (about 6 medium cloves)

½ fresh medium-spicy red chile, such as Korean (sometimes called fresh cayenne), red serrano, or Fresno (about ¼ ounce/7 g), optional

1 red or green bird's-eye chile, optional

1 teaspoon Diamond Crystal kosher salt

3 tablespoons kecap manis (recipe follows)

For the omelet

1 14-ounce (400 g) package firm or extra-firm tofu

⅛ pound (60 g) scallions (about 2 medium)

6 large eggs

½ teaspoon Diamond Crystal kosher salt

10 ounces (285 g) bean sprouts, washed and drained

2 cups (475 ml) boiling water

2 tablespoons coconut or neutral oil

Fried shallots (page 116), optional

Kecap manis (recipe follows), for drizzling

Sambal rawit (page 116), or another hot sauce, optional

1   **Fry the peanuts:** Heat 2 tablespoons of the coconut or neutral oil in an 8-inch (20 cm) nonstick skillet over medium heat. Add the ½ cup (85 g) peanuts and adjust the heat so that they're sizzling a little but not burning as you cook.

Continued

113

If you've made the optional fried shallots (page 116), you can use the shallot frying oil instead of coconut or neutral oil for any part of this dish.

2   Fry the peanuts until they're just a little brown on all sides, stirring them constantly with a wooden spoon or spatula so all sides cook evenly and they don't burn. This usually takes a minute or two at most. Turn off the heat and remove the peanuts with a slotted spoon from the pan to a mixing bowl to cool. Set the pan aside, but don't clean it.

3   **Prepare the bumbu kacang (peanut sauce):** Peel and roughly chop the ¾ ounce (20 g) garlic (about 6 medium cloves). You'll have about 2 tablespoons. Set the garlic aside, then stem the ½ fresh medium-spicy red chile (about ¼ ounce/7 g) and the 1 red or green bird's-eye chile, if using, and slice them into rough chunks.

4   Add the last ½ tablespoon of the coconut oil or neutral oil to the frying pan (the same one you fried the peanuts in) and turn the heat to medium. Once the oil is hot, fry the garlic, stirring constantly, just until it's no longer raw (a minute at most). If you're using the chiles, add them and do the same thing—the chiles should brighten in color. (If you're not adding chiles, fry the garlic for another minute, or until it's golden in color.) Remove the pan from the heat and transfer the garlic and chiles to the bowl with the peanuts to cool slightly.

5   When the garlic and chiles are no longer hot, put them and the peanuts in a blender (preferably a smaller "bullet" style blender). Add the 1 teaspoon Diamond Crystal kosher salt, the 3 tablespoons of kecap manis, and ½ cup (120 ml) tap water. Process until smooth and then transfer to a small serving bowl. (The mixture should be velvety smooth like peanut butter, though a few pieces of peanut are fine.)

6   Stir in ½ cup (120 ml) more tap water to thin the mixture into a sauce and set it aside while you make the omelet.

You can make the bumbu kacang up to three days in advance and refrigerate it—just stir in the second ½ cup (120 ml) water when you're ready to make the omelet.

7   **Prepare the ingredients for the omelet:** Rinse the 1 14-ounce (400 g) package firm or extra-firm tofu and cut it into ½-inch (1.3 cm) square-rectangular cubes and set them aside. (The cubes don't have to be perfect.)

8   Trim the end of the ⅛ pound (60 g) scallions (about 2 medium). Reserve a 6-inch (15 cm) piece of the green part for garnishing, and then cut the rest into ¼-inch (0.6 cm) slices. You'll have about a heaping ½ cup. Set the scallions aside.

9   Beat the 6 large eggs in a medium mixing bowl with the ½ teaspoon Diamond Crystal kosher salt.

10 Drain any water that might have collected under your tofu cubes, then add them to the bowl with the eggs. Add the scallion to the bowl with the eggs and tofu, then stir everything gently so that the tofu is covered in egg and the scallion is mixed through. Set this aside while you prepare the bean sprouts.

11 **Prepare the bean sprouts:** Bring 2 cups (475 ml) of water to a boil, if you haven't already.

12 Put the 10 ounces (285 g) bean sprouts in a heatproof bowl in the sink. When the water reaches a boil, pour it over the sprouts. Move the sprouts around a bit with a spoon so that they all touch the hot water. Let them sit for 20 seconds (or until they're still very crunchy but no longer raw), then transfer them to a colander or strainer in the sink to fully drain.

13 **Finish the omelet:** Heat a 9½-inch (24 cm) nonstick skillet over medium-high heat. Add the 2 tablespoons coconut oil or neutral oil. When the oil is hot, add the eggs and tofu and use a spoon or spatula to make sure the tofu is all in one layer. Lower the heat to medium.

14 Cook the omelet, tilting the pan up slightly on one edge so that the runny eggs from the center go to the sides to cook. Flip the omelet after about 3 to 4 minutes, or when the bottom is lightly browned and you can easily take a thin spatula and run it around the edges of the omelet and lift it from the pan. The top will still be wet.

15 Use two spatulas to gently flip it over. It might break—that's okay. Just use your two spatulas to put it back into place while it finishes cooking, still on medium.

16 Cook until the other side is browned and the eggs are cooked through, again lifting the pan to let the runny parts and any water from the tofu move to the side as it cooks. This should take about 3 to 4 more minutes.

17 When the omelet is done, turn off the heat and lift it out onto a serving plate. If it's broken or in pieces, just use your hands or a spatula to press it into place: You're going to completely cover it with toppings.

18 **Garnish the dish:** Use your hands to cover the top of the omelet with half of the bean sprouts, leaving just a little border of omelet peeking out on the outer edge. Use a spoon to drizzle the bumbu kacang (peanut sauce) over the omelet so that it's almost entirely covered with sauce. Then sprinkle over the rest of the bean sprouts, and then sprinkle the fried shallots (page 116) over the top of the dish, if using.

19 Use a pair of kitchen scissors to cut the reserved scallion top into fine slivers right onto the top of the omelet. Drizzle on the kecap manis (page 115) in thin lines over the top, like chocolate syrup on a sundae.

20 **Serve the tahu telor:** Serve with hot jasmine rice. Put any extra bumbu kacang or fried shallots on the table, along with the sambal rawit (page 116) or another hot sauce, if using.

21 Serve the omelet hot or room temperature. It's easiest to put it on the table and to serve it family style. Ideally you take a bit of rice, and then a bit of the omelet and chew them together.

Homemade Kecap Manis

(INDONESIAN SWEET SOY SAUCE)

MAKES 1½ CUPS (350 ML)

If you can't easily find kecap manis, or Indonesian sweet soy sauce, you can make your own. There are sweeter and saltier versions: Shandra says this version is close to the ABC brand of kecap manis she often buys, which has a flavor profile somewhere in the middle.

> ¼ cup (60 ml) water
> 3 tablespoons molasses
> 6 tablespoons soy sauce
> 1 cup (9.7 oz/275 g) coconut sugar or dark brown sugar
> 2 teaspoons Diamond Crystal kosher salt

Put all of the ingredients in a small saucepan over low heat, stirring just until the sugar dissolves. Turn off the heat and let the mixture cool completely, then store in a covered jar at room temperature for up to 3 months.

Continued

Sambal Rawit

(INDONESIAN RED CHILE SAUCE)

MAKES ABOUT ½ CUP (120 ML)

This quick chile sambal, or sauce, is easy to make and you can use it with any dish where you would want a little fresh chile flavor. (When you're done, just be careful to wash out your blender with a strong dish soap, like Dawn, so that your smoothies don't taste spicy!)

⅛ pound (60 g) fresh red bird's-eye chiles (about 30)
¼ teaspoon Diamond Crystal kosher salt
¼ teaspoon white vinegar

Remove the stems from the ⅛ pound (60 g) fresh red bird's-eye chiles (about 30) and put them in a small saucepan with ½ cup (120 ml) of water and bring to a boil. Adjust the heat so the liquid is at a low simmer and let the chiles cook for 10 minutes. Turn off the heat. Puree the chiles and the cooking water in a blender. Open it away from your face—the chile fumes will be strong. Transfer the mixture to a clean storage jar and stir in the ¼ teaspoon Diamond Crystal kosher salt and ¼ teaspoon white vinegar. When the mixture has fully cooled, cover the jar and store it in the refrigerator for up to 2 weeks.

Indonesian Fried Shallots

MAKES ABOUT ¼ CUP (4 TABLESPOONS)

You can also use the shallot frying oil for salad dressing or for cooking the bumbu kacang (peanut sauce) in the Indonesian omelet (page 113). Just strain the oil before you store it.

⅛ pound (60 g) shallot (about 1 medium)
Pinch Diamond Crystal kosher salt
1 cup (240 ml) coconut or neutral oil

1. Slice the ⅛ pound (60 g) shallot (about 1 medium) into rings, making them as thin as you can, or use a mandoline. (You will end up with about ⅔ cup shallots.) Put the sliced shallots in a small mixing bowl and sprinkle them with the pinch of Diamond Crystal kosher salt. Cover the shallots with ½ cup (120 ml) tap water and set them aside. (The water will just barely cover the shallots.)

2. Prepare a large plate or baking sheet lined with paper towels. Heat 1 cup (240 ml) coconut or neutral oil in a 9½-inch (24 cm) nonstick skillet over medium to medium-high heat. You want the oil to shimmer, but you don't want big bubbles—if it's too hot when you fry the shallots, they'll burn and taste bitter.

3. When the oil is hot, drain the shallots and separate the rings with your fingers. Carefully add them to the hot oil—the oil will bubble and splatter—and lower the heat a little to medium. Stir them frequently as they cook—stirring them around and moving the ones from the outer edge to the middle. Fry the shallots until they're barely golden, watching the pan at all times, then remove them with a slotted spoon to the paper towels, making sure they're spread out and not overlapping. (If they're piled up, they'll steam and lose their crunch.) They will continue to darken and brown. Let them cool completely before using or storing. These are better fresh, as they lose their crispiness when stored, but they will still hold on to their flavor for up to a week.

Huevos con Tocino y Habanero

(MEXICAN EGGS WITH BACON AND HABANERO CHILES)

Instructor: Angelica Vargas

"My auntie loved eggs and bacon, and my mom used to prepare it for her when she went to school. And because I like spicy food so much, my mom started adding jalapeño when she made it for me, and I said, 'No, I want habanero.'" —Angie

Angie usually makes these eggs for breakfast (along with black beans and flour tortillas), but I like to make them for dinner. They're fast and easy, but also satisfying, and I love how the heat of the chiles cuts the richness of the bacon fat. Plus, Angie uses several cool techniques that make this quick scramble a more luxurious, full-flavored combination of bacon and eggs than you may have tried before.

First, she cuts a few strips of bacon into pieces and then sautes them just until the edges are starting to get a little crispy and golden brown, so they're still very soft and juicy. Then she scrambles the eggs right in the pan, only draining out any extra bacon fat at the end. The best tip she learned from her mother: When Angie adds the eggs to the pan, she doesn't beat them first in a separate bowl, but cracks them right in as if she were making eggs sunny-side up. As they cook, she breaks up the whites and scrambles those first, before breaking up and mixing in the yellows. When everything is about 80 percent done, she turns off the heat and lets the eggs finish cooking over the residual heat of the skillet. This ensures the whites are fully cooked but the yolks are not overcooked, which I always feel is a difficult balance. Plus, you end up having whole bits of both the yolks and the whites, which is even more delicious.

Angie loves chiles, and if she's making this for herself, she often uses 2 or 3 habanero chiles, which are really hot. For just a little heat, try about 1 teaspoon of diced chiles, which is about half a small habanero. (Just be careful as you cut them—I always wear disposable gloves when I cut habaneros.) If you're serving kids or anyone who doesn't like chiles, you can also leave them out and instead make the very easy and delicious onion and habanero relish on page 118 to serve on the side. (Angie actually likes to put chiles in her bacon and eggs *and* eat them with the onion and habanero relish.)

Serve with: flour or corn tortillas, the onion-habanero relish on page 118, if desired, and the black beans on page 144.

½ pound (225 g) sliced bacon (about 5 to 7 strips)
½ to 3 habanero chiles, to taste
4 large eggs
8 to 12 flour or corn tortillas (page 165)
Diamond crystal kosher salt, for the table

1   **Prepare the ingredients:** Use a large sharp knife to slice the ½ pound (225 g) sliced bacon (about 5 to 7 strips) crosswise into ½-inch (1.3 cm) wide pieces. (You can stack the slices up to do them all at the same time.)

Angie puts any leftover bacon in the freezer to use for another time—she often cuts the unopened plastic pack in half, wraps up one half and puts it in the freezer, and uses the other half for one batch of eggs. When you want to use the frozen bacon, just take it out of the package and cut the frozen block into strips—they will come apart and defrost as you cook them in the pan.

2   Remove the stem(s) from the ½ to 3 habanero chiles, and then slice them in half lengthwise.

Continued

117   EGGS

Remove the stems and the seeds, then cut them into a fine dice, about ⅛ inch (0.3 cm). (Be careful not to touch your eyes or face.)

3 **Cook the eggs:** Heat a 12-inch (30 cm) nonstick pan over medium-high heat. Add the bacon and stir it around with a spoon or spatula so that it's distributed evenly over the bottom. As it sizzles, turn it and spread it around frequently so it cooks evenly. (Be careful of splatters.) Cook just until the edges turn golden brown and begin to crisp but the bacon is not fully crispy, 3 to 4 minutes. Lower the heat to medium and add the diced habanero to your liking.

4 Cook the chiles for 1 full minute, stirring frequently, then break the 4 large eggs into the pan, keeping them near the middle. Use a nonstick spoon or spatula to gently stir the whites, but leave the yolks intact (it's okay if you break one). When the whites are 80 to 90 percent cooked (after about 1 minute), break the yolk and gently mix them in—don't overmix.

5 Let the eggs cook for 1 more minute, then, with a nonstick spatula, flip them over piece by piece so the less-cooked top continues to cook from the heat of the pan, and turn off the heat. Let the eggs sit on the stove to stay warm while you heat the tortillas.

6 **Prepare the tortillas:** Warm the 8 to 12 flour or corn tortillas (page 165). You can place them directly over a flame on a gas stove or on a very hot, preheated griddle. Cook them until they get at least a few spots of brown on either side, flipping them once or twice. Keep them warm wrapped in clean kitchen towels.

7 **Serve the eggs.** Put the salt on the table—you may want a pinch or two on your eggs, depending on how salty the bacon is. (If you left out the chiles to serve this to kids or others who don't like chiles, you can also put out the onion and habanero relish.) Serve the eggs hot,

scooping them out of the pan with a spatula, leaving any extra bacon fat in the pan. You can either make tacos with the tortillas as you eat or tear off a bit of tortilla and use it to scoop up some eggs, eating them together.

Onion and Habanero Relish

MAKES 1 CUP (330 G)

Serve this on top of eggs, beans, grilled meats, or anything else where you'd like something spicy and acidic. Once you've eaten all the onions and chiles, you can use the leftover lime juice itself as a dressing on cabbage slaw or other vegetables. (I've even made this with just the onions, without the chiles, and it's still delicious.)

⅓ pound (150 g) red or white onion (about 1 small)

½ to 2 large habanero chiles (or 3 small)

¾ cup (180 ml) fresh lime juice (from about 5 to 6 limes)

1½ teaspoons Diamond Crystal kosher salt

1 Peel the ⅓ pound (150 g) red or white onion (about 1 small) and cut it in half through the root and stem ends. Slice each side crosswise as thinly as you can along the equator to make paper-thin half-moon-shaped slices of onion. You should end up with about 1 cup.

2 Stem the ½ to 2 large habanero chiles (or 3 small) and then slice them in half lengthwise. Remove the membrane and the seeds, then slice the chiles as thinly as you can into long strips. Set them aside, separate from the onions.

3 Prepare the ¾ cup (180 ml) fresh lime juice (from 5 to 6 limes). It's better not to try to get the last little bits of juice from the limes

by over-squeezing them, or you'll end up with bitter notes from the lime peel.

4   Put the onion slices in a small serving bowl and spread them along the bottom of the bowl so that they are not mounded in the middle. Layer the sliced habaneros on top, then sprinkle the 1½ teaspoons Diamond Crystal kosher salt across the top of the habaneros. Add the lime juice. Then mix the onions and the habanero with two forks, like you're tossing a salad, so that everything is mixed together.

5   Let the relish sit for at least 15 minutes at room temperature before serving—a few hours is even better. It will continue to get softer as the lime juice "cooks" the onions, and the flavors will continue to meld. Stored in a jar with a lid, it will last for a week or so in the refrigerator.

6   To serve, use a fork to remove the onions and habaneros from the lime juice before you add them to a dish, shaking off any extra juice as you do.

Angelica (Angie) Vargas

Angie grew up in Monterrey, a northern Mexican city near the US southern border. It's a region famous for its cowboys, cattle, and barbecue—on both sides of the Rio Grande. Her grandparents lived on a ranch next to the river, and she loved spending time there when she was a kid. The house was surrounded by all kinds of fruit trees—avocado, lime, papaya, pomegranate, and pecan. She loved watching her mom and grandmother make fresh flour tortillas or cook in the outdoor kitchen, where they often grilled meat and fresh cactus paddles, which they harvested from their land. She and her two siblings often helped their busy, working mom with the cooking, and whenever Angie was over at a friend's house, she would usually end up in their kitchen asking questions.

At fifteen, Angie moved with her mother and her sister to New York City. At eighteen, she started working as a bartender at a Mexican restaurant, where, of course, she also helped out in the kitchen. Since then, Angie has worked as a model, an actor, and a photographer and helped run the Mariachi Academy of New York, a nonprofit school that offers free music lessons to children. She is passionate about preserving Mexican traditions of all kinds, the color pink, and being a very proud mom to her son, Alexander, and her daughter, Angelina.

What is the secret to being a great cook? Cooking with love. There's no other secret. When I cook and I'm not happy, believe me, even the eggs are going to taste horrible. It's cooking happy and with lots of love, and I think that's the magic, secret ingredient. And that's for everything in life, not just for cooking. I really feel like when you cook a meal with lots of love and good energy, you're giving that to your family, to the people you love.

If someone is a total beginner in the kitchen, what advice would you give them? It's never too late or too early to start cooking. I started cooking very young, at seven. My daughter, officially, she's been making tortillas since she was three years old. But one of the best pieces of advice that I can give is don't be scared. Don't be afraid of doing something wrong, because there's always a way to fix it—unless you've added too much salt!

If you want to cook something fast, easy, and very delicious just for yourself, what do you make? I like a ham, mayo, and avocado sandwich with a soda. Or I will just grill a steak. I'm a meat lover—I love meat, and I always have. I go for good steaks, so I always have a rib eye in my fridge. It's a must. When I make a steak, I'll saute some onions and have all that with some flour tortillas and slices of avocado. That will be my perfect meal.

If you want to have something sweet after a meal, but you don't want to make a whole dessert, what do you eat? I always go for peanut butter and strawberry jam on bread. And I actually love Mexican bread, the conchas, so I always have them in the house. So I'll grab a concha with hot chocolate or a soda.

What are some of your favorite home remedies? Garlic. My mom used to add garlic to everything every time we got sick. Even if a mosquito bit us, she would put garlic on the bite. My mom used to fill a bottle of tequila with garlic and drink some of that when she felt she was getting sick.

What foods do you like to grow yourself? I have a lot of peppers. I have habaneros, jalapeños, and arbol chiles. I have mint. I have the best mint in the world. I like to plant papalo because it's a very Mexican, traditional herb that you don't find often outside of Mexico. I have a peach tree that my mom planted, and I'm so excited about it. I have strawberries and tomatoes and tomatillos. I have aloe vera. I planted some little cactuses, too, and hopefully they'll grow bigger.

What do you like about teaching for the League of Kitchens? The opportunity to share my culture. I am very proud of who I am, and where I come from, and I'm very proud of my food. And I love being able to share the same way that I learned from my mother, so I try to be a mother to my students. I feel like all of us, all the teachers, we love to be mothers, and we love to give love in a motherly way. I really feel that I make an impact when I love somebody and when I teach them how I'm cooking or how easy it is to make a homemade meal. And when students see that they did it, they get so excited—and then they get to share that with their loved ones.

What do you feel like you've learned from being part of this community of women from around the world? Even though we are from different cultures and from different parts of the world, we are very similar. We eat in very similar environments; we cook in a very similar way. All these other instructors, who I love to the moon and back, I really feel like they're my mothers and my friends. I feel that even though we are from different backgrounds, from different parts of this beautiful world that we live in, we are all the same. We have beautiful hearts.

Angelica Vargas

Deem Vaji

(BANGLADESHI SUMMER AND WINTER OMELETS)

Instructor: Afsari Jahan

"This is my lazy-day meal." —Afsari

Once you learn the basic technique and flavor structure of these omelets, you can make them with any vegetables you have on hand. First, you bloom cumin seeds in oil—that's the foundation of the flavor. Then you add your vegetables, along with chopped green chiles and cilantro. Those three ingredients—cumin seeds, green chiles, and cilantro—are what give these omelets a Bangladeshi flavor.

These specific vegetable combos are outstanding, however. Before I made these with Afsari, I had never thought to put long beans or green beans, daikon, or cauliflower in an omelet, and they're all delicious. Both omelets also include peas, chopped onion, scallions, and tomato.

The summer omelet features long beans, because that's when they grow. Afsari says dark green long beans have more flavor. You can use green beans too, as both are cut into tiny pieces, and they taste similar. For the winter omelet, the shredded daikon releases a little water as it cooks, which helps to soften the chopped cauliflower.

Afsari prefers to defrost things as slowly as possible in the refrigerator, so if you can plan in advance, let the peas defrost overnight or over a few hours. Your ingredients will lose less flavor and water this way.

In both omelets, Afsari puts three green chiles. I use one. She also serves them with homemade roti (page 173), but if I'm in a hurry, I eat these with good-quality flour tortillas.

Serve with: the roti on page 173 (or any warm bread) for a light dinner. For a larger brunch, Afsari often serves this with the Bangladeshi version of the vegetarian rice and grain dish called khichari—we have a version from Yamini, our Indian instructor, on page 146.

For the summer omelet

2½ ounces (70 g) long beans or green beans (about 6 long beans or 12 green beans)

For the winter omelet

¼ pound (115 g) cauliflower (about ¼ medium head)

¼ pound (115 g) daikon radish (about 1 3-inch/7.5 cm piece)

For the omelet base

½ cup (70 g) frozen or fresh sweet green peas

1 ounce (30 g) scallions (about 1 medium)

⅛ pound (60 g) fresh cilantro (about ½ bunch)

1 ounce (30 g) yellow onion (about ¼ small)

⅛ pound (60 g) plum tomato (about ½ medium)

1 to 3 green bird's-eye chiles

4 large eggs

1 teaspoon Diamond Crystal kosher salt

¼ cup (60 ml) neutral oil

1 teaspoon whole cumin seeds

Roti (page 173) or warm bread, for serving

1 **Defrost the peas:** If you're using frozen peas, measure ½ cup (70 g) into a small bowl and set them aside to defrost.

2 **If you're making the summer omelet:** Cut the 2½ ounces (70 g) long beans or green beans (about 6 long beans or 12 green beans) into thin (⅛-inch/0.3 cm) slices. You should end up with about ½ cup. Put them into a large mixing bowl.

3 **If you're making the winter omelet:** Remove any stems from the ¼ pound (115 g) cauliflower

Continued

(about ¼ medium head). Finely chop the florets—you should have about ½ cup. Put them in a large mixing bowl.

4   Peel the ¼ pound (115 g) daikon radish (about 1 3-inch/7.5 cm piece). Cut it into julienne or grate it using the medium holes of a box grater. You should have about ½ cup. Add it to the bowl with the cauliflower.

5   **Prepare the rest of the omelet ingredients:** Trim the ends of the 1 ounce (30 g) scallion (about 1 medium) and cut it into thin (⅛-inch/0.3 cm) slices. You should have about ¼ cup. Add them to the bowl with the other vegetables.

6   Trim away all but the tender stems and leaves from the ⅛ pound (60 g) fresh cilantro (about ½ bunch) and finely mince it. You should have about ¼ cup. Add it to the bowl with the rest of the vegetables.

7   Peel the 1 ounce (30 g) yellow onion (about ¼ small) and cut it into ⅛-inch (0.3 cm) dice. You should have about ¼ cup. Add it to the mixing bowl.

8   Cut the ⅛ pound (60 g) plum tomato (about ½ medium) into ⅛-inch (0.3 cm) dice. You should have about ¼ cup. Add it to the mixing bowl.

9   Remove the stem(s) from the 1 to 3 green bird's-eye chiles and cut the chiles into ⅛-inch (0.3 cm) slices, then add them to the bowl with the rest of the vegetables. Set the bowl aside.

10 Beat the 4 large eggs in another small bowl with a whisk until they're frothy, then set them aside.

11 **Cook the omelet:** Add the ½ cup (70 g) defrosted or fresh peas and 1 teaspoon Diamond Crystal kosher salt to the bowl with the vegetables and gently mix everything together with your hands. (Don't do this step until you're

ready to cook the omelet, or the vegetables will start to release too much water before you add them to the pan.)

12 Heat the ¼ cup (60 ml) neutral oil in a 12-inch (30 cm) skillet, preferably nonstick, over medium heat. When the oil is shimmering, swirl it around so it coats the pan and sprinkle the 1 teaspoon cumin seeds across the bottom. (They should crackle a bit—that's normal.)

13 Spread the vegetable mixture evenly over the bottom of the pan. Cook over medium heat, stirring occasionally then spreading them all out again, until the vegetables are still a little crunchy but nothing is still raw, about 5 minutes.

14 Add the beaten eggs to the skillet, shaking the pan a bit to make sure the eggs are all in one layer.

15 When the bottom is light brown and there is no vegetable liquid on the top of the omelet (the eggs may not yet be fully cooked on top), run your spatula around the edge of the omelet to loosen it, then gently flip it. Light browning usually takes 3 to 5 minutes.

16 It's okay if the omelet breaks—just put it back together in the pan. (You can also flip it into a plate and then slide it back into the skillet, if you want to keep it in one piece.) When the other side of the omelet is light brown, usually about 2 more minutes, turn off the heat.

17 **Serve and eat the omelet:** Serve the omelet hot, warm, or at room temperature. Use your spatula to cut it into wedges right in the pan and transfer them to a serving platter or individual plates. Tear off a piece of roti or warm bread and use it to grab a bit of omelet, and then eat them together in the same bite.

Orak-Arik Sayuran

SERVES 4 TO 6

(INDONESIAN STIR-FRIED GREEN BEANS AND CARROTS WITH EGGS)

Instructor: Shandra Woworuntu

"When I was in school my siblings and I always got home late. One day my family served us this dish, and we all ate it together. I was too young to identify what was inside it myself, so I got my mom to show me how to make it."
—Shandra

This egg stir-fry feels so light and easy to eat because the vegetables are cut to the same thin size and shape—everything just kind of blends together. Beyond a few chiles, its primary seasoning is just a little finely ground white pepper, which also makes it interesting—it's peppery but complex. If you can use coconut oil, it also adds a ton of flavor. It's traditional in Indonesia, but Shandra uses it less often in the United States because it's so much more expensive here.

Cutting the carrots into matchsticks and slicing the green beans so thinly—you're basically frenching them—takes a little bit of time, but it's a big part of what makes this dish taste so good and feel so special. (Shandra says she likes to listen to music while she cuts them!) But I've also made orak-arik with a food processor slicer attachment—just cut the beans in half so you can lay them horizontally in the feeding tube. It's super-fast, and still excellent. You can also cut the carrots in the food processor with the shredding attachment, if you really want to save time.

Because this is traditionally served with jasmine rice, it's made just a little on the salty side so that the stir-fry and the rice balance each other out as you eat them. But this version holds up either with rice or on its own.

Serve with: any meal as a vegetable side, or as a main with jasmine rice. Shandra says leftovers are great with the corn fritters on page 96 or even fried chicken.

½ pound (225 g) green beans

½ pound (225 g) carrots (about 4 medium)

¾ ounce (20 g) garlic (about 6 medium cloves)

⅛ pound (60 g) shallot (about 1 medium)

1 fresh medium-spicy red chile, such as Korean (sometimes called fresh cayenne), red serrano, or Fresno (about ½ ounce/15 g), optional or seeds removed, if desired

3 large eggs

2 tablespoons coconut or neutral oil

1½ teaspoons Diamond Crystal kosher salt

¼ teaspoon finely ground white pepper

1   **Prepare the green beans and carrots:** Stem the ½ pound (225 g) green beans. Peel and trim the ends of the ½ pound (225 g) carrots (about 4 medium).

2   If you're using a food processor, fit it with the slicing blade and process the green beans and carrots separately, setting them aside in separate bowls.

3   If you're cutting them by hand, use a large knife to slice each green bean on the bias into multiple long, diagonal slivers—just as thin as you can get them, so they look like frenched green beans. (Most should end up about 1½ inches/3.8 cm long and ⅛ inch/0.3 cm thick.) As you cut the green beans, put them in a mixing bowl. Then cut the peeled and trimmed carrots into matchsticks about the same width

Continued

EGGS

of the green beans—about ⅛ inch (0.3 cm) thick. Put them in another mixing bowl.

If you intend to cut the green beans and carrots by hand, try to find one of those oversized carrots in your supermarket, which will make cutting carrot matchsticks easier. (Shandra's mother always taught her not to get the big ones, because they aren't as sweet and have less flavor, but for this dish she breaks the rule.) Cut about half the carrot into ⅛-inch (0.3 cm) thick coins, and then cut the coins into ⅛-inch (0.3 cm) thick sticks.

4   **Prepare the rest of the ingredients:** Peel the ¾ ounce (20 g) garlic (about 6 medium cloves) and finely chop it. You should end up with about 1 tablespoon. Then peel, slice, and roughly chop the ⅛ pound (60 g) shallot (about 1 medium); you should end up with about 5 tablespoons. If using, slice the medium-spicy red chile (about ½ ounce/15 g) on the diagonal into ⅛-inch (0.3 cm) thick slivers; you should end up with about 4 tablespoons. Keep the garlic, shallot, and chile separate and set them aside.

5   Beat the 3 large eggs in a small bowl or measuring cup and set them aside.

6   Measure out ½ cup (120 ml) water and set it by the stove.

7   **Cook the vegetables:** Add the 2 tablespoons coconut or neutral oil to a 12-inch (30 cm) wok or skillet, preferably nonstick, and turn the heat to medium-high (you want the oil to get hot but not burn or smoke). When the oil is hot, add the chopped garlic.

8   Cook and stir-fry the garlic, watching carefully, until it's just a little bit golden, then add the chopped shallots. Stir-fry them for a minute or so, until the shallots are soft and a little browned, then stir in the slivered chile, if using.

Add the carrots and stir-fry them for about 20 seconds, then add the ½ cup (120 ml) water to the wok.

9   Cook and stir the carrots for a minute or so over high heat, just until they begin to soften slightly and deepen in color. Then add the green beans, stirring frequently for a few seconds. Stir in the 1½ teaspoons Diamond Crystal kosher salt and ¼ teaspoon finely ground white pepper, tossing and stirring so everything is mixed together.

10   Continue to cook over high heat, stirring often, until the carrots have just cooked through— they should still have some bite and not be soft. This takes about 2 to 3 minutes.

11   **Add the eggs:** When the carrots are cooked through, lower the heat slightly and make a small well (about 3 inches/8 cm wide) in the center with your spatula.

12   Drizzle part of the 3 beaten large eggs around the edge of the pan on top of the vegetables, and then pour the rest into the well in the center. Wait 5 seconds, and then gently stir the contents of the pan with a spatula. Wait 5 seconds more, then gently stir. Repeat once or twice more if necessary, until the egg is cooked through and mixed into the beans and carrots. This is usually just 30 seconds to a minute in a wok. Remove from the heat immediately.

13   **Serve the orak-arik:** You can serve this hot, warm, or even at room temperature—it's usually served with rice on the side, as opposed to on top of it on the same plate. Leftovers are best at room temperature—you don't really want to reheat the eggs or they'll get tough.

Arroz Blanco con Huevos

(ARGENTINIAN RICE WITH BUTTER, PARMESAN CHEESE, AND FRIED EGGS)

Instructor: Mirta Rinaldi

"I used to always come home and say 'Mom, would you make me the rice?'" —Mirta

This is pure Argentinian comfort food. It merges a Latin American favorite—fried eggs over white rice—with a Northern Italian riso in cagnone (rice with butter and cheese). Much of Argentinian food is a merging of those two influences, and many of Mirta's ancestors came to Argentina from Northern Italy. There is so much to love about this dish—it's so simple but so good, and maybe something you wouldn't think to make unless someone made it for you first. It's basically a pantry recipe—just rice, butter, Parmesan cheese, and eggs. Mirta stirs cubed butter and grated cheese right into the rice when it's still steaming, piping hot—and it really becomes a cheater's risotto, just as rich and nearly as creamy. The yolk from the over-easy eggs also adds some richness. When Mirta went to university, she would often come home at midnight from her night classes. Her mom would always wait at the bus stop to meet her, and make this dish for her when they got home.

Mirta sometimes uses pre-grated store-bought Parmesan cheese, and sometimes grates real Parmigiano-Reggiano from scratch, depending on how much time she has or what she has—feel free to do the same. Mirta uses a lot of butter here (she says her brother uses even more!), and you could of course use less, if you really wanted—but it won't taste quite as delicious.

2 cups (400 g) extra-long-grain white rice

1 teaspoon Diamond Crystal kosher salt, plus extra for finishing

8 tablespoons (115 g) unsalted butter (1 stick)

1½ ounces (40 g) grated Parmesan cheese (about 1 loosely filled cup, freshly grated), plus extra for sprinkling

3 tablespoons olive oil

4 large eggs

1   Put the 2 cups (400 g) extra-long-grain white rice in a medium (3-quart/3 L) saucepan (it should have a cover) and wash it under running water in the sink three or four times until the water is almost clear. Drain the rice (there will still be a little water left in the pot—that's fine). Add 4 cups (950 ml) water to the pot and then add the 1 teaspoon Diamond Crystal kosher salt.

2   Put the pan over high heat just until the water comes to a boil. Then cover the pot, reduce the heat to low, and let the rice cook for around 15 minutes, or until it's soft and cooked through (you can taste a grain to make sure). Some of the water may not yet be absorbed—that's okay.

3   When the rice is fully done, turn off the heat and fluff and stir the rice with a fork. Cut the 8 tablespoons (115 g) unsalted butter (1 stick) into cubes and stir them into the rice until they're fully melted and mixed in. The rice will be mushy and creamy—that's what you want. Add the 1½ ounces (40 g) grated Parmesan cheese (about 1 loosely filled cup, freshly grated), again stirring until it's all mixed

Continued

together. Cover the pot and let it sit on the stove so it stays warm while you make the eggs.

4 **Fry the eggs:** Heat the 3 tablespoons olive oil in a 10-inch (25 cm) nonstick skillet over medium heat. When the oil begins to shimmer, crack the 4 large eggs into the pan. (It's okay if they're touching.) Let the eggs cook until the whites are set and the yolks are no longer fully runny but just a little set, usually about 3½ minutes over medium heat. As the eggs cook, tilt the pan and spoon some of the hot oil just over the whites to help them cook before the yolks are fully done.

My kids are wary of any raw egg, so I flip these eggs for one second at the end—the yolks stay a little soft, but there's no rawness left.

5 **Serve and eat the rice and eggs:** Divide the rice into four bowls, sprinkle the tops with a little more of the grated Parmesan to taste and salt to taste, and then put one of the eggs on top of the grated cheese. Break the egg up, mix it into the rice, and eat immediately, while everything is still hot.

Ejjeh Bi Koussa

(LEBANESE ZUCCHINI AND EGG SCRAMBLE WITH GARLIC AND CUMIN)

Instructor: Jeanette Chawki

"It's a very fast and easy meal, and you can enjoy it at any time of the day. This is the best." —Jeanette

Ejjeh is a kind of Middle Eastern country omelet or scramble that can be made with many types of fillings. This version is my favorite kind of recipe—something fast and simple, cheap to make, but also delicious and interesting. Instead of just sauteing the zucchini, Jeanette grates the squash (she prefers to use cousa or gray squash, but zucchini works great, too) and then she salts it and squeezes out all the liquid, which intensifies the flavor of the squash and prevents the eggs from getting too watery. She seasons the eggs with roasted cumin powder, and then at the very end, she adds raw grated garlic, both of which add an incredible amount of savory flavor.

But what really makes this special, and makes it a meal, is how she serves the ejjeh: with mint-sprinkled labneh, warm pita, and wedges of tomato. That combo—the hot, garlicky zucchini eggs with the cold creamy yogurt and the little bit of mint, all scooped up in pieces of warm pita, with a taste of juicy tomato in between bites—is just so satisfying.

1½ pounds (680 g) zucchini or gray squash, preferably small (about 4 small)

2 teaspoons plus ½ teaspoon Diamond Crystal kosher salt, divided

¼ pound (115 g) yellow onion (about ½ medium)

4 large eggs

¼ ounce (7 g) garlic (about 2 medium cloves)

3 tablespoons olive oil

½ teaspoon roasted cumin powder (page 23)

Freshly ground black pepper

2 cups (475 ml) labneh or plain whole milk Greek yogurt

½ teaspoon dried mint

2 large tomatoes on the vine

Pita, for serving

1 **Prepare the ingredients:** Trim the bottom of the 1½ pounds (680 g) zucchini or gray squash (about 4 small). Leave the stem ends so you can use them as a handle when you get close to the end of the squash. Grate them on the large holes of a grater into a bowl. Use your hands to mix the shreds well with 2 teaspoons of the Diamond Crystal kosher salt. Put the salted squash in a strainer over the bowl and knead and squeeze the squash with your hands to get out as much of the liquid as you can, about 2 minutes. You should have about 2 cups. Let the strainer sit over the bowl and continue to drain while you prepare the rest of the ingredients. (You can keep the liquid and add it to vegetable soup, if you like, or discard it.)

2 Peel the ¼ pound (115 g) yellow onion (about ½ medium) and cut it into small pieces about ⅛ inch (0.3 cm) wide. You should have about 1 cup. Set it aside.

3 Beat the 4 large eggs with the remaining ½ teaspoon Diamond Crystal kosher salt in a small bowl.

4 Peel the ¼ ounce (7 g) garlic (about 2 medium cloves) and grate it over the fine holes of a box grater. You should end up with ½ tablespoon.

Continued

5 **Cook the ejjeh:** Put the 3 tablespoons olive oil in a 12-inch (30 cm) frying pan or skillet, preferably nonstick, with deep sides and turn the heat to medium. Add the chopped onion and cook, stirring constantly at first so that it cooks evenly, for 4 to 5 minutes, until soft and translucent.

6 Give the squash another squeeze to get out any remaining water, and then use your hands to sprinkle the shreds over the onions. Stir the squash and onion in the pan for about 45 seconds, then turn the heat to low and cover the pan. Cook, checking and stirring occasionally to make sure the squash doesn't stick, for about 10 minutes, until nearly all the liquid has bubbled away and the oil starts to bubble up around the edges of the squash. (Some liquid is fine.) Stir in the ½ teaspoon roasted cumin powder.

7 Turn the heat to medium-high and then, working quickly, stir in the beaten and salted eggs, using a fork or spatula to gently stir them into the squash and onion mixture so that it's all mixed together. Immediately reduce the heat to low, give the pan a shake to make sure the egg and squash mixture is evenly distributed in the pan, and then cover the pot with the lid set slightly ajar to let out a little steam.

8 After 2 to 3 minutes, or when the bottom of the eggs are a little set but the top is still jiggly, use the spatula to scramble it all together.

9 Sprinkle the grated garlic across the top of the eggs. Put the lid back on the pan, again slightly ajar, and turn the heat as low as it will go. Let it cook for another 30 seconds, then dust the top with freshly ground black pepper.

10 Turn off the heat, then use your spatula to scramble it all again and move the eggs and squash from the pan to a serving platter or large plate.

11 **Prepare the accompaniments:** Put the 2 cups (475 ml) labneh or Greek yogurt in a small serving bowl and stir until smooth. Dust the top with ½ teaspoon dried mint, crumbling it between your fingers as you do.

12 Slice the tomato into wedges and put them on a small serving plate. Sprinkle the wedges with a little bit of freshly ground black pepper.

13 Warm the pita bread.

14 **To serve and eat the egg scramble:** Put the yogurt, tomatoes, and pita bread on the table with the scrambled eggs, or even right on the serving platter with the eggs.

15 Each person should take a serving of eggs, along with some yogurt or labneh, and a few wedges of tomato. Ideally, you put a little yogurt and dried mint on a piece of pita, then top it with a bite of egg. In between bites, you take a bite of juicy tomato.

Mirta Rinaldi

Mirta was born in Mendoza, Argentina, a mountainous region she will proudly tell you is known for its wines (Malbec!), gorgeous landscapes, and fabulous barbecues. She moved to New York City with her husband in 1975 but has retained a passion for her country that impresses every student who attends a class in her home, which is filled wall to wall with Argentinian art, crafts, and artisan-made cookware. Mirta, who had a long career planning elaborate events for world leaders, politicians, musicians, and actors, greets everyone with yerba mate, the traditional herbal tea of Argentina. Like many Argentinian families, Mirta's has Italian, Spanish, and Indigenous roots. She grew up learning to cook from her grandmother, who had owned a small hotel in an area south of Mendoza and who had cooked all the meals for the guests, as well as from her mother, aunts, and friends. She lives in Queens and her grown daughter, Paola, lives nearby.

What makes Argentinian cuisine special? It all revolves around asado, which means barbecue. This is unique and comes from the culture of the gauchos, or the South American cowboys of the Pampas. Also, in Argentina, it is always a good time to stop for mate, a traditional herbal tea that is also the national drink. We usually enjoy snacks with mate. Argentinians respect the culinary legacy of the country and mate time has become a tradition for all Argentinians, including the diaspora, in which we feel connected to our cultural roots.

How did you learn to cook? I learned to cook from my family. All the women of my family were lovers of food and each one had their own specialty. We would get together every weekend to cook together—we would prepare pasta, or make big batches of membrillo, or quince paste, or spend a whole weekend canning tomato sauce.

What do you enjoy about cooking? What I enjoy about cooking is that I can play, and I feel really free to do it. I experiment with ingredients. And the most rewarding part is when I hear people say "mmm, mmm . . ." I love all those different "mmms" that I hear after they have a first or second bite. That is happiness for me. It's music.

What do you think is the secret to being a great cook? If someone is just starting out and you're giving them

advice, what would you say? The advice that I would give to people who start cooking is to first focus on the flavors—good sazón, good flavors in the food. And don't be afraid to mix ingredients, especially native ingredients that belong to your culture. Mixing and experimenting is how you get a good meal.

How did your mother plan out her cooking when you were growing up? When I was growing up, my mom cooked whatever was in season. And my father was the person who shopped in the big market, and he did all the food shopping. One thing that we made twice a week in my house was pasta. Thursdays and Sundays were always pasta days. It's very Italian. And so, out of that tradition, for me, I like pasta on Sundays. I skip Thursdays, but pasta on Sunday sounds like the perfect meal. A bagel in the morning, pasta at night—that's a super Sunday.

If you want something sweet after a meal, but you don't want to make a whole dessert, what do you have? One sweet bite that I always have available is membrillo—I always make a big batch of quince paste every year—and I always have cheese. Membrillo and Manchego, that's a perfect bite.

What do you enjoy about teaching for the League of Kitchens? What I enjoy about teaching for the League of Kitchens is the opportunity to meet people, because it creates such a community. And when you're with your students in person and you spend three or five hours cooking, talking, and sharing, it's an experience that is very unique. The students become friends. At the end of the class, we sit for dinner and share the food that we all prepared, and they're proud of what they made, and eating that food together is such a beautiful ending to the class.

What have you learned from your fellow instructors and from being part of this community of women from around the world? What I've learned from my colleagues, from this whole experience, is that if you cook with love, you make the best meals. All of my colleagues have that in their souls. They have different professions, different cultures, different religions, and they had different lives in their countries, but here, we're all dedicated to teaching about food and culture. We're so good together—there's no competition between us, it's all sharing.

Mirta Susana Rinaldi

ビーンズ

豆

Frijoles

ছোলা

صويا

Frijoles

कठोल

BEANS

Haricots

Ловия

Φασόλια

حبوب

Бобовые

لوبيا

Kacang-kacangan

Foul Moudammas

(LEBANESE MASHED FAVA BEANS)

Instructor: Jeanette Chawki

"A pot of foul cooking is the smell of a family gathering for me—I remember I would wake up to the smell of this cooking, because my mother had started it earlier in the morning." —Jeanette

Jeanette learned her method for making foul moudammas, or stewed fava beans, from her sister, who loves making (and eating) it. But a Lebanese friend recently taught her the trick of adding both whole and crushed chickpeas—the whole chickpeas give it a little more texture, while the crushed chickpeas help to make the foul richer and thicker. Seasoned with cumin (good for preventing gas!), allspice, sumac, Aleppo pepper, and garlic, these beans are full of flavor. And because you cook the onions and tomato just long enough to soften them, the dish is also still very fresh-tasting—and extra-delicious when you eat it with crunchy raw vegetables and fresh mint leaves, as Jeanette always does.

The plate of raw vegetables that's eaten with foul is actually a really important part of the experience. The extra yummy bonus items you serve on the side that act as an accent to the meal are a big part of Lebanese cuisine, and Jeanette feels very strongly about serving adequate "extras" with her meals. For her, making sure these extras are both plentiful and varied is a sign of a good cook and a good host. The fresh, juicy crunchiness of the vegetables helps to balance and contrast with the smooth, creamy texture of the beans. And when you serve foul with pita and a big plate of vegetables, it becomes a very satisfying and complete meal.

Jeanette eats this dish hot, warm, at room temperature, or cold from the refrigerator, either as a side or often all by itself for breakfast. The latter is traditional in Lebanon, because it keeps you full for a long time, and is also full of vitamins and protein. But it's also often set out at the start of a meal as an appetizer like hummus or baba ganoush.

For the foul

2 15.5-ounce (440 g each) cans fava beans

1 15.5-ounce (440 g) can chickpeas

¼ pound (115 g) yellow onion (about ½ medium)

½ pound (225 g) tomatoes on the vine (about 2 medium)

1 teaspoon Diamond Crystal kosher salt, plus more to taste

1 teaspoon crushed Aleppo or Marash pepper flakes

1 teaspoon ground sumac

½ teaspoon roasted cumin powder (page 23)

½ ounce (15 g) garlic (about 4 medium cloves)

2 tablespoons fresh lemon juice (from 1 to 2 lemons), or more to taste

¼ teaspoon ground allspice

3 tablespoons extra-virgin olive oil

Pita bread, for serving

For the "extras"

A mix of at least 2 or 3 raw vegetables and herbs, such as whole scallions, sliced onion, wedges of tomato, slices of bell pepper, whole cayenne peppers, sliced radishes, fresh mint, and fresh parsley

1   **Prepare the ingredients:** Drain the 2 15.5-ounce (440 g each) cans of fava beans into a strainer and rinse the beans under running water in the sink—you don't have to really wash them, just rinse them off. Transfer the beans to a 5-quart (3.5 to 5 L) Dutch oven or saucepan and set it aside.

2   Drain the 1 15.5-ounce (440 g) can of chickpeas into the strainer and rinse them. Measure out

Continued

1 cup (160 g) chickpeas and put them on a plate or in a bowl. Use a fork to roughly crush them. Keep the remaining chickpeas whole and set them aside separately from the mashed chickpeas. (You can also set aside about 5 whole chickpeas to use as garnish, if you like.)

3   Peel the ¼ pound (115 g) yellow onion (about ½ medium) and then cut it into small pieces about ⅛ inch (0.3 cm) wide. You should have about 1 cup. Add the onion to the bowl with the smashed chickpeas. (You can also set aside about 1 tablespoon of chopped onion to use as garnish, if you like.)

4   Remove the stem ends from the ½ pound (225 g) tomatoes on the vine (about 2 medium). Cut the tomatoes into pieces about ⅓ inch (1 cm) wide. You should have about 1 cup. Add it to the bowl with the onion and chickpeas. (You can also set aside about 1 tablespoon chopped tomatoes to use as garnish, if you like.)

5   Measure out the 1 teaspoon Diamond Crystal kosher salt, 1 teaspoon crushed Aleppo or Marash pepper flakes, 1 teaspoon ground sumac, and ½ teaspoon roasted cumin powder into a small bowl and set it aside. (Do not add the allspice.)

6   Peel the ½ ounce (15 g) garlic (about 4 medium cloves) and grate it over the fine holes of a box grater. You should end up with a scant tablespoon. Set it aside in a separate bowl.

7   Prepare 2 tablespoons fresh lemon juice (from 1 to 2 lemons), if you haven't already, and set it aside in a small bowl.

Jeanette always keeps her lemons on the countertop for a few days to soften them before she puts them in the refrigerator, so they're easier to juice. She also rolls them on the counter before she juices them, for the same reason.

8   **Cook the fava beans:** Add 2 cups (475 ml) water to the Dutch oven with the fava beans and bring to a boil over medium-high heat. Reduce the temperature to low and cook the fava beans for 10 minutes, stirring occasionally.

9   Use a fork to press and roughly crush about a quarter of the beans in the pot. Stir in the whole chickpeas, then let the beans and whole chickpeas continue to cook for another 10 minutes.

10 Add the smashed chickpeas, onion, and tomatoes and the bowl with all the spices, then stir until everything is incorporated. Add enough water so that everything is covered, usually at least 1 cup (120 ml), then increase the heat to medium-high to bring the pot to a strong simmer. Reduce the heat to medium-low so that there are a few bubbles around the edge of the pot, and cook for about 10 minutes. The tomatoes won't be fully cooked, but the onions will be translucent and soft and the liquid should have thickened slightly.

11 Turn off the heat and stir in the ¼ teaspoon ground allspice and the grated garlic. Add the lemon juice. Stir everything until it's well mixed. Taste for lemon and salt and add more if needed. Set the foul aside until you're ready to serve it.

12 **Serve and eat the foul:** Prepare the vegetables for the "extras" and arrange them on a large platter. You can serve foul hot, warm, at room temperature, or cold. You can put the foul in a large serving bowl to serve family-style or give everyone an individual small bowl. If desired, garnish the center of the serving bowl or individual bowls just before serving with the reserved chickpeas, chopped onions, and/or chopped tomatoes. Then drizzle the 3 tablespoons extra-virgin olive oil across the top of the foul. Serve with the "extras" and pita.

Pahelo Dal

(NEPALI YELLOW DAL)

Instructor: Rachana Rimal

"In Nepal we make a different kind of dal almost every day. It is so important." —Rachana

Dal is so central to the South Asian table—we have three South Asian instructors in the League of Kitchens and between them we probably could have packed this book with at least fifteen different fabulous dal recipes. Rachana is vegetarian (although her family eats meat—having a mix of both in one household is quite common in Nepal), so dal is one of her main sources of protein, and there is dal at every Nepali meal she serves. This one is made with split yellow pigeon peas, also known as toor or rahar ko dal, and flavored with cardamom, cinnamon, cloves, cumin, and fresh ginger added at the end. The spices blend together beautifully, and no flavor is overpowering. Rachana cooks this dal (and many other dishes) with a dried Nepali herb called jimbu. Like garlic and onions, jimbu is in the allium family—when it's still fresh it looks a little like garlic chives, with long skinny leaves. In the United States, you'll most likely have to buy this online, unless you live in a city with a large Nepali population. But if you can't find jimbu, don't worry, this will still be one of the best dals you've ever tasted.

Rachana says to try not to stir the dal while you cook it—it will slow the cooking process by lowering the temperature. And when you pour the hot ghee and tempered spices—the janne—onto the top at the end, be careful, as it will splatter. Rachana uses a pot lid to protect herself as she does it.

I recommend that when you serve the dal, you put an extra dollop of ghee on your rice, top it with a spoonful of dal, and then mix it together with your hand before taking a bite. Eating South Asian food with your hand makes it even more delicious! You can also serve the dal in small bowls and drink it like soup, directly from the bowl.

Serve with: white basmati rice, the greens on page 266, and the cauliflower and potato on page 278.

For the dal

1 cup (200 g) toor dal (split yellow pigeon peas)

2 Indian bay leaves (page 21) or
    4 bay laurel leaves

1 2-inch (5 cm) cinnamon stick (about 2 g),
    or 1 3-inch (7.5 cm) piece Indian flat cinnamon

2 teaspoons Diamond Crystal kosher salt

½ teaspoon ground turmeric

2 green cardamom pods

2 whole cloves

2 pinches asafetida

½ ounce (15 g) fresh ginger root (about
    1-inch/2.5 cm square)

1 tablespoon ghee, plus more straight from the jar
    for serving

For the janne

1 teaspoon jimbu, optional

1 teaspoon whole cumin seeds

1 pinch asafetida

1 tablespoon ghee

1   **Prepare the ingredients:** Put the 1 cup (200 g) toor dal (split yellow pigeon peas) in a bowl in the sink. Fill up the bowl with water and use your hands to swirl and scrub the pigeon peas between your hands to wash them. Pour off the water and refill the bowl

Continued

two or three more times, until the water runs clear.

2   Put the 2 Indian bay leaves or 4 bay laurel leaves, the 1 2-inch (5 cm) cinnamon stick (about 2 g) or 1 3-inch (7.5 cm) piece Indian flat cinnamon, 2 teaspoons Diamond Crystal kosher salt, ½ teaspoon ground turmeric, 2 green cardamom pods, 2 whole cloves, and 2 pinches asafetida in a bowl.

3   Peel the ½ ounce (15 g) fresh ginger root (about 1-inch/2.5 cm square) with a spoon. Cut it into slices about ⅛ inch (0.3 cm) thick, then smash them in a mortar and pestle until they are a fine paste. (If you don't have a mortar and pestle, grate them on the fine holes of a box grater.) You should have about 1 tablespoon. Set the ginger aside.

4   Bring 6 cups (1.4 L) water to a boil in a kettle or large saucepan. (Once it comes to a boil, you can turn off the heat, but cover it so it stays hot.)

5   **Cook the dal:** Put the washed toor dal into a 5-quart (4.8 L) Dutch oven or saucepan or small stockpot with a heavy bottom. Add 2 cups (475 ml) tap water, the 1 tablespoon ghee, and the combined spices, then bring the pot to a boil over high heat. Lower the heat to medium or medium-high so that the pot cooks at a simmer—you have many small bubbles—but doesn't boil over or burn at the bottom.

6   Cook, without stirring, until most of the water has been absorbed by the toor dal, 7 to 10 minutes. Add 1 cup (240 ml) of the hot water. Simmer until most of the water has been absorbed, another 7 to 10 minutes, then add 1 more cup (240 ml) of the hot water. Cook the dal, adding 1 cup (240 ml) more water as needed in this manner, until the dal is soft and tender and completely cooked through.

It depends on your peas, but it usually takes about 60 minutes for the dal to finish cooking after it comes to a boil. Generally, you need to add 3 more cups (700 ml) of water (for a total of 5 cups/1.2 L), waiting about 10 minutes between each cup—then let it cook for an additional 10 to 15 minutes at the end.

7   Add more hot water as needed at the end so that the dal is the consistency of thin soup, not porridge.

8   Turn off the heat, then stir in the crushed or grated ginger. Cover the pot to keep the dal warm while you prepare the janne.

9   **Prepare the janne:** When you're ready to serve the dal, measure out the 1 teaspoon jimbu, if using, 1 teaspoon whole cumin seeds, and a pinch of asafetida into a small bowl or measuring cup.

10   Heat the 1 tablespoon ghee in a small saucepan over medium-high heat. As soon as it begins to bubble, stir in the combined spices and fry them, stirring constantly so they don't burn, just until they begin to color and pop, usually 10 to 15 seconds. Pour the janne right onto the top of the dal, being careful of splattering oil, then stir it in.

11   **Serve and eat the dal:** Serve the dal immediately, while the janne is still hot, preferably with basmati rice. Put out a jar of ghee so everyone can top their rice with a spoonful before mixing in some dal.

Frijoles Negros

(MEXICAN BLACK BEANS)

Instructor: Angelica Vargas

"People ask me why I don't soak my beans overnight. I am always running between my kids and my jobs, and I never have time. I find that it really doesn't make a difference, I just cook them a little longer!" —Angie

These flavorful beans are an everyday type of dish in Mexico, eaten with almost every meal. They freeze well, too, says Angie, and she always makes sure she has some in the freezer so she doesn't have to buy canned beans.

You can find fresh epazote—it has a jagged thin leaf—in nearly all Mexican grocery stores, and it also grows as a weed in most of the American continent. It has such a strong chemical flavor when it's raw—almost like gasoline—that you might be afraid to use so much, but don't worry, it becomes both mild and delicious when cooked down with the beans. Plus, adding it to the beans helps reduce gas! But if you can't get epazote, these beans are still fabulous.

Angie typically serves a scoop of these beans with a scoop of Mexican tomato rice (page 176) as the partner to many meals, especially the picadillo on page 78. She also uses these to make black bean tostadas, which are a really easy dinner—she just purees some of the beans with enough of their cooking liquid to cover them in a blender and spreads it across fried corn tostadas (page 93). She then adds toppings like crumbled queso fresco, one of the salsas on pages 65 and 66, slices of avocado, shredded iceberg lettuce, and sour cream thinned with milk and seasoned with a little salt.

Serve with: the Mexican rice on page 176, the steak tacos on page 63, the eggs with habaneros on page 117, or with just a few corn tortillas (page 165).

¾ pound (340 g) white onion (about 1 medium)

3 ounces (85 g) garlic (about 1 large head)

1 pound (450 g) dried black beans

⅛ pound (60 g) fresh epazote (about ½ bunch), optional

1 tablespoon neutral oil

1½ tablespoons Diamond Crystal kosher salt

1 **Prepare the ingredients:** Wash the ¾ pound (340 g) white onion (about 1 medium). Trim the ends and remove the outer papery peel, but keep the onion whole. Set it aside.

2 Wash the 3 ounces (85 g) garlic (about 1 large head) and scrub away any damaged or dirty roots at the root end. Use a large knife to cut about ¾ inch (2 cm) off the stem end of the head in one big slice, so you expose some of the garlic but leave the rest of the head intact.

3 Spread the 1 pound (450 g) dried black beans on the counter or on a large plate and look them over for small stones. (Even mass-produced bags often have little stones in them.)

4 Put the beans in a large mixing bowl and rinse them in the sink under running water, swirling them with your hands until the water runs fairly clear. Drain the beans and set them aside.

5 Rinse the ⅛ pound (60 g) fresh epazote (about ½ bunch), if using, making sure to remove any dirt clinging to the bottom of the leaves (it's often fairly gritty). Trim any dry or damaged ends from the stems.

6 **Cook the beans:** Fill a 5-quart (4.8 L) Dutch oven or saucepan with 10 cups (2.4 L) of water.

Add the washed beans, the whole peeled white onion, and the garlic head. (The garlic and onion may float—that's okay.)

7   Add the 1 tablespoon neutral oil and 1½ tablespoons Diamond Crystal kosher salt and bring to a boil over high heat. Reduce the heat slightly, to medium or medium-high, so that the beans cook at a strong simmer—there will be lots of smaller bubbles, but the pot shouldn't boil over. After about 30 minutes, add the ½ bunch of epazote, if using.

8   Simmer the beans, stirring occasionally with a wooden spoon, until they're fully soft all the way through, usually at least another hour, and often more than two.

9   If the water sinks below the beans as they cook, add 2 to 3 cups (475 to 700 ml) more tap water so that the beans stay submerged as they simmer.

10 When the beans are done, keep them warm until you're ready to serve them. You can also refrigerate them in their cooking liquid, or even freeze them. (You don't need to remove the whole onion and garlic, but you can if you want to.)

11 **Serve and eat the beans:** When you're ready to serve the beans, gently reheat them, if needed, in their cooking liquid, then use a slotted spoon to transfer them to each plate or a serving bowl. You can also serve them in a bowl with a little bit of the liquid. Angie usually puts a few sprigs of cooked epazote in each serving, as well.

Khichari

(INDIAN SPLIT MUNG BEAN AND RICE PORRIDGE)

Instructor: Yamini Joshi

"When I was ten years old I was already cooking khichari—so it's a lifelong memory of my childhood." —Yamini

When Yamini was small, she lived in Mumbai in a chawl, a kind of multifamily apartment building that was shared with many relatives. There were around fifty family members living all together and sharing one kitchen. They ate a varied and complex lunch meal that changed every day and with the seasons, but dinner was always khichari, usually with a pickle and pappadum, a kind of crispy flatbread. Khichari is basically a rice and split mung bean porridge spiced with a mix of ingredients, which always includes cumin seeds, ginger, turmeric, and asafetida, but beyond that, there are many variations. Yamini's version also includes curry leaves, fenugreek seeds, ground coriander, and green chiles.

In Ayurveda—a traditional Indian system of healing—it's recommended that lunch should be your main meal of the day, and that dinner should be something light, nourishing, and easily digestible—like khichari. Plus, it makes a lot of sense when you're feeding so many people to make one big pot of something for dinner! Yamini says it's also what you eat when you're sick, when you're old, or when you've just given birth. But, really, it's great anytime.

As with every recipe in this book, what makes this khichari so spectacular is in the details of how Yamini cooks it. Instead of bringing a separate pot of water to a boil in advance, Yamini puts the water she'll need to add during cooking in a bowl directly on top of the pot of cooking rice and split mung beans. The bowl serves as a lid for the pot, and the pot heats the water. Yamini says the bowl on top also helps draw some of the heat away from the pot, preventing the rice and beans from absorbing the water too quickly—which results in better khichari. It's an ingenious technique that really works. (But you can just heat the water separately, too.)

For more about all the spices in this dish, see page 21. You can use basmati rice or long-grain white rice or any broken rice—rice grains broken during the milling process—which is beginning to be more widely available. Using aged or very-long-grain basmati rice is not important here, as everything turns to mush. In fact, there is a stage where the rice grains are distinct but cooked—you want to go past that. As long as you keep adding hot water and stirring occasionally so it doesn't burn, you can't overcook it!

Yamini keeps the chiles whole in this dish and just cuts a small slit near the top. You get the flavor of the chiles but very little heat. If you want just a hint of chile flavor, use just one, without a slit.

Serve with: the Indian cucumber salad on page 226, the lemon pickle on page 149, fresh crisped pappadum, and a bowl of plain whole milk yogurt stirred smooth and sprinkled with roasted cumin powder.

1 cup (200 g) basmati or long-grain white rice

1 cup (200 g) moong dal (split mung beans)

2 tablespoons whole cumin seeds, divided

1 teaspoon whole fenugreek seeds

⅛ teaspoon asafetida

12 medium fresh, frozen, or dried curry leaves

2 teaspoons ground turmeric

1 or 2 green bird's-eye chiles

2 tablespoons roasted coriander powder (page 24)

2 teaspoons Diamond Crystal kosher salt

⅓ ounce (10 g) fresh ginger (about 1 inch/2.5 cm)

Continued

¼ cup (60 ml) ghee, plus more straight from the jar for serving

2 cups (475 ml) plain whole milk yogurt

1 teaspoon roasted cumin powder (page 23)

Lemon pickle (recipe follows), for serving, optional

Toasted prepackaged pappadum, for serving, optional

1 **Wash and soak the grains:** Combine the 1 cup (200 g) basmati or long-grain white rice and the 1 cup (200 g) moong dal (split mung beans) in a large mixing bowl. Put the bowl in the sink under cool running tap water. Use your hands to swirl the grains and gently rub them between your hands under the water until the water runs fairly clear.

2 Drain the grains as much as you can, then add about 1 cup (240 ml) water—the water should be just covering the grains. Set the bowl aside to let the grains soak for at least 15 minutes or up to 1 hour.

Don't let the grains soak overnight, or they'll begin to ferment.

3 **Prepare the spices while the grains soak:** Measure out the following into a small bowl: 1 tablespoon of the whole cumin seeds, the 1 teaspoon whole fenugreek seeds, ⅛ teaspoon asafetida, the 12 medium fresh, frozen, or dried curry leaves, and 2 teaspoons ground turmeric.

4 Remove any long stems from the 1 or 2 green bird's-eye chiles and then use a paring knife to make a small slit near the tip of the chile. Add them to the bowl with the spices and curry leaves. Set the bowl aside.

5 In another small bowl, measure out 2 tablespoons roasted coriander powder (see page 24) and 2 teaspoons Diamond Crystal kosher salt.

6 Use the edge of a soup spoon to scrape off just the rough parts of the skin from the

⅓ ounce (10 g) piece of fresh ginger (about 1 inch/2.5 cm). Roughly chop the ginger into small pieces. You should end up with about 1 tablespoon of diced ginger. Add it to the bowl with the coriander powder and salt and set it aside.

7 Keep everything close by the stove so it's ready when you need it.

8 **Cook the khichari:** Measure the ¼ cup (60 ml) ghee into a 5-quart (4.8 L) Dutch oven or saucepan, preferably nonstick.

9 Put 3 cups (700 ml) of water in a large measuring cup and put it by the stove.

10 Heat the ghee in the pot over medium-low heat until the ghee begins to smell fragrant and smoke just a little, usually less than a minute—if you add 1 cumin seed, it should sizzle immediately—then add the bowl of spices, curry leaves, and chiles to the pot. Use a wooden spoon or spatula to stir everything in the oil for 10 seconds or so, until it's fragrant and everything is spattering and popping. Stir in 2 cups (475 ml) of the tap water from the measuring cup.

11 Raise the heat to medium-high. Stir in the remaining 1 cup (240 ml) of water, and then the combined coriander powder, salt, and diced fresh ginger.

12 Let the liquid come up to a boil, then stir in the washed and soaked grains. Let it come back to a boil, give the grains a stir so that they don't stick to the bottom, then reduce the heat to medium or medium-low so that the pot cooks at a simmer. (You don't need to skim any foam.)

13 Put 3 cups (700 ml) tap water in a metal, heatproof mixing bowl that will fit on the top of the Dutch oven and set it on the top of the pot to form a lid. Let everything cook for 7 minutes, then carefully remove the bowl (use an oven

mitt or dry dish towel to touch it) and check the grains to see if the liquid has all been absorbed. If it has, use a ladle to scoop about ½ cup (120 ml) hot water from the hot bowl into the pot. Give the grains a stir so that they don't stick to the bottom, then return the bowl to the top of the pot and cook for about 3 minutes, until the liquid has been absorbed.

14 Add ½ cup (120 ml) hot water from the hot bowl every 10 minutes until the khichari is done—everything will be broken down and mushy, where the grains and rice are no longer really recognizable—usually about 1 hour. Start testing for doneness about 40 minutes into the process. Remember that as long as you continue to add water and stir to keep it from sticking, you can't really overcook it, but you can undercook it. (Depending on your grains and rice, you may not need to use all of the water, or you may need to add more tap water to the pot, if you're running low.)

15 When the khichari is done, it should still be a little softer and soupier than cooked rice. If it's completely dry, stir in another ¼ cup (60 ml) of hot water from the hot bowl. Stir in the remaining 1 tablespoon of whole cumin seeds, cover the pot, turn off the heat, and let it sit until you're ready to eat.

16 **Prepare the accompaniments:** Put the 2 cups (475 ml) whole milk yogurt into a bowl. Whisk it until it's smooth. Keep it in one serving bowl to share, or put it in separate individual bowls. Sprinkle the top of the yogurt with 1 teaspoon roasted cumin powder (page 23).

17 Put out the jar of ghee and the lemon pickle (recipe follows), if using, and the toasted pappadum, if using.

18 **To serve and eat the khichari:** Serve the khichari hot or warm on a plate or in a bowl. Each person should top their khichari with a dollop of ghee and then mix it in. If you're serving this with lemon pickle and pappadum, traditionally you would have a bite of each of those between bites of khichari, so you have some flavor and textural contrast, or you could even scoop up some of the khichari or pickle with the pappadum. (If you're not eating it with the pickle, you may want to add more salt, to taste, to the khichari at the table.) You would also generally have a bite of yogurt in between, too.

Like all South Asian foods, khichari is meant to be eaten with your hands, and I strongly recommend that you try that—it really changes the taste and experience of the dish. Spoon some khichari on a plate, top it with a dollop of ghee, and then take the hand you eat with and mush and mix the ghee into the khichari. Take a small amount with your hand and mush it into a loose ball, then put it in your mouth.

Nimbu Ka Achar Mitha

(INDIAN SWEET LEMON PICKLE)

MAKES ABOUT 2 CUPS (475 ML)

This is one of the more labor-intensive recipes in the book, but this pickle, or achar, is truly worth it because it's so delicious. Yamini learned this recipe from her maternal grandmother, and it's one of the best South Asian condiments I've ever had. It also lasts for a long time. Because it's quite potent, you usually eat just a few tablespoons per person in a given meal—it's meant to be an accent, and one that helps with digestion. It's particularly good with khichari, providing a spicy, sweet, and tangy contrast to the smooth simple flavor of the porridge. It's also great alongside Yamini's dal on page 157.

Continued

Picking out great lemons at the store is important here—the skin of the lemons should be silky and soft to the touch, and not thick, which would take a lot longer to cook. For more about the spices in this dish, see page 21. If you want your pickle to be spicy, add the highest amount of chile powder; for just a little heat, add the lowest amount.

2 tablespoons plus 1 teaspoon whole fenugreek seeds, divided

1 pound (450 g) lemons (about 4 large)

2 tablespoons roasted coriander powder (page 24)

1 tablespoon roasted cumin powder (page 23)

1 teaspoon black pepper powder

¼ to 2½ teaspoons Kashmiri chile powder or another red chile powder

1 teaspoon black salt

½ teaspoon ground turmeric

3 tablespoons untoasted sesame oil

1 teaspoon asafetida

1 teaspoon Diamond Crystal kosher salt

10 ounces (285 g) jaggery (see page 22) or dark brown sugar, about 2 cups

1 **Toast and crush the fenugreek:** Heat a 9½-inch (24 cm) skillet over medium heat, then wipe out any moisture. Add 2 tablespoons of the whole fenugreek seeds and toast them, watching carefully, just until they become fragrant (the time varies, but it's usually within a minute or so). Let the seeds cool completely in the pan. Then very coarsely grind the seeds in a spice mill or grinder just until all the seeds are broken—you don't want them to become a powder. Set these aside.

2 **Prepare the lemons:** Wash the 1 pound (450 g) lemons (about 4 large). With a small knife, cut the peel (including the white pith) away from the pulp, the same way you'd cut a grapefruit into supremes. (The peel doesn't have to look

pretty or stay in one piece.) Set the flesh aside and then cut the pieces of skin roughly into ½-inch (1.3 cm) chunks; set the lemon peel aside.

3 Cut the pulp of the lemons roughly into 4 or 5 pieces, removing and discarding the seeds. Use your fingers to tear apart the pulp, then set it aside separate from the peel.

4 Put the lemon peels in 1 cup (240 ml) of water in a medium saute pan and bring to a boil. When the water comes to a boil, lower the heat to a simmer and cover the pot. Let the mixture cook, stirring occasionally, until it's so soft that you can break a piece of peel with a spoon or mush it between your thumb and forefinger, often about 45 minutes if your peels are on the thicker side. (If you need to cook your peels for a long time, you may need to add water so that they stay covered.) When the skins are soft, turn off the heat and set the pot aside.

5 **Prepare the spice blend** (**masala**): Measure the following out into a small bowl: 2 tablespoons roasted coriander powder, 1 tablespoon roasted cumin powder, 1 teaspoon black pepper powder, ¼ to 2½ teaspoons Kashmiri chile powder or another red chile powder, 1 teaspoon black salt, and ½ teaspoon ground turmeric. Set this aside.

6 **Make the achar:** Put 3 tablespoons untoasted sesame oil in a 12-inch (30 cm) skillet, preferably nonstick. Heat the oil over medium heat until it's sizzling, then add the remaining 1 teaspoon whole fenugreek seeds (not the crushed). Cook for about 2 minutes, stirring occasionally, until they turn light brown, about 1 minute.

7 Stir in 1 teaspoon asafetida, and then add the boiled lemon peel with any water still left in the pot. Stir everything together for about 20 seconds, then stir in the crushed roasted fenugreek seeds and 1 teaspoon Diamond

Crystal kosher salt. Cook, stirring frequently, for 2 minutes.

8 Stir in the spice blend (masala) and the reserved lemon pulp, making sure that everything is mixed together. The pot will be fairly dry at this point—that's fine—but cook, stirring constantly, for 1 minute.

9 Add the 10 ounces (285 g) jaggery or dark brown sugar (about 2 cups), using your fingers to crumble it as necessary (you don't want any big pieces because they won't break down). As it begins to soften and melt, stir it into the lemon peel and flesh so everything is coated. Cook over medium to medium-high heat so that the mixture bubbles, stirring frequently to make sure the bottom doesn't scorch, until the mixture has thickened and most of the liquid has evaporated, about 10 minutes. Turn off the heat, remove the pot from the stove, and let it cool completely.

10 **Ripen the achar:** Once the achar has cooled completely, put it in a glass storage container or canning jar with a tight-fitting lid. It can be eaten right away, but it's even better after it sits for at least a few days, and preferably about a week. Let it sit out on the counter at room temperature for 1 week to let the flavors meld and ripen, then refrigerate. It will last in the refrigerator for at least 1 month.

11 **Serve the achar:** Lemon pickle is generally served in a small bowl on the table as a condiment. Put a spoonful on your plate and eat it in between bites of other food.

Lubya

(AFGHAN RED BEANS AND GRAVY)

Instructor: Nawida Saidhosin

"Lubya and challow—or red beans and rice—is every Afghan child's favorite food." —Nawida

These beans are super-delicious, savory, and saucy, and I feel that way even though I'm often ambivalent about beans. These are so flavorful, stewed with a rich and thick gravy, thanks to all the spices and tomato and onion, which essentially melt into the sauce. This is considered a proper main dish, and when served with the rice with cloves and garlic on page 179 called challow, it's like the macaroni and cheese of Afghanistan, meaning it's the dish all kids from Afghanistan love, says Nawida. You can eat these beans with bread, too, or serve them over pasta with a garlicky yogurt sauce (that recipe follows).

Lubya is typically served with large slices of raw onion that are sprinkled with lemon juice and dried mint and/or red chile powder, and this is a great combination, with that pungent-but-sweet, juicy, crisp raw onion cutting through the richness of the beans. In addition, Nawida likes to put out slices of raw jalapeño for a spicy accent.

There is also so much technique in these beans that makes them extra delicious. Once the beans are in the process of cooking, Nawida adds only hot water to make sure they fully soften, and she also blanches the beans before they cook, which ensures the beans end up a beautiful bright red in the finished dish, and their flavor is less muddied, too.

Serve with: the rice with garlic and cloves on page 179 and the Afghan custard on page 299. These beans are also used in the Afghan macaroni with white sauce on page 155.

For the beans

1 pound (450 g) dried red or kidney beans
¾ pound (340 g) yellow onion (about 1 large)
¼ ounce (7 g) garlic (about 2 medium cloves)
¼ cup (60 ml) ghee, olive oil, or neutral oil
1½ tablespoons tomato paste
2 teaspoons roasted coriander powder (page 24)
1 teaspoon ground turmeric
½ teaspoon black pepper powder
1½ tablespoons Diamond Crystal kosher salt
1 teaspoon roasted cumin powder (page 23)
Challow (page 179), white basmati rice, or bread, for serving

For the onion

1 pound (450 g) white onion (about 1 large)
1 large lemon
½ teaspoon dried mint, optional
½ teaspoon red chile powder, optional
1 jalapeño chile, optional

1 **Prepare the bean cooking water:** Bring 10 cups (2.4 L) of water to a boil in a large saucepan. (Once it comes to a boil, you can turn off the heat, but cover it so it stays hot.)

2 **Blanch the beans:** In a stockpot or 5-quart (4.8 L) Dutch oven or saucepan with a lid, cover the 1 pound (450 g) dried red or kidney beans with tap water to cover by 1 inch (2.5 cm). Bring to a boil, then cook for 1 minute, stirring once or twice to make sure all of the beans are mixed in the boiling water.

Continued

3   Turn off the heat and drain the beans into a colander in the sink. Rinse them with very hot water from the tap or some of the heated water from your saucepan and set them aside in the sink to drain.

4   **Cook the beans:** Peel the ¾ pound (340 g) yellow onion (about 1 large). Cut it in half from root to stem, trim the ends, and then slice each half from root to stem into thin slices about ⅛ inch (0.3 cm) thick. You should end up with about 2 cups. Put the onions in the pot you used to blanch the beans.

5   Peel the ¼ ounce (7 g) garlic (about 2 medium cloves), trim the ends if they're especially damaged or dirty, and then cut it into about 4 equal slices. Add them to the pot with the onions.

6   Put the blanched beans on top of the onions and garlic, then add 6 cups (1.4 L) of the very hot water. Give everything a stir so that the onions and garlic get mixed into the beans, then put the pot over medium-high heat and bring to a heavy simmer. Cover the pot and lower the heat slightly so that the beans cook at a steady simmer but the pot doesn't boil over.

7   **Prepare the seasoning:** While the beans are cooking, heat ¼ cup (60 ml) ghee, olive oil, or neutral oil in a small saucepan over medium-high heat. When the oil is hot (but not smoking) stir in the 1½ tablespoons tomato paste, turn the heat to low (so you don't burn it), and stir and fry it for just a few seconds, until its color changes and it breaks apart slightly. Then stir in the 2 teaspoons roasted coriander powder, 1 teaspoon ground turmeric, and ½ teaspoon black pepper powder.

8   Stir in ¼ cup (60 ml) of the hot water and 1½ tablespoons Diamond Crystal kosher salt. Let everything just heat through, then turn off the heat and set aside.

9   **Add the seasoning to the beans:** Stir the seasoning mixture into the pot with the beans once the beans have begun to soften just a little—they will still be fairly al dente in the middle if you taste one. (This timing varies widely, depending on the age and quality of the beans, but it typically takes 30 to 40 minutes.) Cook for about a minute uncovered, then cover the pot and let the beans simmer over medium-low heat for 20 minutes. (If for some reason your beans are dry, add hot water as necessary so that the beans are covered by liquid by about ¼ inch (0.6 cm).

10 **Finish the beans:** After the beans have cooked with the seasoning mixture for 20 minutes, stir them once or twice and then lower the heat to the lowest heat possible. They should be close to fully soft all the way through when you press them, but if not, cover the pot and let them simmer until they're done. (Again, this time varies widely, depending on your beans, so don't worry if they're not yet done.)

11 When the beans are fully cooked, stir in the 1 teaspoon roasted ground cumin, cover the pot, and let the beans cook for 5 more minutes, then turn off the heat.

12 **Prepare the onion:** When you're ready to serve the beans, peel the 1 pound (450 g) white onion (about 1 large). Cut it in half from the stem to the root, then slice each half parallel to the equator into very thick (½-inch/1.3 cm) half-moons; don't separate the rings. (You can discard the ends once you've cut all the slices.) Put the onion slices in a small serving bowl or plate. Cut the 1 large lemon in half and squeeze the juice over the onion. Crush the ½ teaspoon dried mint between your fingers and sprinkle it over the onion, if using, then sprinkle on the ½ teaspoon red chile powder, if using. Slice the 1 jalapeño chile into thin slices, if using, and add it to the serving bowl.

13 **Serve the beans:** Put the sliced onions out on the table. You can serve the beans hot, warm, or room temperature, either in individual bowls or family style, either on top of challow or basmati rice, or paired with bread. The traditional way to eat them is to take a bite of onion with each bite of beans, often with or in between a bite of rice or bread.

Lubya with Macaroni and White Sauce

(AFGHAN RED BEANS AND PASTA)

SERVES 4

The combination of the red beans and their rich gravy mixed with garlicky yogurt and dried mint is comforting and delicious—kids really love it. You serve it with pasta all together in a large dish or casserole topped with a sprinkle of cilantro. Make sure to use both the beans and their cooking liquid, or gravy—the liquid is super flavorful and is part of what makes this pasta dish so good. Use small pasta so that you can eat this dish with a spoon.

> 1 pound (450 g) ridged elbow macaroni or another similar-sized pasta
>
> 3 cups (700 ml) lubya and gravy (page 153)
>
> ½ cup (120 ml) labne or plain whole milk Greek yogurt, at room temperature
>
> ½ ounce (15 g) garlic (about 4 medium cloves)
>
> 1 teaspoon Diamond Crystal kosher salt
>
> 1 tablespoon neutral oil
>
> ½ teaspoon dried mint
>
> ⅛ to ½ teaspoon red chile powder, optional
>
> 1 handful minced fresh cilantro

1 **Cook the pasta and warm the beans:** Cook the 1 pound (450 g) elbow macaroni or other similar-sized pasta according to the package directions and drain it through a colander in the sink. While the pasta cooks, heat the 3 cups (700 ml) lubya and gravy over medium heat and keep it warm on the stove.

2 **Make the garlic yogurt sauce:** While the pasta cooks and the beans are reheating, put ½ cup (120 ml) labne or plain whole milk Greek yogurt in a small mixing bowl. Finely grate the ½ ounce (15 g) garlic (about 4 medium cloves) into the bowl with the yogurt using a Microplane or a grater with star-shaped holes. Add the 1 teaspoon Diamond Crystal kosher salt and ¼ cup (60 ml) tap water and stir until the yogurt is very smooth, like a thick sauce. Set this aside.

You can use regular yogurt for this dish if that's what you have on hand, but you'll need to reduce the amount of water you add to the sauce, or even omit it.

3 **Compose the dish:** Get a large serving platter or casserole dish that will hold all the pasta. Spread a thin layer of the yogurt sauce on the bottom of the dish: You just want it to lightly cover the bottom. Use a serving spoon to mound the hot, drained pasta on top of the yogurt, then spoon the rest of the yogurt sauce over the pasta. (It will not cover the pasta completely—that's fine.)

4 Sprinkle the ½ teaspoon dried mint over the top of the pasta, then the ⅛ to ½ teaspoon red chile powder, if using: You just want a light dusting of both. Then use a spoon to layer the lubya and gravy on top of the pasta, the same way you'd spoon chili over nachos. (It will not cover the top completely—that's fine.) Sprinkle the 1 handful minced fresh cilantro over the top.

Panchvati Dal

(INDIAN MIXED DAL WITH TOMATO AND GARLIC)

Instructor: Yamini Joshi

"This is a special dal from Rajasthan and a favorite of my family. It's very flavorful and it matches with everything."
—Yamini

What sets apart this dal—a slow-cooked mix of lentils and beans that's made all over South Asia—is Yamini's delicious tarka. A tarka is a combination of whole and ground spices, chiles, and aromatics bloomed in hot ghee or oil, then poured over the top of a dish at the end. This one has umami from tomato and garlic and texture from whole cumin seeds and fragrant curry leaves (see page 21). If you don't want a lot of chile heat in your dal, use just one chile.

Dal, served along with rice, a pickle, and at least one vegetable, is an essential part of most meals in India. Usually you would have a bowl of rice and a bowl of dal, which is a little bit soupy. You'd put a dollop of ghee on your pile of rice, and then spoon the dal on top. Then you mix it all together and eat it with your fingers. Adding the ghee to the mix might seem optional, but it really makes it extra yummy. Or you can dip a piece of bread like roti (page 173) into the bowl of dal, and then just sip the rest like soup, directly from the bowl. (It's especially good if you spread some ghee and jaggery on the roti also, like you see in the photo, opposite, to eat in between bites of dal.)

Just as she does with her khichari (page 146), Yamini warms the water she needs to add to the dal in a bowl set on top of the cooking pot. This technique draws some of the heat out of the pot, keeping the lentils and beans from absorbing the water in the pot too quickly, and results in better-tasting dal. She is also very careful not to stir the pot too often, because stirring lowers the temperature of the dal and makes it take longer to cook. (Yamini uses a wooden spoon instead of a metal one, for the same reason.)

Yamini uses a traditional Indian cooking vessel that narrows at the opening, which makes it easier to cook the dal slowly without burning it—but the rest of us can use any heavy-bottomed pot or Dutch oven, and if it's designed to be nonstick, even better.

Yamini first discovered this kind of mixed dal at a family wedding feast. If you don't want to buy five kinds of dal to mix yourself, you can make a really delicious version of this with just masoor dal (split red lentils, which are readily available at most health food stores) or moong dal (split mung beans). You would just use an equal amount, or 14 tablespoons. (Preferably, you wouldn't use a mix of both: For good luck, Yamini only combines pulses for dal in odd numbers. In other words, one, three, or five kinds is fine, but not two or four.) Sometimes you can find bags of mixed dal at South Asian supermarkets.

Serve with: basmati rice and/or roti (page 173) and at least one other vegetable dish, such as the sweet potatoes on page 242 or the cucumber salad on page 226. You can also eat this with the sweet lemon pickle on page 149 or the mango yogurt parfait on page 291. Traditionally, you would eat the yogurt parfait as part of the meal, getting a sweet accent between savory bites, rather than eating it at the end as dessert.

For the dal

2 tablespoons toor dal (split pigeon peas)

1 tablespoon urad dal (black mung beans, preferably without skin)

1 tablespoon chana dal (split chickpeas)

Continued

2 tablespoons masoor dal (split red lentils)

8 tablespoons moong dal (split mung beans)

2 tablespoons ghee

1 teaspoon whole cumin seeds

2½ teaspoons Diamond Crystal kosher salt

1 teaspoon ground turmeric

⅛ pound (60 g) fresh cilantro (about ½ bunch)

For the tarka

½ ounce (15 g) garlic (about 4 medium cloves)

½ pound (225 g) plum tomatoes (about 2 medium)

1 to 3 green bird's-eye chiles

2 tablespoons ghee

2 teaspoons whole cumin seeds

11 fresh, frozen, or dried medium curry leaves

⅛ teaspoon asafetida

⅛ to 1½ teaspoons Kashmiri chile powder

1   **Prepare the dal:** Measure 2 tablespoons toor dal (split pigeon peas), 1 tablespoon urad dal (black mung beans, preferably without skin), 1 tablespoon chana dal (split chickpeas), 2 tablespoons masoor dal (split red lentils), and 8 tablespoons moong dal (split mung beans) into a mixing bowl.

2   Put the bowl in the sink under running tap water. Once the water covers the pulses, swirl them gently once or twice, then pour off the water and refill the bowl. Repeat this 6 or 7 times, until the water runs clear. Cover the pulses with 1½ cups (350 ml) of water and set them aside to soak for 30 minutes.

3   **Cook the dal:** Put the soaked lentils and beans and their soaking water into a 5-quart (4.8 L) Dutch oven or saucepan, preferably nonstick, then add 2 cups (475 ml) more water to the pot. (Don't stir them.) Turn the heat to high. When the water starts to boil, stir nearly constantly with a wooden spoon until the foam rises to the top, then skim off and discard as much of the foam as you can.

4   Once you've removed most of the foam, stir in the 2 tablespoons ghee, 1 teaspoon whole cumin seeds, 2½ teaspoons Diamond Crystal kosher salt, and 1 teaspoon ground turmeric.

5   Lower the heat to medium so that everything cooks at a simmer. Put 4 cups (945 ml) tap water in a metal heatproof mixing bowl that will fit on the top of the Dutch oven and set it on the top of the pot to form a lid.

6   Let the dal simmer for 10 minutes, then carefully remove the bowl from the top of the pot (using a towel or potholder) and use a ladle to pour ½ cup (120 ml) hot water from the bowl into the pot—don't stir it in.

7   Again, let the dal simmer for 10 minutes, then carefully remove the bowl from the top of the pot and pour in another ½ cup (120 ml) hot water from the bowl—don't stir it in.

8   Replace the bowl on the pot and continue to cook for 10 more minutes, then check to see if all the lentils and beans are soft. (The toor dal, or split pigeon peas, usually take the longest.) If they're not yet soft, pour in another ½ cup (120 ml) hot water from the bowl, replace the bowl, and cook for another 10 minutes. If needed, reduce the heat to low, keep the pot covered, and continue to cook, checking every 5 minutes or so. You want the dal to be a little soupy when it's done, and not thick and fully dry, so add a little hot water as needed, even if the lentils and beans are done. Turn off the heat under the pot, but keep it covered.

At some point you may need to add more water to the bowl on top of the pot if you're running low.

9   **Make the tarka:** Peel the ½ ounce (15 g) garlic (about 4 medium cloves) and finely chop it into ⅛-inch (0.3 cm) pieces. You should have about a scant tablespoon. Set this aside.

10 Remove the hard white stem end from ½ pound (225 g) plum tomatoes (about 2 medium) and cut them into ⅓-inch (1 cm) dice. You should have about 1 heaping packed cup. Set this aside.

11 Remove any damaged stems from the 1 to 3 green bird's-eye chiles and cut a small slit near the tip. Set aside.

12 Heat a 9½-inch (24 cm) skillet or wok over high heat until your hand is immediately hot when you hold it over the pan. Add the 2 tablespoons ghee, let it melt, and then the 2 teaspoons whole cumin seeds right on top of the ghee. (Test the ghee with one cumin seed. If the ghee is hot enough, the cumin seed should float and bubble immediately.) As soon as the cumin seeds begin to foam, add the chopped garlic.

Ghee pools more deeply in Yamini's traditional Indian pot, and when you use a flatter pan like a skillet, it's much easier to burn everything. One trick Yamini taught me is to make sure to add the spices to the spot in your pan right where the ghee is pooled, even if it's not the middle. Then they're less likely to burn.

13 Let the garlic cook for about 10 seconds, then add the 1 to 3 slit green bird's-eye chiles and 11 fresh, frozen, or dried medium curry leaves (they will begin to pop a little). Stir in the ⅛ teaspoon asafetida, ⅛ teaspoon to 1½ teaspoons Kashmiri chile powder, if using, and the chopped tomatoes.

14 Mix everything together and fry for about 2 minutes, stirring constantly, until you see bubbles around the edge of the pan and the tomatoes soften. Add the tarka to the dal and mix it gently into the pot. Cover the pot and keep it warm until you're ready to serve it.

15 Trim away all but the tender stems and leaves from the ⅛ pound (60 g) fresh cilantro (about ½ bunch). Finely mince the cilantro and set it aside. You should have about ½ cup.

16 **Serve and eat the dal:** Serve the dal in small individual bowls garnished with a spoonful of chopped cilantro, alongside cooked basmati rice and extra ghee, or roti.

Mahboubeh (Mab) Abbasgholizadeh

Mab was born and raised in Khorramshahr, a city with a large Arab population in southern Iran. Her father owned a restaurant, a grocery store, and a tea importing company, and he taught her about picking the best ingredients for every recipe. Her mother taught her how to cook, often dishes from the Azeri region of northern Iran, where both of Mab's parents grew up. She learned to go "low and slow" to bring out the incredible flavors and smells of the food that would transport them back to Azeri. Mab is both a documentary filmmaker and an activist—involved in the Iranian Revolution in the late 1970s, she was later persecuted by the Islamic Republic as a vocal advocate for women's rights. After being imprisoned three times during the 2000s for organizing peaceful protests, she fled Iran and moved to New York City as a political refugee. She now lives in Oakland, California, with one of her two adult daughters and also teaches mindfulness meditation.

Do you have a cooking philosophy? For me, cooking is the intersection between my culture, my memories, medicinal food, nature, and art. My cooking philosophy is about re-creating the concept of home in an exile situation. When I cook and re-create that home feeling, I feel empowered. Because part of me is an activist, I love serving the community, I love working for community, I love changing my community. And I want to contribute to my new community here. When you feed people, at the same time, you can tell your story and share your culture.

What do you enjoy most about cooking? The thing I enjoy most is my power to transform different ingredients into very delicious different foods. Sometimes we think that thinking is the most incredible thing about being human, but I think the biggest difference between humans and other beings is cooking. No other beings can cook.

What advice would you give to someone who's just starting to cook? My advice would be to start with very simple foods, with not too many ingredients.

What do you think is the secret to becoming a great cook? The secret to becoming a great cook is love. I like to cook for someone else, a loved one, my family, my friends, and I think they give me more motivation to put more creativity in my cooking. Love is very helpful because you want to show how you are creative, you want to show your love, you want to say, "I am taking care of you." That's my first secret, but there is another one. I cook when I am hungry because I have more of a sense of the ingredients. I don't recommend grocery shopping when hungry, but when we are hungry we can sense more, smell more, taste more strongly.

How did your mom plan out what she cooked? How do you do that? It's part of our art to plan for weekly cooking. Three days a week we should have protein—meat, fish, or chicken. Then two days we should have rice, not more. We love rice. That's why we are very careful not to have too much rice. Then the other days we have vegetarian food. Persian culture is very close to a vegetarian diet, I think, and it's getting a little bit more protein recently because of modernization, but the traditional way is we don't do animal protein more than two or three days a week. On the weekend, when we are with family, we love to have a stew with lots of meat, with rice with saffron and tahdig. The day before the weekend we have one type of dish that is a cleaning of the kitchen and refrigerator: We take all the vegetables and make a sauteed kind of stew or soup.

When you want to make something easy and fast but delicious, what do you make? I make white basmati rice with scrambled eggs and a little bowl of yogurt mixed with crumbled walnuts and dried mint. Together they are very delicious. Or I will boil a potato, cut it up, and mix it with sauteed onions and lots of turmeric, black pepper, red pepper flakes, and salt. I put that in lavash and roll it up and eat it. It's very good.

If you want to have something sweet after a meal, but you don't want to make a dessert, what do you eat? After a meal, I like to have one big Medjool date with a nice Persian tea—that is the simplest way and very good for digestion. Another thing I like is plain yogurt with rose petal jam.

What is your favorite food to eat that's not Persian? Pizza. I also love Italian food and Mexican food. I never had guacamole or avocado before I came to the United States. And I love sushi, especially raw salmon. It's like a revolution in my eating because there is no connection between having raw fish and rice in this way in my culture. It's like, "Oh, my God, this is so different, but it's so delicious."

What do you like about teaching for the League of Kitchens? I love teaching with the League of Kitchens because of the feeling of community, because all the students want to learn something, and they want to use their own hands, and they are very open for any adventure of the food. They are curious and open. The other thing is the community we have together. Maybe we are very different and we are from different countries, different backgrounds, different cultures, but when it comes to cooking and teaching and enjoying food, I feel that I am with my sisters here. There is a deeper connection. We share with each other and really enjoy it. But it's not all just sharing our kitchen or our family things. We share our concerns about our countries, conflicts, war, and also happiness, Eids, celebration days, everything. Happiness, that is one of the things that I always feel with my friends, my colleagues in the League of Kitchens—happiness.

Mahboubeh Abbasgholizadeh

ライスと 他のグレインズ
米と他の穀物

Arroz y granos

চাউল, ভাত ও শস্যদানা

Гурýч ва бошқа
дон маҳсулотлари.

Ρύζι και άλλα Δημητριακά

رز ومختلف انواع الحبوب

Рис и другие
крупы

RICE AND
OTHER GRAINS

برنج و سایر غلات

پاسخ و غلات.

चामल, फापर, मकै, अरु अन्न

Arroz y Otros granos

Beras dan biji-bijian
lainnya.

चावल और ओट की
रोटीयाँ

Riz et autres céréales

Tortillas de Maiz

(MEXICAN CORN TORTILLAS)

Instructor: Angelica Vargas

"There's nothing better than a homemade tortilla." —Angie

Fresh, homemade corn tortillas and store-bought corn tortillas, even good ones, are completely different animals. I never really liked corn tortillas until I tried my first made by Angie, hot off the comal. It made me do a total 180 when I saw how soft and aromatic it was. But I would never have thought to try making my own until I watched Angie make them and saw how simple it could be. In fact, her daughter has been making tortillas since the age of three! Angie loves to eat these right off the griddle with a few slices of avocado mashed inside and a sprinkle of salt. And they're fantastic with any of her recipes in this book, especially the steak tacos on page 63.

I encourage you to consider buying a Mexican tortilla press, or a tortillera, to make these—they're not expensive, and they make the tortilla-making process so much easier. (You can also use it to make perfectly round rotis! See page 173.) If you don't have a tortilla press, you can either roll them out with a rolling pin or use a pot to press down on the circle of dough. Corn tortillas become hard after a day, so Angie tries to make just enough for one day's meals.

The masa harina, or instant corn masa flour, is made from ground corn that's been cooked and soaked in an alkaline solution, a process called nixtamalization. This gives the corn flour a nuttier flavor and makes it more nutritious, as well. It's increasingly easy to find in supermarkets (Bob's Red Mill produces it, and that's Angie's favorite), and it's also available in any Mexican market or online. Don't make the mistake of using regular cornmeal—it won't work.

Serve with: the Mexican ground beef and potatoes on page 78, the steak tacos on page 63, the black beans on page 144, or just wrapped around a slice of Mexican cheese or avocado.

> 2 cups (260 g) masa harina (instant corn masa flour)
> 1 tablespoon neutral oil
> 2 teaspoons Diamond Crystal kosher salt
> Tortilla press, rolling pin, or large flat-bottomed pan
> 1 large thin plastic bag (such as a shopping bag or a heavy-weight zip-top plastic bag)

1   **Heat the griddle:** Heat a large comal, cast-iron griddle, or cast-iron pan over medium heat for at least 10 minutes.

2   **Make the masa:** While the cooking surface is heating, put the 2 cups (260 g) masa harina (instant corn masa flour), 1 tablespoon neutral oil, and 2 teaspoons Diamond Crystal kosher salt into a large mixing bowl. Use your fingertips to work the oil and salt into the flour—take your time and try to touch every bit of the flour in the bowl.

3   Fill a large measuring cup or pitcher with 3 cups (700 ml) water. Add about ½ cup (120 ml) of water to the bowl and mix with your hands. Knead and squeeze the dough, using your fingertips and turning the bowl from time to time. Continue adding water ½ cup (120 ml) at a time, kneading well after each addition, until the dough comes together, is soft like Play-Doh, and doesn't stick to your hands. You probably won't

Continued

165   RICE AND OTHER GRAINS

use the entire 3 cups (700 ml) of water. If you've added too much water, just mix in a little more masa harina—but you don't want the dough to be too dry, or the tortillas will crack. Cover the bowl with plastic wrap and set it aside.

4 **Cook the tortillas:** Cut two 10-inch (25 cm) squares from a clean plastic shopping bag or heavy-weight zip-top plastic bag. Set them aside.

5 Get a clean large kitchen towel and set it aside.

6 Take about a golf-ball-size piece of dough from the bowl and roll it between your palms into a ball that's about 2 inches (5 cm) wide, then gently press it flat into a circle with your hands. (Keep the bowl covered in between making tortillas.)

7 Put one of the plastic squares on the bottom of your tortilla press. Place the flattened ball of masa in the center and place the other plastic square on top. Press down the top of the tortilla press to form a tortilla. Alternatively, you can roll the dough between the plastic with a rolling pin into a thin circle, or press down very hard with the flat bottom of a pan. (If your tortilla is jagged around the edges, put the dough back with the rest, dribble on a little bit more water, knead it for a few seconds, and then try again.)

8 Open the tortilla press and remove the top piece of plastic. Put the other piece of plastic, still supporting the tortilla, flat in one hand. Then flip it over into your other open hand, so you end up holding the tortilla flat in one hand without the plastic.

9 Now gently flip the tortilla from your hand onto the preheated cooking surface. Let it cook for 30 to 45 seconds per side, flipping it with a spatula when brown spots begin to appear, and pressing it down if it puffs up. When the tortilla is done, place it in the clean cotton kitchen towel and keep the tortilla stack wrapped until you're ready to serve the tortillas.

Angie flips the tortillas on the comal with her hand—the sign of a truly experienced tortilla maker!

10 Repeat with the rest of the masa until all of the tortillas are formed and cooked. Eventually, you can begin to form a tortilla while another one cooks.

11 **Serve and eat the tortillas:** Place the tortillas in a serving bowl or basket, still wrapped in the kitchen towel, and serve hot or warm.

Roz Bil Shaghrieh

(LEBANESE RICE WITH VERMICELLI)

Instructor: Jeanette Chawki

"If you follow this way, you're going to have the best rice ever, and the best taste." —Jeanette

This mix of rice and broken vermicelli is a little like Rice-A-Roni, but much more delicious. The key is using a very wide pan to make it—at least 12 inches (30 cm) in diameter, and if you have one that's wider, even better. Jeanette says the secret to making this rice without breaking the grains or having them turn to mush is giving everything plenty of room. She likes to say that the rice needs a lot of room to be happy.

She uses Turkish baldo rice, which is creamy and starchy like arborio or carnaroli, and you can substitute either. If you can't find short vermicelli, which are very fine, very short wheat noodles, you could break longer vermicelli into pieces about ³/₄ inch (2 cm) long. She also says that the ideal soaking time for the rice is about an hour or two, though 30 minutes will work if you're in a rush. Or you can soak it overnight in the refrigerator if you want to do it in advance. Jeanette will also sometimes toast the vermicelli in advance and keep it in a sealed jar so she can put this together more quickly for dinner. The butter added at the end makes the rice extra delicious. If she has them, Jeanette will also add a few whole nuts to the top of the dish when she serves it. She uses pine nuts, cashews, almonds, pistachios, or a mix, and toasts them in butter until they are golden-brown. Just be sure to cook them separately, she says, as they brown at different speeds.

Serve with: the stewed green beans on page 263.

2 cups (420 g) baldo, arborio, or carnaroli rice

1 cup (120 g) short vermicelli

1 tablespoon extra-virgin olive oil

1 tablespoon Diamond Crystal kosher salt

2 tablespoons unsalted butter

1   **Wash and soak the rice:** At least 30 minutes, and ideally 1 to 2 hours, before you want to make the dish, put the 2 cups (420 g) baldo, arborio, or carnaroli rice in a mixing bowl with tap water in the sink and gently scrub it and swirl it with your hands. Drain the water and repeat the process two or three more times until the water is mostly clear. Drain the bowl again, then fill it up and let it sit at room temperature for at least 30 minutes and preferably 1 to 2 hours. (You can also soak it overnight in the refrigerator.)

2   **Cook the rice and vermicelli:** When you're ready to make the rice with vermicelli, bring 4 cups (945 ml) water to a boil in a kettle or stockpot.

3   Drain the rice, rinse it under running water, and set it aside.

4   Put the 1 cup (120 g) short vermicelli noodles in a dry skillet or wok at least 12 inches (30 cm) in diameter, ideally nonstick, and turn the heat to medium-high. Stir the noodles gently but continuously in the pan until they are deep golden brown, 3 to 4 minutes.

5   Stir in the 1 tablespoon extra-virgin olive oil, then add the drained and rinsed rice. Stir the rice gently with the spatula so that it's mixed in with the vermicelli, being careful not to break the grains.

Continued

6 Stir in the 1 tablespoon Diamond Crystal kosher salt. Cover the pot and cook over medium-low heat, stirring occasionally, for about 2 minutes, until the rice and vermicelli gets completely dry. They will begin to make sizzling sounds.

7 Stir the rice and vermicelli gently to make sure nothing is sticking, then add the 4 cups (945 ml) boiling water. Stir very gently, then raise the heat to medium-high and cook, stirring frequently, until the liquid comes to a strong simmer.

8 Cover the pot and cook for about 10 minutes, until there's no more water in the pan. The grains might still have a little moisture clinging to them—that's okay.

9 Cut the 2 tablespoons unsalted butter into smaller pieces.

10 When the rice is done, turn off the heat and scatter the pieces of butter across the top of the rice. Wait until just before serving to stir in the butter.

11 **Serve and eat the rice and vermicelli:** Stir in the butter and serve the rice and vermicelli while it's still hot, in a large bowl in the middle of the table or on individual plates as a side with other dishes.

Saffron Polo Ba Tah-dig

SERVES 6

(PERSIAN BASMATI RICE WITH SAFFRON AND TAHDIG)

Instructor: Mahboubeh Abbasgholizadeh

"Rice is an important food for us, like pasta for Italians, so we have to use good ingredients for everything. Washing is a big deal with rice. We are very respectful of rice. This is the secret of having delicious Persian rice." —Mab

My daughters love rice tahdig, and I love this technique because it's so easy—you just need patience, as Mab says. Tahdig refers to something crispy that's cooked on the bottom of the rice pot. You can make a tahdig with lavash or potatoes, but the simplest version is made by crisping up the rice itself. Tahdig can seem intimidating, but this technique is pretty foolproof. Plus, the rice itself turns out fluffy and light. Persian cuisine is full of amazing, complex rice dishes. This is a basic everyday rice that's elevated by the drizzle of saffron water.

This rice is best when left to steam for 40 minutes before you serve it, but if you need to hurry, says Mab, you can steam it for as little as 20 minutes. Traditionally, you would start the rice well before you started making anything else for dinner so that it could steam while you were doing the rest of your cooking.

As with Nawida's challow on page 179, another secret is to look for aged, extra-long-grain basmati rice, which will stand up to the long cooking time without getting mushy. You can usually find it in Indian or Middle Eastern markets. Mab also prefers to use filtered water when making grains like rice, because it improves the flavor of the finished dish. If you have it on hand, use it both for the saffron water and for cooking the rice.

Serve with: the Persian chicken kabobs on page 29.

¼ teaspoon (0.25 g) saffron threads (about 1 large pinch)

3 cups (700 ml) plus 2½ teaspoons room-temperature filtered water, divided

2 cups (400 g) extra-long-grain basmati rice (preferably aged)

1 tablespoon ghee or unsalted butter

1 tablespoon plus 2 teaspoons olive oil, divided

1 teaspoon Diamond Crystal kosher salt

1 **Make the saffron water:** Grind the ¼ teaspoon (0.25 g) saffron threads (about 1 large pinch) with a mortar and pestle into a fine powder (you can also use the end of the handle of a wooden spoon and a small bowl). Put the ground saffron in a small glass jar or drinking glass (a 4 ounce/120 ml mason jar is perfect) and add 1½ teaspoons room-temperature filtered water. Cover the glass and set it aside in a warm (or at least not cold) place.

Mab soaks the saffron in a small amount of liquid in a small container in order to keep as much of the aroma intact as possible.

2 **Wash the rice:** Put the 2 cups (400 g) extra-long-grain basmati rice in a 5-quart (4.8 L) Dutch oven or saucepan, preferably nonstick.

3 Place the pot in the sink and cover the rice with room temperature tap water. Gently drag your fingers through the rice, moving it around just a little, then drain it. Repeat this until the water is mostly clear, 2 to 4 more times depending on your rice.

Continued

The LEAGUE OF KITCHENS Cookbook   170

4   Drain the rice as well as you can without straining it. Usually there's a little water left in the pot when you're done—that's okay.

5   **Cook the rice:** Pour 3 cups (700 ml) of room-temperature filtered water into the pot with the rice. Add the 1 tablespoon ghee or unsalted butter, 1 tablespoon olive oil, and 1 teaspoon Diamond Crystal kosher salt and put the pot over high heat.

You want to bring the rice to a boil as fast as you can to prevent clumping—you can use the largest burner on your stove, or, if you're using an electric stove that takes a while to heat up, preheat it.

6   Once the water boils, shake the pot to redistribute the rice, then lower the heat to medium. Cover the pot, and then as soon as the rice foams up to the top of the pot and steam comes out the sides (usually after less than a minute), open the lid slightly. Let the rice cook until all the water boils away and small holes have appeared in the top (you can open the lid to peek), usually 2 to 4 minutes. The rice will be al dente.

7   Turn the heat as low as it will go, then wrap the lid carefully in a clean cotton kitchen cloth or thick organic paper towel. (Fold or tie up the edges, so they don't droop down and accidentally catch on fire.) Then cover the rice and let it steam for at least 20 minutes, but preferably 40 minutes, before you move on to the next step.

8   **Add the oil and saffron:** When you're nearly ready to serve the rice, slowly drizzle the remaining 2 teaspoons olive oil on top of the rice around the edges of the pot. The heat should still be on low.

9   Drizzle the saffron water over the top of the rice—it won't cover the whole top or may look splotchy—that's okay. Add the remaining 1 teaspoon of filtered water to the glass that held the saffron water, swirl it to get all the last bits of saffron, then drizzle that into the pot as well. Cover the pot, let the rice cook for 10 minutes more, then turn off the heat and remove the lid.

10 **Serve and eat the rice:** Use a large plate (slightly larger than your pot) to cover the top of your pot, then, holding the plate tightly on the pot, flip the pot onto the plate so that the rice and tahdig slide out. The bottom may not be evenly golden brown—it may be light or even very dark in some spots, but it should be crunchy and crispy.

11 Use a spatula or large serving spoon to give everyone both a piece of the tahdig and the fluffy rice inside.

Roti

MAKES ABOUT 12 ROTI

(INDIAN FLATBREAD)

Instructor: Yamini Joshi

"In India, every girl has to learn to make roti! When I was eight or nine my mom made me sit next to her and said, 'Make roti.' At first I would roll them halfway, then she would roll them out the rest of the way." —Yamini

I love making homemade roti—they're delicious, and it feels really empowering to make them. It can be tricky to shape them into even circles—Yamini can turn out roti after roti that are all perfect circles and all the same size. When Yamini learned how to make tortillas from Angie, she realized that you could also use a tortilla press to make rotis, and so that's what I do—it makes them super easy to shape. (Though I aspire to one day be able to roll out a perfect circle by hand, just like Yamini!)

After every two roti she makes, she puts a dollop of ghee in the middle and rubs them together to spread the ghee before she stacks them. The ghee in between keeps the roti soft and moist (and makes them extra delicious). For her grandchildren, she'll make fresh roti, add ghee and a sprinkle of jaggery, then roll them up and serve them while they're still warm. I tried it with my girls and, of course, they loved it. What's not to love?

One thing to note is that proper roti are made with atta, a coarsely ground type of whole-grain flour used in South Asia for flatbreads like roti, paratha, and chapati—it's not the same thing as the whole-wheat flour more commonly found in the United States. It's very high in gluten, which gives the roti its fantastic stretchiness and softness. If you don't live near a South Asian grocery, you can also order it online. Some cooks suggest blending equal parts white whole wheat (not regular whole wheat) flour with bread flour, though it won't have quite the same texture or flavor.

Serve with: Yamini's dal (page 157) or Indian spiced sweet potatoes (page 242), Afsari's ground beef curry (page 82), chicken curry (page 53), or summer and winter omelets (page 123). They're also great with ghee and a little crumbled jaggery, a dark brown unrefined cane sugar, or brown sugar or honey, if you don't have jaggery.

2 cups (325 g) atta flour, plus more for dusting
1 teaspoon Diamond Crystal kosher salt
½ cup (120 ml) ghee

1 **Mix the dough:** Measure out the 2 cups (325 g) atta flour into a large mixing bowl, spooning it into the measuring cup and then leveling it off with a knife, if you're not weighing the flour. Add the 1 teaspoon Diamond Crystal kosher salt to the bowl.

2 Fill a large, easy-to-pour measuring cup or small bowl with 1½ cups (355 ml) tap water.

3 Pour a little of the water into your hand over the bowl, then sprinkle it over the flour in the bowl. Use your hands to pinch and crumble all of the flour in the bowl so that you break up the wet parts and fully distribute the water into the dry parts. Repeat this process, pinching and crumbling thoroughly. By the third or fourth addition of water, you should be able to squeeze some of the dough in your hands and it will begin to hang together, with none of the flour feeling fully dry. If not, keep adding water just a little at a time, mixing thoroughly each time you add it.

4 Once the dough comes together, continue to knead and turn the dough in the bowl, folding

Continued

173   RICE AND OTHER GRAINS

and pressing it, and using your hands and the dough to scrape the loose flour from the sides and bottom of the bowl. Add just a sprinkle of water, as necessary, as you go, kneading and mixing very well after each addition. Continue to knead until the dough is no longer sticky, lightens in color, and becomes stretchy and eventually becomes smooth. The whole process usually takes at least 10 minutes, and usually you end up using all of the water in the measuring cup.

5   **Make the roti:** Clear a place on your counter to roll out the roti. Put several scoops of atta flour on a plate or in a mixing bowl and set it aside, then put the ½ cup (120 ml) ghee in a small bowl, with a small spoon for spreading it at the ready.

6   Rub a little ghee on your hands. Remove the dough from the mixing bowl and roll it onto the counter into a long, thick log, about 15 inches (38 cm) long. Cut the log into two equal 7½-inch (19 cm) lengths, then cut each half into 6 equal pieces (about 1.8 ounces/51 g each), so you have 12 pieces of dough.

7   Roll each piece in your hands into a smooth ball and then flatten it with your palms into a disc.

8   As you finish them, put them into the bowl you used to knead the dough and cover the bowl with a clean kitchen towel or plastic wrap so they don't dry out. When all the dough is rolled and flattened, set the bowl aside and heat the griddle.

9   **Cook the roti:** Heat a 10- or 12-inch (25 or 30 cm) nonstick or cast-iron skillet or flat griddle over low heat. Prepare a dish for stacking the cooked roti when they come off the griddle, such as a deep-dish pie pan, by lining it with a clean dish towel.

10 Take one of the pressed discs of dough and dip both sides into the flour on the plate or bowl, shaking off the excess. Using a rolling pin, gently roll out the ball into a circle, using the rolling pin in such a way that the dough turns in a circle as you roll it, until it's 7 inches (18 cm) in diameter. (You can also press it in a tortilla maker.)

11 Put the roti in the skillet. As soon as you see small white spots form on the surface, after about 1 minute, flip and cook the other side until white spots form on the surface and there are a few brown spots on the bottom of the roti, usually a minute or less.

12 If you have a gas or even a coil electric stovetop, at this point you can remove the pan from the heat and place the roti directly on the burner or heating element of the stovetop. Use tongs to very quickly flip it back and forth, cooking for a few seconds on either side until it puffs up and develops a few brown spots on each side; use the tongs to press down the puffed bread before you flip it.

   If you have a smooth-top stove, just continue to cook the roti in the pan, flipping it several times until it develops a few brown spots on both sides—it may even puff a little.

13 Put the cooked roti into the towel-lined pie pan. Repeat to cook the second roti. After the second roti is cooked, put a spoonful of ghee on the first roti and rub the two together to spread the ghee while the second roti is still hot, then place them down in the pie pan. Repeat until all the roti are cooked, adding ghee after every other one. Eventually, you can try rolling out one roti while you cook another.

14 **Serve the roti:** You can serve the roti right away while they're still warm, or at room temperature. You can also keep them wrapped in the refrigerator for a week or more, and gently reheat them on a hot skillet or griddle on the stovetop.

(MEXICAN TOMATO RICE)

Instructor: Angelica Vargas

"Anything homemade is always better. This rice is so much better than what you would get at a restaurant." —Angie

This is a classic Mexican red rice seasoned with pureed tomatoes, onion, and garlic, perfect with the wonderful black beans on page 144. It's somewhat similar in technique to the Mexican tomato soup and pasta on page 199, in that you toast the grains in oil before you slowly simmer them in the sauce. Note that this rice is on the wetter side—it's not totally dry and fluffy like some other ways of cooking rice. As with the soup, Angie grew up seasoning the tomato sauce with bouillon cubes, and prefers that flavor, but it's also very tasty without them.

Angie prefers to use basmati rice to make this dish, as opposed to the long-grain white rice that's the tradition in most of Mexico. Basmati stands up to the multipart cooking process without getting mushy, she says, and she also really likes its floral flavor.

You can add all of the frozen vegetables as you like, or none—Angie makes this rice in several variations, depending on whether she's serving any other vegetables with the meal. If she's making this to serve with the picadillo on page 78, she will usually add them.

When Angie's babysitter would make this rice, she would add a few slices of ripe banana to the top—a combination Angie still craves today. The sweet goes really well with the savory, especially when serving this rice with the spicy picadillo.

Serve with: the black beans on page 144, as well as the Mexican ground beef and potatoes on page 78 or the steak tacos on page 63. You can also use the remaining half of the onion to make the onion-habanero relish on page 118.

1 pound (450 g) plum tomatoes (about 4 medium)

¼ ounce (7 g) garlic (about 2 medium cloves)

⅓ pound (150 g) white onion (about ½ medium)

2 chicken or tomato bouillon cubes, or one of each, optional

1 to 3½ teaspoons Diamond Crystal kosher salt, depending on if you're using the bouillon cubes

2 cups (400 g) basmati or other long-grain white rice

1 cup (140 g) frozen or canned corn kernels, optional

½ cup (70 g) frozen sweet peas, optional

½ cup (70 g) frozen cubed carrots, optional

3 tablespoons neutral oil

1 **Prepare the tomato sauce:** Cut the 1 pound (450 g) plum tomatoes (about 4 medium) in half lengthwise and put them in a blender. Peel the ¼ ounce (7 g) garlic (about 2 medium cloves) and add it to the blender with the tomatoes. Trim the stem ends of the ⅓ pound (150 g) white onion (about ½ medium), then peel it, cut it in half, and add it to the blender, along with the 2 chicken or tomato bouillon cubes (or one of each), if using. Add 1 teaspoon Diamond Crystal kosher salt if you added the bouillon cubes, or add 3½ teaspoons Diamond Crystal kosher salt if you didn't.

2 Add 1½ cups water (350 ml) to the blender and puree everything on high speed until the mixture is smooth, fluffy, and lighter in color. Set the sauce aside, still in the blender. If you did not use a high-speed blender, get a sieve or strainer ready for when it's time to add the sauce to the rice.

I will sometimes use chicken bone broth instead of water and bouillon cubes—I buy a frozen version that comes in 3-cup (700 ml) packages and keep it in the freezer. You could also use chicken stock.

3 **Prepare the rest of the ingredients:** Put the 2 cups (400 g) basmati or other long-grain white rice in a strainer and wash it under running water in the sink, swirling it with your hands until the water runs clear. Drain it and set it aside.

4 Measure out the 1 cup (140 g) frozen or canned corn kernels, ½ cup (70 g) frozen sweet peas, and ½ cup (70 g) frozen cubed carrots, if using, into one small bowl and set them aside. (They do not need to fully defrost before you add them to the rice.)

5 **Cook the rice:** Put the 3 tablespoons neutral oil in a 5-quart (4.8 L) Dutch oven or saucepan, preferably nonstick, and heat it over medium-high heat. When the oil begins to shimmer, add the washed and drained rice, using a wooden spoon or spatula to gently spread it out across the bottom, being careful, as it may spatter.

6 Lower the heat to medium, then fry the rice until it turns light golden in color, usually about 10 minutes—you don't want it to brown, so be sure to stay by the stove. When you hear the bottom of the rice begin to sizzle as it cooks, use the spatula to gently move it around so that it doesn't burn.

Continued

RICE AND OTHER GRAINS

7   When the rice is golden in color, reduce the heat to as low as it will go. If you didn't use a high-speed blender, pour the reserved tomato sauce through the sieve or strainer directly into the rice, using a spoon to press most of the sauce through the strainer. (There won't be much left in the strainer—you're mainly just getting rid of skin and any whole seeds.) If you used a high-speed blender, pour the sauce directly into the rice.

8   Gently stir in the tomato sauce so it's fully incorporated, then increase the heat to medium-high so that the tomato sauce begins to simmer strongly—you should see many bubbles. Once you see the bubbles, gently scrape once around the bottom of the pan with a spoon or spatula to make sure the bottom doesn't stick.

9   Let the sauce bubble for 1 full minute, scraping gently along the bottom once or twice, then add 1½ cups (350 ml) of tap water. (You can also swirl the water around in the blender first to pick up any remaining bits of sauce, if you like.) Gently stir the water into the rice, then stir in the frozen vegetables, if using, and let the sauce come back to a strong simmer.

10 Once the sauce begins to bubble again, stir once around the pot to make sure it isn't sticking to the bottom, then cook for 2 full minutes. Cover the pot, lower the heat to medium, and let it simmer until the liquid has reduced to where it's just at the very bottom of the pot, usually about 15 minutes.

11 Reduce the heat as low as it will go, return the cover to the pot, and continue to cook until all of the liquid is completely absorbed by the rice, usually about 30 to 40 minutes. Turn off the heat and let the rice sit covered on the stove until you're ready to serve it.

12 **Serve and eat the rice:** Serve the rice while it's still hot, either piled into a serving bowl on the table or scooped onto individual plates. (If some of the rice has stuck to the bottom of the pan, just leave it there and scoop up only the soft and fluffy rice on top.)

Challow

(AFGHAN BASMATI RICE WITH GARLIC AND CLOVES)

Instructor: Nawida Saidhosin

"You add the garlic and the cloves, and this rice is going to taste so different and delicious." —Nawida

This method of cooking basmati rice is central to Afghan cuisine. The rice can be flavored in various ways, but this combo—two whole heads of garlic, unpeeled, plus some whole cloves—is extra delicious and complements so many of Nawida's recipes, especially the red beans on page 153.

The garlic and clove flavor are really subtle—they add a delicious savoriness you almost don't notice, except for in how good it tastes. Nawida also heats some oil until it sizzles right at the end and pours it on top of the rice, mixing it all in so that the grains of rice don't stick together. That slight oil coating also adds another layer of flavor.

To get the full experience—super-fluffy rice that doesn't stick or break—it's very important to find aged, extra-long basmati rice. It cooks totally differently from standard American grocery-store basmati rice. You can find it at any South Asian or Middle Eastern market. Nawida prefers the Aahu Barah brand. You can soak the rice for longer than three hours—such as overnight or while you're at work. (Nawida has even let hers soak for a day or two and it still comes out great.) Keep it covered in the refrigerator, so it doesn't ferment, and then pay attention to the rice as it cooks so it doesn't get mushy: It should cook more quickly the longer you have let it soak.

Serve with: the Afghan red beans on page 153, the Afghan chicken on page 39, or the Afghan okra on page 249.

3 cups (600 g) extra-long-grain basmati rice (preferably aged)

3 tablespoons Diamond Crystal kosher salt, divided

2 tablespoons neutral oil, olive oil, or melted ghee

¼ pound (115 g) whole garlic heads (about 2 medium)

4 whole cloves

¼ cup (60 ml) neutral oil

1   **Soak the rice:** Put the 3 cups (600 g) extra-long-grain basmati rice (preferably aged) in a large pot or bowl and cover it with about 2 inches (5 cm) of cold tap water. Let the rice soak, covered with a lid or a large plate, for at least 3 hours. (If you're soaking the rice for longer than 3 hours, put it in the refrigerator.) After the rice has finished soaking, transfer the rice to a colander in the sink, run water over it for just a few seconds to rinse it, and then let it drain while you bring the water to a boil.

2   **Parboil the rice:** Fill a 5-quart (4.8 L) Dutch oven or saucepan with 10 cups (2.4 L) water and bring it to boil over high heat. Add 2 tablespoons of the Diamond Crystal kosher salt and gently stir in the soaked and drained rice.

3   Let the pot come back to a boil and then lower the heat to medium or medium-high so the rice cooks at a strong simmer but isn't fully boiling. Cook until the rice is just al dente (you can bite through a grain but it's not yet fully cooked in the middle), stirring gently once or twice with a spatula to make sure all the grains are evenly cooked. This should take around 2 minutes if

Continued

your rice has been soaked for 3 to 4 hours but could be faster or longer depending on the age and quality of the rice. Turn off the heat.

4   Drain the al dente rice through a colander into the sink (if a few grains remain stuck to the bottom of the pot, that's fine), and then return it to the pot. (The heat should still be off.) Pour the 2 tablespoons neutral oil, olive oil, or melted ghee over the top of the rice and set the pot aside.

If the rice is getting too soft or almost mushy, cool it in the sink under cold running water before adding it back to the pot.

5   **Season the rice:** In a small saucepan, bring 1 cup (240 ml) water just to a boil and add the remaining 1 tablespoon Diamond Crystal kosher salt. Stir until the salt dissolves, turn off the heat, then pour this all over the top of the rice. Use a spatula to very gently mix the salted water and the oil into the rice.

6   Wash the 2 heads of garlic under running water in the sink. Make 2 holes about the size of the garlic with the end of your spatula handle in the rice (one on each side of the pot), then press one head of garlic into each of the holes, almost like you're planting bulbs. Use your spatula to cover the heads of garlic with rice. Then tuck the 4 cloves into the rice evenly around the garlic in the same manner (2 on each side of the pot), making sure they're covered with the rice, too.

7   Once the garlic heads and cloves are buried, use the end of the spatula handle to make 6 or 7 little holes in the rice around the edges of the pot about 1 inch (2.5 cm) in from the edge— almost like you're marking every other number on the face of a clock. (The holes may not stay fully open—that's okay.)

8   **Cook the rice:** Cover the pot with a large clean kitchen towel, place the pot lid on top of the towel, and then wrap the towel around the lid, tying the corners into a knot, so it creates a tight seal with the pot and so the edges of the towel don't droop down and accidentally catch on fire. (If your lid is wobbly, try turning it upside down for a tighter seal.)

9   Put the covered and sealed pot on the stove and turn the heat to high. Cook until you begin to hear crackling sounds from the rice drying out on the bottom—3 to 5 minutes—then turn the heat as low as it will possibly go. (Move it to the smallest burner on your stove, if you can.)

10 Let the rice continue to steam over the lowest heat for 40 minutes, then turn off the heat and let it sit, covered, for up to 20 minutes. Make the sizzling oil just before serving.

11 **Make the sizzling oil:** When you're ready to serve the rice, heat the ¼ cup (60 ml) neutral oil in a small saucepan until it's bubbling and shimmering, but don't let it smoke (if it does, start over). Turn off the heat, open the pot of rice, pour the oil around the pot, and use a spatula to gently mix it all together and fluff the rice, discarding any cloves, if you find them. Remove the garlic to a plate to serve with dinner.

12 **Serve and eat the rice:** Put the rice and the steamed garlic out on the table so that each person can serve themselves. Use your fingers to squeeze the garlic out of the husk onto your plate to eat separately or mix it into the rice, as you choose.

Khachapuri and Pirog s Kapustoy

(GEORGIAN CHEESE AND SPINACH PIE AND RUSSIAN CABBAGE PIE)

Instructor: Larisa Frumkin

"I learned this recipe for the dough quite recently from my niece when I was in Moscow. I started using it instead of my old one because it's good for any Russian baking: bread, buns, sweet or savory. It's great, great, great." —Larisa

Larisa calls this dough recipe a "lazy housewife recipe" because it needs only twenty minutes to rest before you use it, but it's also fine if you let it sit for an hour or two. She learned it from her niece in Russia, where it's a very popular recipe. Even if the pies end up misshapen or even split open along the seams while baking, they still look impressive.

The cheese pie is based on the Georgian khachapuri, says Larisa, but the spinach is her own addition. Both of these fillings are equally delicious, and it's really special to have both at one meal, which is why Larisa always makes and serves both at the same time. If you make them both, you also get a combination of vegetables and protein, from the cheeses, so it's a very satisfying meal. But you could easily double one of the fillings, if you wanted, and make two of the same kind. The cheese and spinach filling, in particular, comes together very quickly and requires no extra seasoning, says Larisa, because the salt, sweetness, and flavor is all in the cheeses.

Serve with: the cold beet soup on page 202, the hot beet and vegetable soup on page 207, and/or a simple salad, or by itself for lunch or a snack.

For the dough for two pies

    3 cups (360 g) all-purpose flour
    1 teaspoon Diamond Crystal kosher salt
    1 teaspoon white sugar
    ¼-ounce (7 g) package dry instant yeast
    1 cup (240 ml) buttermilk
    ½ cup (120 ml) neutral oil

For the cabbage filling for one pie

    2 large eggs
    ¾ pound (340 g) yellow onion (about 1 large)

    6 ounces (170 g) green cabbage (about ⅓ small cabbage)
    ¼ pound (115 g) carrots (about 1 medium)
    1 ounce (30 g) scallion (about 1 medium)
    ½ ounce (15 g) fresh dill (about 7 sprigs)
    2 tablespoons neutral oil
    1½ tablespoons unsalted butter
    1½ teaspoons Diamond Crystal kosher salt
    1 teaspoon sweet paprika
    Freshly ground black pepper

For the cheese filling for one pie

    1 cup (225 g) cottage or farmer's cheese
    1 cup (160 g) crumbled feta cheese
    ½ cup (40 g) grated mozzarella cheese
    ¼ pound (115 g) baby spinach
    2 large eggs, divided
    ¼ teaspoon neutral oil

1   **Make the dough:** Measure the 3 cups (360 g) all-purpose flour into a very large mixing bowl. Add the 1 teaspoon Diamond Crystal kosher salt, 1 teaspoon white sugar, and ¼-ounce (7 g) package dry instant yeast. Stir everything together and set aside.

2   Put a few inches of water in a 9½-inch (24 cm) skillet and heat it over medium-low. Put the 1 cup (240 ml) buttermilk in a small saucepan, add the ½ cup (120 ml) neutral oil, and place it into the skillet, so the pan is sitting in the water. Heat the buttermilk and oil, stirring constantly, until the mixture is just barely

Continued

warm to the touch, usually less than 3 minutes. Remove the pot from the skillet. (If you're using a thermometer, the goal is to warm the mixture but to keep it below 100°F/38°C—a few degrees above is fine, just let it cool slightly.)

If you have a double boiler, you could use that to heat the buttermilk-oil mixture, but Larisa's method is even easier!

3   Pour about a third of the buttermilk-oil mixture from the pot into the bowl with the flour and use a rubber spatula to mix it fully into the dough. Repeat—adding the liquid a few tablespoons at a time and then mixing it in—until you have used up all the liquid.

4   Use your hands to knead the dough in the bowl for about 2 minutes, until it forms a ball and you have taken up most of the flour on the sides of the bowl. The dough will be very sticky and soft and easy to form into a round but not perfectly smooth or dry. Cover the bowl with a clean kitchen towel and let it sit while you prepare the fillings. (The dough needs to sit for just 20 minutes, but it will be fine for up to 2 hours.)

5   **Prepare the cabbage filling:** Fill a small saucepan with water and bring it to a boil over high heat, then lower the heat so that the water is at a strong simmer. Add the 2 large eggs and let them simmer for 11 minutes. Drain them immediately and then transfer them to a bowl of cold water in the sink. Let them sit until they're cool. (You can leave the tap running at a trickle into the bowl to speed up this process.)

6   While the eggs cook and cool, peel the ¾ pound (340 g) yellow onion (about 1 large) and dice it as finely as you can. You should have about 2 cups.

7   Measure out the 6 ounces (170g) green cabbage (about ⅓ small cabbage), if you haven't already, and remove the core. Cut it into pieces about ¼ inch (0.6 cm) square. The easiest way to do

this is to cut it first into slices about ¼ inch (0.6 cm) thick. Then cut the slices into pieces about ¼ inch (0.6 cm) wide. You should have about 2½ cups.

8   Peel and trim the ends from the ¼ pound (115 g) carrots (about 1 medium). Grate them over the large holes of a box grater. You should end up with about ¾ cup. Add it to the cabbage.

You can also substitute an equal amount of shredded cabbage for the carrots, if you prefer.

9   Cut the white and green parts of the 1 ounce (30 g) scallion (about 1 medium) in half lengthwise, and then into ¼-inch (0.6 cm) wide slices. You will end up with about ¼ cup.

10 Trim about 1 inch (2.5 cm) from the stem ends of ½ ounce (15 g) fresh dill (about 7 sprigs). Chop the dill very fine—you should end up with about ¼ cup. Add it to the scallions and set aside.

11 When the eggs have cooled, peel them, and then grate them over the large holes of a box grater. Set the eggs aside.

12 **Cook the cabbage filling:** Heat the 2 tablespoons neutral oil and 1½ tablespoons unsalted butter in a 12-inch (30 cm) skillet over medium-high heat just until the butter begins to sizzle.

13 Add the chopped onion and lower the heat to medium. Saute the onion, stirring frequently, until it's very soft and beginning to brown, about 10 minutes. Add the chopped cabbage and carrot. (The pan will be very full.) Cook, stirring occasionally, until the cabbage has wilted, about 5 minutes.

14 Add the 1½ teaspoons Diamond Crystal kosher salt, 1 teaspoon sweet paprika, and a few grinds of black pepper across the top of the pan and then stir until everything is mixed together. Cook for about 5 minutes, until the onions and

cabbage are very soft, translucent, and lightly browned.

15 Stir in the diced scallions and dill. Cook for 5 minutes, stirring occasionally, then stir in the grated eggs. Turn off the heat and transfer the contents to another bowl or dish and set the filling aside to cool.

16 **Prepare the cheese filling:** Put the 1 cup (225 g) cottage or farmer's cheese, 1 cup (160 g) crumbled feta cheese, and ½ cup (40 g) grated mozzarella cheese in a large bowl and set it aside.

17 Roughly chop the ¼ pound (115 g) baby spinach. You should end up with about 2 heaping cups. Add it to the bowl with the cheese.

18 Take 1 of the eggs and separate the yolk and white. Set the yolk aside in a small bowl and add the white to the bowl with the spinach, then add the other whole egg.

19 Use your hands to mix the cheese, spinach, and eggs together in the bowl.

20 **Prepare the glaze for the top of the pies:** Whisk the yolk with the ¼ teaspoon neutral oil and set it aside.

21 **Roll out the dough:** Preheat the oven to 400°F (200°C) with the rack one setting above the middle. Clear out enough space on the counter to roll out the dough. Get two 9-inch (23 cm) diameter pie pans or cake pans (of any depth), or similar sized pans. Cut three 12-inch (30 cm) wide pieces of parchment paper.

You can roll out the dough on a silicone mat or clean cutting board and place it right into the pan. But parchment paper makes it easy to remove after baking.

22 Cut the dough into 4 equal pieces. Put one on a piece of parchment paper, and keep the 3 you're not rolling out loosely covered in the bowl the dough was in.

23 Roll out the dough on the parchment paper into a circle that is about 10 inches (25 cm) wide. Lift the parchment paper with the dough circle into the pan, pressing it in so that it fits snugly into the bottom and goes a bit up the sides. Use a spoon or spatula to pile one of the fillings into a mound in the middle of the dough, then, working from the center, spread it evenly over the bottom.

24 Roll out another piece of dough on a second piece of parchment paper to the same size as the bottom crust. Lift the dough on the paper and flip it over the pie so it's lying over the top of the filling. Peel off the parchment paper. Tuck in the top dough around the sides of the pan like a sheet—push the top dough down to the bottom dough and press them shut.

25 Repeat this process with the other two dough quarters and the second filling (you will reuse one of the pieces of parchment).

26 **Bake the pies:** When both pies are filled and formed, brush the tops with the egg yolk glaze. Prick the top of each pie 3 times evenly across the top with the tines of a fork. (Larisa usually does them in different patterns, so she can tell them apart once they're baked.) Bake them both at the same time, for 25 to 30 minutes, until the tops are browned.

27 Remove the pies still in their pans to a wire rack to cool for at least an hour, or until they're warm or even very warm but not hot. Then use the parchment paper to lift them out of the pan onto a serving plate or cutting board.

28 **Serve and eat the pies:** Serve the pies warm or room temperature—but not cold—sliced into wedges.

Instructor Spotlight

Jeanette Chawki

Jeanette grew up in the hilltop city of Zahle in Lebanon—the largest predominantly Christian community in the Middle East. She was one of seven children, and her grandparents and aunt also lived with her family. Her father was a farmer, and every day he would bring home the freshest, most delicious vegetables for her mom to cook. Jeanette learned to cook from her mom, her grandmother, her aunts, and her friends. After she got married at nineteen, she also learned her mother-in-law's recipes. Jeanette worked as an elementary school French teacher in Lebanon before moving to the United States in 2006. Today, she lives with her husband on Staten Island near her three grown children and one grandchild. She is an active member of her Lebanese Catholic church and is known as one of the best cooks in the community. She often caters small parties and events.

Why do you love to cook? Because it keeps me busy and engaged with life. My passion is baking. I love how small the dough is when it starts, and then seeing how it takes shape and changes color in the oven. I feel happier and more positive when I'm baking sweets.

Do you have a cooking philosophy? I think we eat with our eyes as well as our mouths. So I don't like to just cut a cucumber. I like to think about how to design it on the plate and make it look special. It's important to cook with love.

What advice would you give to someone who's just starting out? When you go in the kitchen, you need to feel comfortable and relaxed. Don't go in stressed, or your food is not going to come out well. Don't go to your kitchen without knowing what you want to do. You're going to mess up your kitchen for nothing. So think first about what you want to do and prepare all your ingredients around you first, then you'll be comfortable and the food will taste better.

What are some of your favorite home remedies from the kitchen? If you have a sore throat, mix one tablespoon tahini sauce with a little honey and a squeeze of lemon juice and just swallow it little by little and it will help. If you ever have any problem with your stomach or you don't have an appetite, the best thing to do, just go bake a potato, add a pinch of salt, and enjoy it.

What are some of your favorite self-care tips from the kitchen? If you have leftover tomato, rub some on your face, then rinse it off with water, and it will make your skin clearer. If you have a party the next day and you want your skin to look nice, make a mask of yogurt. Put about four or five tablespoons of yogurt in a bowl outside the fridge for two to three days until it dries out a lot. Then put that on your face as a mask for fifteen to twenty minutes. After you wash it, your face will be bright and shiny and all the redness will be gone. Lemon juice is very important. When you use a lemon, for any salad or something like that, always take it and rub it on your skin. You can also sprinkle some sugar on top and use it to scrub your face.

If you have very dry hair, if it's not shiny, it's broken sometimes on the end, just mix one egg very well and squeeze in a little lemon and one or two tablespoons of olive oil. Put it on your hair for about one hour before you shower. Then rinse it out. You're going to see your hair shine beautifully, like a diamond. I used to do this every week when I was young.

How do you plan out your cooking every week? The first thing I do is ask my husband and kids what they would like because I want everyone in my family to have the food they like. Then I have my plan: On Sundays we eat outside the house—we treat ourselves and eat with family and friends. For the other days, three days we have meat, and three days we have vegetarian. On Wednesdays I have vegetarian food and Fridays we have fish because those are the days in the church that you don't eat meat. Saturdays we always have leftovers—we have to empty the fridge. And I always buy whatever vegetables are freshest and in season and cook based on what I find at the store.

What foods and herbs do you grow yourself in your garden? I love growing green beans. I love picking them by hand—sometimes a plant gives you twenty-one, sometimes thirty. So I collect them for a week and then I make lubiyeh (page 263). I also grow tomatoes, cucumbers, and green peppers. I have two fig trees—I love eating them fresh but also making fig jam. Mint, always I have mint. I grow Lebanese mint from seeds I brought from Lebanon—it's so nice, and softer, sweeter. I always dry my own mint because it's cleaner and the taste is better. I pick the leaves off the stems, and I dry it on a tray in my oven with just the light on.

What do you like about teaching for the League of Kitchens? It's a beautiful experience for me. You learn every day something new from the people you meet. League of Kitchens is something unique in the world. It's not complicated. With the League of Kitchens, we have really honest recipes, very homemade, very real, home-sweet-home. This is the food of the League of Kitchens. And I learned to enjoy other cuisines, because before I ate only Lebanese food. I learned from the League of Kitchens how really all other kitchens have something good.

Jeanette Chawki

جانيت شوكي

スープ
汁

sopas

চচড়া

шӯрвалар

soupes

شوربا

cупе

SOUPS

سوپ

شوربا

झोल

sopas

sup.

सूप

soupes

Mashhurda

(UZBEK MUNG BEAN SOUP WITH RICE, FRESH HERBS, CARROTS, AND DRIED APRICOTS)

Instructor: Damira Inatullaeva

"I like to use lots and lots of chopped herbs and dried apricots in this soup. That's what my mother-in-law did, and I do everything according to her recipe." —Damira

This is an amazing one-pot vegetarian dish that is also a complete meal because it includes beans, rice, vegetables, and yogurt. When you get a bite of dried apricot, it's just a wonderful sweet surprise that perfectly accents the heartiness of the soup.

In Samarkand, the unsulfured, darker brown apricots used in this soup are called gulyunk. Damira says that when she was growing up, in rural areas they were left to dry right on the trees, then spread out on the rooftops to finish drying, so at a certain time of year, you would see drying apricots across the landscape.

Damira learned this particular version from her mother-in-law, who was Tajik (in the Tajik language, mashhurda means something like "mung bean food"). There are two interesting techniques hidden in this soup: One is simmering the generous quantities of herbs in the soup along with the vegetables, and the other is adding small amounts of hot water little by little over time as needed, rather than cooking everything in one big pot of boiling water. The flavors remain concentrated and the ingredients don't get soggy. The Turkish baldo rice used in this soup is creamy and starchy like arborio or carnaroli, both of which make a great substitute.

Note that the chopped fresh herbs, black pepper, and labne—a thick strained yogurt—are key components. They add an extra creaminess and brightness that make this soup so incredibly satisfying. Damira often serves this with bread—ideally Uzbek non, most typically a circular white bread with a patterned indentation in the center.

Serve with: The Uzbek radish salad on page 218 or the Uzbek tomato and onion salad on page 231, and plenty of bread.

1 cup (200 g) green mung beans

⅓ cup (65 g) baldo, arborio, or carnaroli rice

½ pound (225 g) yellow onion (about 1 medium)

⅓ pound (150 g) carrots (2 to 3 medium)

½ pound (225 g) dill (about 2 bunches)

½ pound (225 g) cilantro (about 2 bunches)

¼ cup (60 ml) neutral oil

2 tablespoons unseasoned tomato sauce

2 teaspoons Diamond Crystal kosher salt, divided, plus more if needed

4 bay leaves

¾ cup (140 g) dried apricots, preferably unsulfured

2 cups (475 ml) labne or plain whole milk Greek yogurt

Black pepper powder

1   **Prepare the ingredients:** Put the 1 cup (200 g) green mung beans in a small saucepan and rinse them with cold running water in the sink, stirring them a bit with your fingers. Drain off as much water as you can, then add clean water to cover them by about ½ inch (1.3 cm) or so. Bring the pot just to a boil over high heat. Reduce the heat slightly so that the beans cook at a simmer, and cook for about 6 minutes—the

Continued

water should turn green. Drain them and set them aside.

In Uzbekistan, Damira bought freshly dried mung beans at the farmers market, where they would arrive with many small stones and sticks, one of the reasons she always rinses and par-cooks them. But this step also makes the soup come together faster, especially if your mung beans have been sitting around in the supermarket, and it releases some of the starches and gas-causing oligosaccharides.

2   Wash the ⅓ cup (65 g) baldo, arborio, or carnaroli rice with cold running water in a small mixing bowl 2 or 3 times until the water runs nearly clear, then drain the water and set the bowl aside. It's okay if there's a little water left in the bowl.

3   Peel the ½ pound (225 g) yellow onion (about 1 medium). Cut it into ¼-inch (0.6 cm) dice. You should have about 1½ cups.

4   Peel the ⅓ pound (150 g) carrots (2 to 3 medium) and cut them into ⅓-inch (1 cm) dice. You should have about 1 cup.

5   Trim away just the ends of the stalks of the ½ pound (225 g) dill (about 2 bunches). Finely chop the dill. Set aside 1½ cups for the soup and reserve the rest for garnish.

6   Trim away just the ends of the stalks of the ½ pound (225 g) cilantro (about 2 bunches). Finely chop the cilantro. Set aside 2 cups for the soup and reserve the rest for garnish.

7   Bring 8 cups (2 L) water to a boil in a kettle or large saucepan. Keep it at a simmer or just keep it warm.

8   **Cook the soup:** Heat the ¼ cup (60 ml) neutral oil in a 5-quart (4.8 L) Dutch oven or saucepan over medium-high heat just until it warms.

9   Add the onions and cook, stirring, just until they begin to change color and soften, about 2 minutes—if you end up with a tiny bit of color around the edges, that's fine, but don't let them fully brown.

10 Reduce the heat to medium and add the diced carrots. Let them cook for about 1 minute to soften just a bit, stirring them once or twice, then stir in the 2 tablespoons tomato sauce so that it's completely mixed in with the vegetables. Add 1½ cups (355 ml) of hot water from the kettle and increase the heat to medium-high so that the water comes back to a boil.

11 Add the drained mung beans to the pot, then another 1½ cups (355 ml) of hot water from the kettle. Stir in 1 teaspoon of the Diamond Crystal kosher salt and the 4 bay leaves, cover the pot, and turn the heat down to medium-low so that the beans cook at a low simmer.

12 Cook for 10 minutes or so, stirring halfway through to make sure the beans are not sticking to the bottom, then add another ½ cup (120 ml) of the hot water. Cook for another 10 minutes or so, stirring halfway through to make sure they're not sticking.

13 At this point, test the mung beans for doneness—if they're soft and some are beginning to split apart, you can go to the next step. If not, add another ½ cup (120 ml) of the hot water and continue cooking. Be patient if they're not ready: The cooking time usually takes between 20 and 45 minutes, depending on the freshness of your beans and the intensity of your simmer. Don't worry about adding too much water, either—the soup will be fine.

14 When the mung beans are soft and splitting, add the washed rice and the herbs to the pot, then add the remaining 1 teaspoon Diamond Crystal kosher salt and 2½ cups (600 ml) hot water. Increase the heat to medium-high to

bring the water back to a boil, then cover the pot and reduce the heat so that the soup cooks at a simmer.

15 Cook, stirring often and adjusting the heat as necessary to make sure the soup doesn't stick or burn—which can happen very easily at this stage—until the rice is soft and creamy. This usually takes 15 to 20 minutes. Check your water level—you want there to still be enough in the pot so that you have a thick soup but not porridge. You'll probably want to add another ½ cup (120 ml) or maybe more of the hot water at this point, but trust your judgment, especially if you added a lot during the cooking process. If you added more water, let the soup come back up to a simmer.

16 Stir in the ¾ cup (140 g) dried apricots, preferably unsulfured, adjust the heat if needed to a low simmer, and cook, stirring often to prevent sticking, for 5 minutes, then turn off the heat. Be careful not to accidentally overcook or boil the soup, as the apricots will begin to melt and lose their sweetness. Cover the pot, let the soup rest for about 10 minutes to let the flavors meld, then taste for salt and add more if needed.

17 **Serve and eat the soup:** Remove and discard any bay leaves. Serve the soup in individual bowls and make sure that each has at least a few apricots. Top each bowl with a hearty pinch of the reserved cilantro and dill, a large dollop of labne or Greek yogurt, and a generous sprinkle of black pepper, and encourage everyone to mix everything together before they take a bite.

18 This soup is best served right away—if you do need to reheat it, add a little water and do so very gently so that the apricots don't get overcooked.

Miso Shiru

(JAPANESE MISO SOUP WITH SOFT TOFU AND ENOKI MUSHROOMS)

Instructor: Aiko Cascio

"Growing up we would have miso soup with rice for dinner almost every day." —Aiko

Aiko makes multiple types of miso soup, including a potato and kelp version that's very special, but her version of the classic is so good, it's the one we wanted to share in this cookbook. It's made with silken tofu, enoki mushrooms, and fresh scallion, and my family says it's the best miso soup they've ever had. If you make a big batch of dashi in advance and freeze it, the soup comes together very quickly.

Aiko prefers to make it with a mix of both white miso and the milder, sweeter saikyo miso, which is fermented for a shorter time and has a higher proportion of koji, the culture used to ferment soybeans into miso paste. She also adds a few slivers of abura age, which is a thin, puffy sheet of Japanese fried bean curd. If you can't easily find abura age or saikyo miso, it will still be delicious. As with making the dashi (recipe follows), the real secret is just to gently simmer the soup.

To that end, if you want to make the miso soup in advance and serve it later, the general rule of thumb is to not let the miso soup come to a boil when you reheat it, because it dulls the flavor of the miso and reduces the amount of probiotics. But it's not a huge deal if you do—in fact, Aiko says that she really likes that flavor, too. She'll often boil her miso soup the next day for a different experience. When she was little, Aiko's mother would add a pat of butter to the top of her soup to melt into her bowl. I love doing that—it adds a little bit of extra-delicious richness to the soup.

Serve with: any of Aiko's dishes, including the vegetable hand rolls on page 253.

For the miso soup

8 cups (2 L) dashi (recipe follows)

6 tablespoons white miso, plus more if needed

4 tablespoons saikyo miso, or more white miso

1 4- by 4-inch (10 cm by 10 cm) thin sheet abura age (Japanese fried bean curd), optional

½ pound (225 g) soft or silken tofu (about ½ block)

¾ ounce (20 g) enoki mushrooms (about 1 large handful)

1 large scallion, for garnishing the soup

1   **Make the soup:** Gently heat the 8 cups (2 L) dashi (recipe follows) in a small soup pot or large stockpot over very low heat.

2   When the dashi is just warm, put 1 cup (240 ml) of it into a bowl and stir in the 6 tablespoons white miso and 4 tablespoons saikyo miso, if using, or add 4 more tablespoons of white miso. Use a whisk or spatula to mix the miso into the dashi—you don't have to worry about lumps, a few are okay. Set this aside.

3   Cut the 4- by 4-inch (10 cm by 10 cm) thin sheet of abura age (Japanese fried bean curd), if using, into ribbons about 1½ inches (4 cm) long and ¼ inch (0.6 cm) wide.

4   Cut the ½ pound (225 g) soft or silken tofu (about ½ block) into ½-inch (1.3 cm) cubes or rectangles: The tofu is fragile, so the easiest way to do this is to place the block of tofu on the cutting board and hold it gently in place

Continued

with one hand the entire time you're cutting it. Use the tip of your knife to cut it into 1½-inch (4 cm) wide strips, then rotate the cutting board 180 degrees and cut the strips into cubes. Set the fried bean curd and the tofu aside.

Any tofu you have left over will last longer in the fridge if you store it in a clean container filled with water or just top off the package with water.

5   Turn the heat under the remaining 7 cups (1.7 L) of dashi to medium-high and add the bean curd slivers, if using, and the soft tofu cubes.

6   While the tofu heats through, trim the roots from the enoki mushrooms and cut the mushrooms in half right across the stem (you will end up with some pieces that are just the stems). Break the mushrooms apart with your fingers if needed and add them to the pot. Then turn the heat to medium-low—the soup should be at a low simmer.

7   Let the soup simmer for about 3 minutes. Stir in the miso mixture, then turn off the heat. (Be careful not to let the pot come to a boil once you add the miso—the heat will change its flavor.) Taste the miso soup for saltiness—if you want a little more, stir in 1 to 2 more tablespoons of white miso. Keep the soup just warm (do not let it simmer or boil) until you're ready to serve.

8   Separate the white and green parts of the 1 large scallion, then cut the white part in half lengthwise. Then slice both white and green parts into very thin rings.

9   **Serve and eat the soup:** Serve the miso soup warm, making sure each bowl has a few enoki mushrooms and pieces of tofu. Top each bowl with a few pieces of scallion.

Dashi

Aiko says that many Japanese cooks just use dashi from a packet, and that works fine, too. But this dashi is so delicious and perfectly flavored, it will really improve any dish that calls for it. It's also easy to make. Just be sure to watch the pot when you begin to heat the kombu, which is the Japanese name for dried kelp. If you don't take it out as soon as you begin to see tiny bubbles form in the pot, the dashi tends to taste like the ocean, says Aiko.

Another tip: Use the cheaper, bigger bags of bonito flakes, or katsuobushi in Japanese, for making dashi. The flakes won't be as large and crispy as those in small bags, but since you'll be simmering them, that doesn't matter. (The small bags are meant to be used for garnishing dishes.) You can also double or even triple this recipe for dashi, and then keep it in the refrigerator for up to 10 days or in the freezer for several months so you'll have it at the ready for making miso soup.

If you want to make vegan dashi without bonito, you can use two dried shiitake mushrooms (trim the ends), but leave them in the pot when it boils and let it cook for two minutes longer. There may be some grit from the mushrooms in the bottom of the pot. When you're done, just leave it there and discard it after you use the dashi.

0.6 ounce (18 g) kombu (about two 4-inch/10 cm square pieces)

0.6 ounce (18 g) bonito flakes (about 1 packed cup)

1   **Soak the kombu:** Soak the 0.6 ounce (18 g) kombu (about two 4-inch/10 cm square pieces) for at least 2 hours or overnight in 8 cups (2 L) water at room temperature. You can use the same pot that you will make the dashi in to soak the kombu.

2 **Cook the kombu:** Have a pair of tongs (or a slotted spoon) ready, then set the pot over medium heat and cook just until you see tiny bubbles forming all over the bottom of the pot. (This will take longer over medium heat than high heat, but with high heat it's much easier to accidentally let the pot come to a full boil.) Turn off the heat and remove the kombu; discard it or save it for another use.

Aiko gathers leftover pieces of kombu in her freezer, wrapped in plastic wrap, until she has several cups' worth, which she'll then use to make kelp chips. After she defrosts the kombu in a bowl of water, she marinates it in tamari and toasted sesame oil for an hour or two, cuts it into small pieces, spreads the pieces on a baking sheet, and bakes them on the middle rack of the oven at 350°F (177°C) for 15 to 20 minutes, until they're very dry. You can also sprinkle them with sesame seeds before you bake them.

3 **Finish the dashi:** Add the 0.6 ounce (18 g) bonito flakes (about 1 packed cup) to the pot—do not stir them—and turn the heat to very low. It should be barely simmering—the top should be steaming. Cook for 5 minutes without stirring. Strain the dashi into a bowl or another pot through a wire strainer and discard the bonito flakes. Set the liquid aside until you need it, or refrigerate it for up to a week or freeze it for several months.

Sopa Aguada

(MEXICAN TOMATO SOUP WITH PASTA)

Instructor: Angelica Vargas

"When I was growing up, I would always make my name around the plate with the letters, or the name of the boy I had a crush on." —Angie

When Angie makes this as the welcome meal for her League of Kitchens classes—the dish she puts out when everyone arrives—her students are always so amazed by how good it tastes and how little work it takes. It has a fresh, bright tomato flavor, and the tiny pasta is so much fun. Angie's kids love it, and so do mine—according to Angie, it's the most popular soup in Mexico.

Any tiny pasta will work for this soup, such as stars, alphabet letters, or tiny cut spaghetti—fidelini, or fideo in Spanish. Sopa agauda essentially means watery soup—but in Mexico you will also find it called sopa de letras if you use the letter-shaped pasta, or sopa de estrillas if you use the stars, and so on. When she can find it, Angie likes to use La Moderna brand pasta, especially the fideo. It's the brand her mother always used. (It comes in 7 ounce/198 g packages—just use the whole thing!)

To Angie, this dish just doesn't taste like home without the extra umami from the bouillon cubes, but even plain water works great, and of course you can use real chicken stock or broth if you have it. I like to buy a brand of frozen chicken bone broth that comes in 3-cup packages, so I just defrost one of those to use for this recipe.

If Angie is in a rush or having this for lunch, she'll often just have sopa aguada with a squeeze of fresh lime juice. But for dinner she'll usually put out warm corn tortillas and slices of fresh Mexican cheese and avocado. While her kids like to put crumbled cheese and cubes of avocado right into the soup, Angie prefers to make simple cheese or avocado tacos to eat in between bites of soup.

Serve with: corn tortillas (page 165), as a main meal, or as an appetizer with the Mexican ground beef and potatoes on page 78 or the steak tacos on page 63.

1 pound (450 g) plum tomatoes (about 4 medium)

¼ ounce (7 g) garlic (about 2 medium cloves)

⅓ pound (150 g) white onion (about ½ medium)

2 chicken or tomato bouillon cubes, or one of each, optional

3 or 4 teaspoons Diamond Crystal kosher salt, depending on if you're using the bouillion cubes

2 tablespoons neutral oil

6 ounces (170 g) small pasta, such as letters, stars, or fideo

3 cups (700 ml) chicken bone broth, chicken stock, or water

1 lime, for cutting into wedges and squeezing over the top of the soup

1 ripe avocado, for serving, optional

Queso blanco and/or queso fresco (page 78), for serving, optional

1 to 2 jalapeño chiles, for serving, optional

1   **Prepare the tomato base:** Cut the 1 pound (450 g) plum tomatoes (about 4 medium) in half lengthwise and put them in a blender. Peel the ¼ ounce (7 g) garlic (about 2 medium cloves) and add it to the blender. Trim the ends of the ⅓ pound (150 g) white onion (about

Continued

½ medium), peel it, then cut it into two pieces and add them to the blender. Add the 2 chicken or tomato bouillon cubes, or one of each, if using. Add 3 teaspoons Diamond Crystal kosher salt, if you're using the bouillon, or 4 teaspoons if you are not.

2   Add 2 cups (475 ml) of tap water to the blender and puree everything on high until it's smooth, fluffy, and lighter in color. Set the mixture aside (you can keep it in the blender, if you like).

3   **Make the soup:** Put the 2 tablespoons neutral oil in a 5-quart (4.8 L) Dutch oven or saucepan and heat it over medium-high heat. When the oil begins to shimmer, add the 6 ounces (170 g) pasta, using a wooden spoon or spatula to gently spread it out across the bottom.

4   Lower the heat to medium, then fry the pasta until it turns golden in color, usually 2 to 3 minutes—you don't want it to brown, so be sure to stay by the stove. When you hear the bottom of the pasta begin to sizzle consistently, stir it constantly with a spatula so that it doesn't burn.

5   When the pasta is golden in color, stir in the pureed tomatoes and onions from the blender. Raise the heat to medium-high and let the liquid come to a strong simmer—where it bubbles as soon as you stop stirring—stirring frequently, but gently, to make sure the pasta doesn't stick to the bottom.

6   Cook for 1 full minute, scraping gently along the bottom once or twice to keep the pasta from sticking, then add the 3 cups (700 ml) chicken bone broth, chicken stock, or water. (You can also swirl the broth or water around in the blender first to pick up any remaining bits of tomato puree, if you like.)

7   Increase the heat to high and bring the soup back up to a strong simmer, making sure to scrape up the bottom with a spoon or spatula occasionally to prevent sticking. As soon as it reaches a simmer, lower the heat to medium and cook, stirring occasionally, just until the pasta is al dente, usually 8 to 10 minutes. (The cooking time will vary depending on the type of pasta.) Turn off the heat and keep the soup warm until it's time to serve it.

8   **Prepare the toppings:** (If you're serving the soup as a main meal, this is a good time to prepare or reheat the tortillas.) Slice the 1 lime into wedges and put them on a serving platter. Cut the 1 ripe avocado into wedges, if using, and add them to the serving platter with the limes. The easiest way to do this is to cut the avocado into wedges with the peel still on, then remove the peel as you eat the avocado.

9   Cut the queso blanco and/or queso fresco into slices about ½ inch (1.3 cm) thick, if using, and put them on the serving platter next to the avocado. Slice the 1 to 2 jalapeño chiles, if using, and add them to the platter with the rest of the toppings.

Though you can just slice some fresh jalapeños and add them to the soup, Angie usually does it in one of two ways. If she's short on time, she'll just slice the jalapeños and put them in a small serving bowl, then sprinkle them with fresh lime juice and salt. But her favorite way is to char the jalapeños on the flame of her gas stove (you could use a broiler), then peel off any blackened skin before she slices them and sprinkles them with the lime juice and salt.

10   **Serve and eat the soup.** This soup is best when served within an hour or so of making it, when the pasta is still al dente—it will continue to expand and soften in the liquid. (You can serve leftovers gently reheated, but you'll need to add

water, as the pasta will have soaked up a lot of the liquid.)

11 Serve everyone a bowl of soup, then put all the toppings on the table so each person can garnish their bowl as they like (or make tacos, if you are also serving tortillas). If you want to add avocado directly to your bowl, use a butter knife to cut cubes from the avocado wedges directly into your soup (see photo, page 198). Just make a cut into the avocado wedge near the tip and then push it off into the soup with your knife.

Svekolnik

(SLAVIC COLD BORSCHT)

Instructor: Larisa Frumkin

"This summer soup is full of vitamins, which were so scarce during the wintertime in the Soviet Union. That is why I use the beet greens and stems. They're a treasure—I want to use every little half-inch of them." —Larisa

This cold borscht is almost like a gazpacho, or even a salad, it's so fresh. I grew up eating cold borscht, too, but we didn't add the chopped cucumber, radish, dill, scallions, and hard-boiled eggs at the end, all of which make this soup extra special and much more substantial. If you serve this with bread and butter, as Larisa does, it's really a whole meal.

Ideally, you would buy beets with the greens still attached and use both for the soup—if you can't find them that way, you can just omit the greens. If your beets end up being a little less or a little more than a half pound each, don't worry—it's fine. Larisa says that many cooks prefer to bake the beets and potatoes separately before adding them to the soup, but she prefers to boil the beets and potato right in the water, for better flavor. And it's true—this is a fantastic, flavorful soup made only with water.

Adding the fresh lemon juice at the end is also very important to this dish, both for flavor and technique. You add it once the potato is fully cooked but before it cools, or else the potato won't soften. (Larisa likes her borscht very tart, but I grew up eating jarred Gold's borscht with my Jewish grandmother, which is quite sweet, and so I like this soup on the sweeter side.)

This can easily be made a day or several hours in advance, especially because it has to cool before you serve it. Then you can just prepare all the garnishes right before serving.

Serve with: the savory pies on page 182, or just bread and butter.

For the soup

1 pound (450 g) beets (about 2 medium), preferably with the greens still attached

1 pound (450 g) russet potatoes (about 2 medium)

2 tablespoons Diamond Crystal kosher salt, or more to taste

1½ teaspoons white sugar, or more to taste

Pinch freshly ground black pepper

½ cup (120 ml) fresh lemon juice (from 2 to 4 lemons), or more to taste

For the toppings

2 large eggs

1 cup (240 ml) sour cream

1 small cucumber, preferably Kirby or Persian

2 red radishes

2 large scallions

2 tablespoons chopped fresh dill

1   **Prepare the vegetables for the soup:** If your 1 pound (450 g) beets (about 2 medium) came with greens, cut them off, wash them, then set them aside to drain.

2   Peel the beets. If they're especially large, cut them into pieces that are easier to handle, then grate them on the large holes of a box grater into a bowl. (You can also use a food processor fitted with the grater attachment.) You should end up with about 3 cups. Set the grated beets aside.

Continued

3   If using, trim any rough stem ends from the beet greens, then separate the stems from leaves. Slice the beet green stems as thinly as you can—about ⅛ inch (0.3 cm) wide—then roughly chop the leaves into pieces about 1 inch (2.5 cm) wide. Set the stems and leaves aside, keeping them separated, since you will add them to the pot at different times.

4   Peel the 1 pound (450 g) russet potatoes (about 2 medium). Cut them into small cubes about ⅓ inch (1 cm) wide. You should have about 3 cups.

5   **Cook the soup:** Put the potato cubes in a 5-quart (4.8 L) Dutch oven or saucepan, add 8½ cups (2 L) of cold tap water, and bring the pot to a boil over high heat.

6   When the water just begins to boil, stir in the grated beets. When the pot returns to a boil, reduce the heat to low and cover the pot, keeping the lid slightly ajar. Let the soup cook for 10 minutes. As the potatoes and beets simmer, remove the lid and skim off and discard any foam that rises to the top of the pot.

7   Stir in the sliced beet stems, if using, then add the 2 tablespoons Diamond Crystal kosher salt. Raise the heat to medium-high to bring the soup back to a boil, then reduce to low and cover the pot, leaving the lid ajar. Cook for about 3 minutes, then check the potatoes for doneness. (When they're done, you should be able to slide a knife or fork easily through a piece.)

8   When the potatoes are done, stir in the beet leaves, raise the heat to medium-high to bring the soup back to a simmer, and simmer for about 5 minutes, until the beet greens have fully cooked through; turn off the heat. Stir in the 1½ teaspoons white sugar and a pinch of ground black pepper. Squeeze enough of the 2 to 4 large lemons to get ½ cup (120 ml) lemon juice and stir it into the pot.

9   Let the soup cool completely before serving. It can be refrigerated for a few hours or overnight and served very cold, or just left to cool to room temperature. Before serving, taste it again for salt, sugar, and lemon juice, as those flavors change as the soup cools.

If you want to speed up this process, you can put the soup pot inside a larger pot filled with very cold water in the sink. Stir the soup occasionally, and it should cool enough to eat in about an hour.

10 **Prepare the toppings:** While the soup is cooling, hard-boil the eggs. Fill a small saucepan with water. Bring the pot to a boil over high heat, then add the 2 large eggs and let them cook for 11 minutes. Immediately drain and transfer them to a bowl of cold water in the sink to cool completely. (You can do this step in advance, or you can speed up this process by putting them in a bowl of ice water or letting the tap run at a trickle into the bowl, to keep the water as cold as possible.)

11 While the eggs cool, put the 1 cup (240 ml) sour cream in a small serving bowl and whisk it until smooth. Set it aside.

12 Cut the 1 small cucumber into ¼-inch (0.6 cm) dice and put it in another small serving bowl. Cut the 2 red radishes into cubes about the same size and add them to the bowl with the cucumber. Trim the ends of the 2 large scallions and cut them into ¼-inch (0.6 cm) slices, or about the same width as the cucumbers and radishes, and add them to the same bowl.

13 Once the eggs are cool, peel them and cut them into pieces the same size as the cucumbers and radishes and add them to the bowl. Then add the 2 tablespoons finely chopped fresh dill. Use a spoon to gently mix everything together.

14 **To serve and eat the soup:** You can serve the soup family style, setting the pot in the middle

of the table with the bowl of sour cream and the bowl of mixed diced vegetables, egg, and dill. Each diner tops their soup to their liking. Or you could prepare individual bowls, topping each one with a spoonful of sour cream and a spoonful of vegetables. Either way, encourage each diner to stir it all in so that everything is mixed together before they take a bite.

The Art of Zakuski

If Larisa is serving guests, she always puts out an assortment of zakuski, or small plates of cold appetizers such as hard-boiled eggs topped with salmon roe, homemade pickles, smoked salmon or pickled herring, chopped chicken liver spread, a platter of raw scallions and cherry tomatoes, and rye bread and butter. These are traditionally consumed with ice-cold vodka, each shot accompanied with a toast from a different guest.

Borshch

SERVES 4 TO 6

(UKRAINIAN HOT BEET AND VEGETABLE BORSCHT)

Instructor: Larisa Frumkin

"There are millions of recipes for borscht. People add all kinds of things. I use apple. Apple gives sweetness and aroma, but you can't recognize it—you will not find it, but you will feel it." —Larisa

This is Larisa's vegetarian version of hot borscht, made extra rich with oil and butter. It's really hard to believe it's made without stock or broth. If her cold borscht is really about freshness, this one is a comforting, hot bowl of mixed vegetable soup that's sweet, sour, and savory, with a tiny bit of heat. Larisa usually uses a pinch of red chile powder, but you could also add a fresh chopped green chile instead of or in addition to the red chile powder, if you prefer.

Larisa adds the cabbage near the end of the cooking process, so it has some bite. The bell pepper is something she started adding when she came to America. She loves the little bit of sweetness that it adds. Garnishes of fresh herbs add extra layers of flavor—but you can serve the borscht without them, as Larisa often did in the winter, growing up in the Soviet Union. This can easily be made a day in advance—in fact, Larisa says that it always tastes better the next day.

Serve with: the savory pies on page 182, or just a tray of zakuski (page 205).

For the soup

¼ pound (115 g) yellow onion (about ½ medium)

¼ pound (115 g) carrot (about 1 medium)

1 6-inch (15 cm) celery rib

⅓ pound (150 g) bell pepper, any color (about ½ large)

½ pound (225 g) tart green apple, like Granny Smith (about 1 medium)

1 ounce (30 g) garlic (about 8 medium cloves)

1 pound (450 g) beets (about 2 medium)

¼ pound (115 g) russet or Yukon Gold potato (about 1 small)

½ pound (225 g) green cabbage (about ⅓ small cabbage)

1 6-ounce (170 g) can tomato paste

2 tablespoons neutral oil

2 tablespoons unsalted butter

1½ tablespoons Diamond Crystal kosher salt

1 tablespoon sweet paprika

¼ teaspoon red or Aleppo chile flakes or hot paprika, optional

Freshly ground black pepper

¼ teaspoon white sugar, or more to taste

2 tablespoons fresh lemon juice (from about 1 lemon), or more to taste

1 large or 2 small bay leaves

For the garnishes

1 cup (240 ml) sour cream

1 large handful finely chopped fresh dill or scallion, or a mix

1   **Prepare the hot water:** Bring 8 cups (2 L) water to a boil in a kettle or large pot and then keep it warm or at a simmer.

2   **Prepare the vegetables:** Peel the ¼ pound (115 g) yellow onion (about ½ medium) and cut it into ⅓-inch (1 cm) dice. You should end up with about 1 cup.

Continued

207   SOUPS

3 Peel the ¼ pound (115 g) carrot (about 1 medium) and grate it over the large holes of a grater. You should end up with about ¾ cup. Set aside separately from the onion.

4 Cut the 6-inch (15 cm) celery rib into quarters lengthwise, then cut it into ⅓-inch (1 cm) dice. You will have about ¼ cup. Set aside.

5 Remove the membrane and seeds from the ⅓ pound (150 g) bell pepper (about ½ large). Cut it into ⅓-inch (1 cm) dice. You should end up with about ¾ cup. Set this aside with the celery.

6 Peel, core, and cut the ½ pound (225 g) tart apple, such as Granny Smith (about 1 medium), into ⅔-inch (1.7 cm) chunks. You should end up with about 1 cup. Set this aside separately.

7 Peel the 1 ounce (30 g) garlic (about 8 medium cloves), then chop it finely. You should end up with about 1½ tablespoons. Put it in a small bowl. Peel the 1 pound (450 g) beets (about 2 medium). Cut them into halves or thirds to make them easier to hold, then grate them on the large holes of a box grater, or use the grating attachment of a food processor. You should have about 3 cups.

8 Peel the ¼ pound (115 g) russet or Yukon Gold potato (about 1 small), and then cut it into ⅔-inch (1.7 cm) chunks. You will have about ¾ cup.

9 Remove any core from the ½ pound (225 g) green cabbage (about ⅓ small cabbage). Slice the cabbage ½ inch (1.3 cm) thick, then cut the slices into ½-inch (1.3 cm) dice. You should have about 3 cups.

10 Put the 6-ounce (170 g) can tomato paste in a small mixing bowl and set it aside.

11 **Cook the soup:** Heat the 2 tablespoons neutral oil in a 5-quart (4.8 L) Dutch oven or saucepan, preferably nonstick, over high heat.

12 When the oil is hot—a piece of onion will sizzle immediately—stir in the onion and add the 2 tablespoons unsalted butter. Stir in the grated carrots and continue to cook the onion and carrot over high heat for about 2 minutes, stirring occasionally, until everything has softened and wilted slightly.

13 Lower the heat to medium, then stir in the chopped celery and peppers. Cook, stirring occasionally, for about 4 minutes, until the vegetables have softened and wilted slightly. Add the chopped apples and cook for about 5 minutes, stirring occasionally.

14 Stir the grated beets into the pot. Cook for 2 minutes, stirring occasionally, then add the potato. Cook for another 2 minutes, stirring occasionally, then add the cabbage. Let everything cook for 5 minutes, stirring occasionally, so all of the vegetables soften.

15 Add the 8 cups (2 L) hot water. Bring the borscht to a heavy simmer over high heat, then lower the heat to medium-high. Simmer for 15 minutes, stirring frequently to mix all the vegetables in. If the pot begins to bubble over or spatter, lower the heat slightly.

16 Reduce the heat to low and cover the pot, leaving the lid ajar. Cook for 3 minutes, then stir in the chopped garlic, 1½ tablespoons Diamond Crystal kosher salt, 1 tablespoon sweet paprika, ¼ teaspoon red or Aleppo chile flakes or hot paprika, if using, and a few grinds of cracked black pepper.

17 Give everything a stir, then check a piece of potato for doneness—it should be soft enough to easily cut through with a spoon or fork. If the potatoes are not yet done, let the soup simmer until they're cooked through.

18 When the potatoes are soft, put about 1 cup (240 ml) of the hot liquid from the soup pot

into the bowl with the tomato paste and blend them together, then add the mixture into the soup pot. Add the ¼ teaspoon white sugar and 2 tablespoons of fresh lemon juice to the soup.

Sour ingredients make things tough—make sure not to add the lemon juice until your potato is fully soft.

19 Cover the pot, leaving the lid ajar, and cook for 2 more minutes. Taste for sugar and lemon juice, adding more to taste. Then stir in the 1 large or 2 small bay leaves, return the lid, leaving it ajar, and let the soup cook for 10 more minutes, then turn off the heat. Keep the soup on the stove to stay warm until you're ready to serve it.

20 **Prepare the garnishes:** Put the 1 cup (120 ml) sour cream in a small serving bowl and whisk it until smooth.

21 Prepare the handful of finely chopped fresh dill or scallion, or a mix, tossing them together in a small bowl if you're using more than one kind.

22 **To serve and eat the borscht:** Serve the soup hot or warm, ladled into individual bowls or served in a covered tureen. Put all the garnishes out on the table so that each person can top their soup to their liking.

Despina Economou

It takes only a few minutes with Despina to understand her enthusiasm for the very freshest ingredients—her students quickly learn this most important facet of Greek cooking. Despina always finds the best: the creamiest feta, the purest extra-virgin olive oil, the freshest oregano. There are stories of the fig, pear, and pomegranate trees that grew in her childhood backyard and the fish in her coastal hometown of Chalcis on the island of Euboea in Greece. She learned to cook as a child from her stepmother and her father, who also worked as a cook in a soup kitchen. She loves to draw and to paint, and her eye for detail is crystal clear in the beautiful appearance of every dish she makes. Despina moved to the US in the 1970s and worked as a registered nurse for more than forty years. Despina and her husband have two grown daughters, and for many years her eldest ran a Greek food stand at one of Manhattan's most famous markets—today they often work together for catering projects. Despina now lives with her husband in Queens; they also have two grandchildren.

Why do you love cooking? It's like therapy. I forget everything when I cook. It's just part of my daily routine. One of the first things I think of when I wake up is, What should I make for dinner?

What advice would you give to someone who is just learning to cook? Be patient, because in the beginning it's difficult. Never give up. Start with simple recipes. Try to have all your utensils, pans, pots, knives, and everything else that you need. And also use fresh ingredients and wash your hands all the time. When you pause to do something and you touch something, when you go back, wash your hands. This is very important.

What are some of your favorite home remedies from the kitchen? When I have a cold, I boil Greek mountain tea, which is called tsai tou vounou. And I add honey because the honey has soothing properties, and lemon, because lemon has vitamin C and it's very good for a cold. When you burn yourself or when you go to the beach and get a sunburn, you put on yogurt, which is cold and very soothing.

What are some of your favorite self-care tips from the kitchen? When I do the tzatziki I save the juice from the cucumber, and I add two, three tablespoons of yogurt and some honey. This is such an amazing mask. For the hair, I put olive oil, and I leave it overnight. And the next day when you wash your hair, it's like silk. It's such an amazing treatment. Even for your skin, olive oil is amazing.

If you're going to cook just for yourself, but you want it to be delicious, what do you make? I like to make french fries or potatoes in the oven, and I beat some eggs and scramble them into the potatoes. Or I make a Greek salad (page 236) with two boiled eggs. I like to make a vegetable omelet. I slice some tomato, some pepper, onions, a little garlic, I saute it, and then I add the eggs. And you can throw some feta on top.

If you want to have something sweet after a meal, but you don't want to make a whole dessert, what do you do? My favorite thing is a piece of toast with almond butter and a little honey. This is so good. Or I make Greek yogurt with honey and some walnuts and a little cinnamon, and this is so satisfying.

What's your favorite thing to eat that's not Greek? Chinese food. The flavors are amazing. Every dish I try, I love it.

Despina Economou
Δέσποινα Οικονόμου

サラダ

Ensaladas

সালাদ

салатар

Salata

салат

Салат

SALADS

سلاد

سلاد

हरी सलाद

Ensaladas

Salads

सलाद

Salades

Vinegret

(RUSSIAN COOKED VEGETABLE SALAD)

Instructor: Larisa Frumkin

"Historically you never saw this in high-society dinners in the Soviet era. If they ate it, it was not with their guests! But I love this salad." —Larisa

Vinegret is a classic pan-Soviet dish with roots in peasant cuisine. It's basically a salad of boiled beets, potatoes, and carrots, but one that's deliciously full of contrasts, thanks to the piquant scallions and fresh dill, the crunchy and sour dill pickles, the tart sauerkraut, and the light mustard vinaigrette. Ideally each of the vegetables is cut into slightly different sizes, says Larisa, which is also a part of vinegret's appeal. Larisa usually makes hers with unrefined sunflower oil, which has a nuttier flavor more like sunflower seeds than refined oil—it's harder to find, but it will give your vinegret even more flavor.

Larisa prefers to bake the beet in the oven, but you could also boil or steam it or even buy precooked beets—preferably whole beets, not those that are sold already sliced. She also always uses canned peas for this dish, instead of fresh or frozen—they were considered a luxury item during the Soviet Era. For those who grew up in the Soviet Union, it's not vinegret without the canned peas!

This is best when made at least two hours before you eat it and left to sit at room temperature so that the flavors meld. Larisa typically makes it earlier in the day and lets it sit until she serves it for dinner. You can also make it the day before, but it'll be even better if you wait to add the herbs once you take it out of the refrigerator. One other trick—do not add the beets to the bowl until you've dressed everything else with the vinaigrette, or else they'll turn the potatoes purple.

Serve with: the pies on page 182, or by itself as a main meal with buttered rye bread and an assortment of the small cold snacks called zakuski (see page 205).

¾ pound (340 g) beet (about 1 large)

1 pound (450 g) russet potatoes (about 2 medium)

⅔ pound (300 g) carrots (about 5 medium)

2 tablespoons plus ½ teaspoon Diamond Crystal kosher salt, divided

1¼ cups (5¼ ounces/150 g) canned or frozen sweet peas

½ pound (225 g) dill pickles (about 4 medium)

1 packed cup (7 ounces/195 g) drained sauerkraut

¼ pound (115 g) scallions (about 4 medium)

⅛ pound (60 g) fresh dill (about ½ bunch)

3 tablespoons fresh lemon juice (from about 1 large lemon)

3 tablespoons unrefined sunflower or neutral oil

1 scant tablespoon spicy brown mustard

1 **Cook the root vegetables:** Preheat the oven to 400°F (200°C). Wrap the ¾ pound (340 g) beet (about 1 large) in foil and bake until you can pierce it all the way through with a knife, usually about 1 hour and 15 minutes for 1 large beet.

2 When the beet is ready, remove it from the oven, open the foil, and let it cool completely, usually about 20 minutes. (You can make the roasted beet a day or two in advance and refrigerate it until you're ready to make the vinegret.)

3 While the beet cooks, fill an 8-quart (7.5 L) stockpot with 4 quarts (16 cups/3.8 L) water and bring it to a boil over high heat. While the water

Continued

comes to a boil, peel the 1 pound (450 g) russet potatoes (about 2 medium) and cut them into quarters lengthwise. Peel the ⅔ pound (300 g) carrots (about 5 medium) and cut each in half crosswise. When the water boils, add the potatoes and carrots to the pot and then add 2 tablespoons of the Diamond Crystal kosher salt.

This may seem like a lot of salt, but a lot of it ends up in the water—you need this much to ensure the carrots and potatoes are well salted in the final dish. (Larisa jokes that she always keeps the cooking water from the carrots and potatoes for vegetable soup and then never uses it, but she is sure it would be good.)

4   Bring the water back up to a boil, then reduce the heat to medium-high to cook at a simmer. Cover the pot, leaving the lid slightly ajar, and cook just until the vegetables are cooked through—they will have some resistance but will not be raw. This is usually about 20 minutes, but don't let them overcook and become mushy. If you're using frozen peas, add the 1¼ cups (5¼ ounces/150 g) peas to the water just before you drain the potatoes and the carrots.

5   Drain the boiled vegetables and set them aside in a large mixing bowl until they're cool enough to handle, 15 to 20 minutes.

6   **Prepare the rest of the ingredients:** While the vegetables cook and cool, prepare everything else for the salad.

7   Trim the stem ends of the ½ pound (225 g) dill pickles (about 4 medium) and cut the pickles into ¼-inch (0.6 cm) cubes. You should end up with about 1½ cups chopped pickles. Put them in a large serving bowl.

8   Drain the sauerkraut if you haven't already, and measure 1 packed cup (195 grams) of drained sauerkraut. Add it to the serving bowl with the pickles.

9   Trim the ends of the ¼ pound (115 g) scallions (about 4 medium) and cut them into ¼-inch (0.6 cm) rounds. You should end up with about 1½ cups sliced scallions. Add them to the bowl with the pickles and sauerkraut.

10 Remove all but the most tender and small stems from ⅛ pound (60 grams) fresh dill (about ½ bunch) and chop it as finely as you can. You should end up with about ½ cup chopped dill. Set the dill aside in a separate bowl.

11 In a small bowl, whisk together the 3 tablespoons lemon juice (from about 1 large lemon), 3 tablespoons unrefined sunflower or neutral oil, 1 scant tablespoon spicy brown mustard, and the remaining ½ teaspoon Diamond Crystal kosher salt. Set this dressing aside.

12 **Prepare the salad:** Cut the cooked and cooled potatoes into rough cubes about ½ inch (1.3 cm) wide. You should end up with about 3 cups chopped potatoes. Add the potatoes to the serving bowl.

13 Cut the cooked and cooled carrots into slightly smaller pieces than the potatoes, just under ½ inch (1.3 cm) wide. You should end up with about 1½ cups cut carrots. Add them to the serving bowl. If using canned peas, drain the 1¼ cups (5¼ ounces/150 g) peas and add them to the serving bowl. (Otherwise, scrape the peas out of the mixing bowl that held the potatoes and carrots and into the serving bowl.)

14 Give the salad dressing a stir and add it to the serving bowl. Use two large spoons to gently toss all the vegetables with the dressing until they're fully coated.

15 Peel the roasted and cooled beets and cut them into small cubes about ½ inch (1.3 cm) or so. You should have about 2 cups. Add them to the serving bowl, then toss everything again

to mix it together. Let the vinegret sit at room temperature for at least 30 minutes, loosely covered, and up to 3 hours before you serve it.

16 **To serve and eat the vinegret:** This is more traditionally considered an appetizer, served in a smaller portion before a meal, but Larisa likes to serve it by itself for supper, often with just a few slices of buttered rye bread. Leftovers will last for up to a week in the refrigerator.

Rediska Salat

(UZBEK RADISH SALAD WITH LABNEH, DILL, CILANTRO, AND GARLIC)

Instructor: Damira Inatullaeva

"Sometimes my students say to me they don't like radishes—until they try this salad!" —Damira

This is a refreshing, light, healthy salad, and a very popular side dish in Uzbekistan. It's especially good with grilled meats. Damira, who was a cardiologist before she retired, says this is great for digestion, especially when served with meat. It's also fantastic in spring, when you can find all kinds of beautiful radishes and young garlic in the market and the dill and cilantro are tender and new. Labne is a thick Middle Eastern–style yogurt. If you can't find it, you can use Greek yogurt or even strain your own. Damira says that some have a sour taste and some have a creamy taste, and eventually you'll find the one you prefer—she likes the Turkish brand called Merve. (If you're serving this to guests, you can also top the bowl with a little freshly ground black pepper or a few strands of dill for extra visual appeal!)

Serve with: the meatballs on page 75, the mung bean and rice soup on page 146, or any kind of roasted or grilled meat, or really any meal as a salad or vegetable side. This is often served as part of a spread of small plates and dishes, including the tomato salad on page 226.

1¼ cups (300 ml) labne or plain whole milk Greek yogurt

¾ pound (340 g) red radishes (about 12 large)

⅛ pound (60 g) fresh cilantro (about ½ bunch)

1 ounce (30 g) fresh dill (about ¼ bunch)

¼ ounce (7 g) garlic (about 2 medium cloves)

1 teaspoon Diamond Crystal kosher salt, or more to taste

⅛ teaspoon finely ground black pepper powder

1   **Prepare the yogurt:** Measure out the 1¼ cups (300 ml) labne or plain whole milk Greek yogurt into a small bowl so that it begins to come to room temperature.

2   **Prepare the vegetables:** Trim the root and stem ends of the ¾ pound (340 g) red radishes (about 12 large). Cut in half lengthwise, then into very thin half-moons. You should have about 2½ cups. Put them in a medium serving bowl.

3   Trim about 2 inches (5 cm) off the ends of the stems of the ⅛ pound (60 g) fresh cilantro (about ½ bunch). Finely chop both the leaves and the remaining stems. You should have about 1 cup. Add it to the bowl with the radishes.

4   Trim about 2 inches (5 cm) off the stems of the 1 ounce (30 g) fresh dill (about ¼ bunch). Finely chop both the leaves and the remaining stems. You should have about ⅓ cup. Add it to the bowl with the radishes.

5   Peel the ¼ ounce (7 g) garlic (about 2 medium cloves) and cut it into ⅛-inch dice (0.3 cm). You should have about 1 tablespoon. Add it to the bowl with the radishes.

6   **Prepare the dressing:** Stir 1 tablespoon water into the labne or Greek yogurt. Add the 1 teaspoon Diamond Crystal kosher salt and ⅛ teaspoon finely ground black pepper powder and stir until the dressing is completely smooth. The texture should be similar to sour cream—if it is still too thick, add a little more water.

7   **Finish the salad:** Stir the seasoned labne or Greek yogurt into the bowl with the radishes and gently fold everything together until it's

well mixed. (If you want to prepare the salad an hour or so in advance, keep the dressing and vegetables separate and combine right before serving.) Taste for salt and add more if needed.

8 **Serve the salad:** Serve the salad at room temperature. It's best eaten right after it's made, or the radishes will release liquid into the dressing.

Sabszi Khordan

(PERSIAN FRESH HERBS WITH FETA, WALNUTS, AND LAVASH)

Instructor: **Mahboubeh Abbasgholizadeh**

"On the traditional Persian table, we always have sabzi khordan. We believe that eating it will make you beautiful and fresh and help you live a long life." —Mab

Served more like a crudité platter than a traditional mixed salad, the ingredients in sabzi khordan should really vary depending on what's at hand: Mab usually tells her students to go to the farmers market and to look at the herbs and scallions—whichever look fresh enough to eat raw, that's your sabzi khordan. In truth, much of the below is optional, because sabzi khordan can be as simple as putting out one fresh herb, a few scallions, and some lavash to eat with your hands in between bites of the rest of your meal. Don't worry about the weight or size of the bunches—the key is to make sure to buy herbs that are very fresh, then to clean them well and fully dry them. Then remove all the parts you don't want to eat raw, like tough stems or wilted leaves.

Sabszi khordan is an essential part of many Persian meals. The fresh kick of the herbs and scallions is like a palate cleanser between bites. Fresh herbs are also considered good for digestion. Many people are used to using fresh herbs in small amounts as a flavoring, but in Persian cuisine, they're considered more like a vegetable or green that you eat in large quantities.

If you add the feta and walnuts and eat it with bread, sabzi khordan can be a small meal or snack on its own, or even an appetizer at a party or picnic. And while the lavash is more traditionally Persian, Mab also likes to serve this with mini pitas.

Serve this with: any of Mab's dishes, including the green bean tahdig on page 170 and the chicken kabobs on page 29. When serving sabzi khordan as part of a larger meal, omit the walnuts, feta, olive oil, dried mint, and bread.

½ bunch fresh parsley

½ bunch fresh cilantro

½ bunch fresh mint

½ bunch fresh purple or green basil

½ bunch thin scallions or chives

1 small bunch round red radishes

¼ pound (115 g) firm feta cheese, optional

2 tablespoons extra-virgin olive oil (if using feta)

1 teaspoon dried mint (if using feta)

1 cup (3 ounces/85 g) shelled walnuts, optional

Lavash or mini pitas, if serving as a snack with feta and walnuts

1   **Prepare the vegetables:** Remove any old, thick, or damaged leaves from the ½ bunch fresh parsley, ½ bunch fresh cilantro, ½ bunch fresh mint, ½ bunch fresh purple or green basil, and ½ bunch thin scallions or chives. Make sure everything is very well washed and fully dried.

2   Pick the leaves from the cilantro, basil, mint, and parsley and discard the stems. Pile the leaves on a large serving platter. Toss the leaves gently with your hands so they're fluffy and mixed together.

If you make this using only one variety of herb, you don't need to pick the leaves—just remove any thick stems and serve the whole sprigs.

3   Use your hands to tear or break the scallions into 3-inch (7.5 cm) long pieces and place them in a pile alongside the herbs.

4   Trim the ends of the 1 small bunch round red radishes and slice them into ¼-inch (0.6 cm) rounds, then arrange them on top of the herbs. (You can also leave them whole, or even score the ends with a crosshatch design.)

5   **If you're adding the feta and walnuts:** Cut the ¼ pound (115 g) firm feta into ¾-inch (2 cm) cubes and sprinkle it over the top of the herbs and radishes, then drizzle the top of the feta with the 2 tablespoons extra-virgin olive oil and sprinkle with the 1 teaspoon dried mint, crumbling it between your fingertips. Pile the 1 cup (3 ounces/85 g) shelled walnuts on the plate.

6   **If eating with bread, prepare the bread:** Cut the lavash into quarters or the mini pita into halves. Set them out next to the salad platter in a basket or on another plate.

7   **Serve and eat the sabzi khordan:** Let each person take what they want from the platter. If you're serving it with other food, eat a bite of herbs, scallion, or radish between bites of other food. If you're serving the sabzi khordan as a light meal or snack, use your fingers to spread the cube of feta across a piece of lavash, add some of each of the other ingredients, then roll the lavash up into a cylinder. If you're serving pita, you can just tuck the ingredients into a pocket, gently crushing the feta in between the bread before you add the rest of the herbs and vegetables.

Salata Sayfieh

(LEBANESE SALAD WITH POMEGRANATE MOLASSES)

Instructor: Jeanette Chawki

"The dried thyme has such a wonderful smell as you sprinkle it over the salad, and once the vegetables marinate in the olive oil, it has such a delicious taste." —Jeanette

This is a simple salad that feels surprising thanks to several unique elements. First, the pieces are all cut a bit bigger than I would normally cut for a salad this style—the cucumbers, peppers, tomatoes, and onions are all about 1 inch (2.5 cm) square—and it makes the salad a pleasure to eat. The dried thyme is something that everyone has on their spice rack, but I would never think to put it on a salad, and it adds such a lovely flavor and aroma. And then there's the refreshing, lip-smacking dressing, with sourness from three sources—lemon juice, sumac, and pomegranate molasses. The pomegranate molasses also adds a touch of sweetness, which balances out the sour flavor. Pomegranate molasses is a thick syrup made from boiling down pomegranate juice. You can find it in any Middle Eastern grocery store, but it's not so hard to find even in regular supermarkets, and it's easily bought online. (Jeanette buys her pomegranate molasses directly from a convent in Lebanon!)

For this salad, Jeanette prefers to use mini Persian cucumbers and pale green Mediterranean sweet peppers, both of which have thinner skins than conventional supermarket varieties, but any peppers or cucumbers will work. This recipe can also easily be multiplied—Jeanette often makes a larger batch, as she loves fresh salads.

Serve: as a fresh salad with any meal.

¾ pound (340 g) cucumbers (about 4 Persian or 1 medium)

¼ pound (115 g) white onion (about ½ medium)

⅔ pound (300 g) bell pepper, any color (about 1 large)

⅔ pound (300 grams) tomatoes on the vine (about 3 medium)

1 tablespoon dried thyme

¼ teaspoon ground sumac

¼ cup (60 ml) fresh lemon juice (from 1 to 3 large lemons), or more to taste

2 teaspoons Diamond Crystal kosher salt, or more to taste

3 tablespoons extra-virgin olive oil

1 tablespoon pomegranate molasses

1   **Prepare the vegetables:** Trim and halve the ¾ pound (340 g) cucumbers (about 4 Persian or 1 medium) lengthwise, and then cut into ½-inch (1.3 cm) half-moons. (If you're using a large cucumber, you should cut it in quarters and then slice it.) You should have about 2½ cups. Put them in a large serving bowl.

2   Peel the ¼ pound (115 g) white onion (about ½ medium) and cut it into 1-inch (2.5 cm) square-ish pieces. You should have about 1 cup. Add the onion to the serving bowl.

3   Remove the seeds and ribs from the ⅔ pound (300 g) bell pepper (about 1 large), then cut it into 1-inch (2.5 cm) pieces. You should have about 2 cups. Add the bell pepper to the serving bowl.

4   Halve the ⅔ pound (300 g) tomatoes on the vine (about 3 medium) and remove the core and any white or pale green parts, then cut them into 1-inch (2.5 cm) chunks. You should have about 2 cups. Add the tomato to the serving bowl.

5   **Dress the salad:** Crush and rub the
    1 tablespoon dried thyme between your hands
    into the bowl, then add the ¼ teaspoon ground
    sumac over the top of the chopped vegetables in
    the bowl.

6   Roll the 1 to 3 lemons on the table to release their
    juices. Juice as many as you need to get ¼ cup
    (60 ml) lemon juice, then drizzle the juice over
    the top of the vegetables in the bowl. Sprinkle
    the 2 teaspoons Diamond Crystal kosher salt
    over the top of the vegetables, then drizzle on the
    3 tablespoons extra-virgin olive oil.

7   Use two spoons to mix everything together well.
    Taste the salad for salt and lemon juice and add
    more to taste. Set the salad aside until you're
    ready to serve it, ideally at least 15 minutes
    to let the flavors meld, and up to 30 minutes.
    (You don't want to let it sit for too long, as the
    vegetables will begin to wilt and release water.)

8   **Serve and eat the salad:** When you're ready
    to serve the salad, drizzle the 1 tablespoon
    pomegranate molasses across the top of the
    bowl, almost as if you were drizzling chocolate
    sauce on the top of ice cream. Do not toss it
    before you serve it—instead encourage everyone
    to take a spoonful with molasses on top.

Damira Inatullaeva

Damira is originally from Samarkand, an ancient city that lies on the Silk Road, which she refers to as "the historic crossroads of East and West." She loved growing up in such a diverse country, where she learned to cook from her mother, grandmother, mother-in-law, and friends of many backgrounds. For Damira, food, family, and culture are inseparable. She fell in love with cooking as a child on her grandmother's farm, helping to prepare meals for her large family, which included many grandchildren. Damira and her husband left Uzbekistan in 2013 to be closer to their three children who were already living in the United States, and to do something new—Damira believes it's always important to try new things and to have many life experiences. While she was still in Uzbekistan, Damira was a doctor until her country's mandatory retirement age of fifty-five. Now, she is doing what she loves most: cooking and hosting people at her dinner table. In 2018, she cooked the first ever Uzbek dinner at the James Beard House, which was also the first halal meal to be offered there. She lives with her husband in Brooklyn. She has three grown children and four grandchildren.

What makes Uzbek cuisine special? It is very delicious, and it smells very delicious. When you eat the food, you can recognize exactly all the ingredients that are inside. In our country, all people love to eat and love to cook. And if people cook something, they do it with love. In our culture it is very common that every time you cook, you share with neighbors and friends. If we have something, we call everyone.

What do you enjoy about cooking? The process of cooking is creative, and I love to create something, to do something new, to learn something. And the process of cooking gives our family strength and tradition—we cook not only to eat, but to form bonds with our family. We love the ritual of cooking together. When our children were younger and lived at home, we usually made dumplings on Sundays. We would sit around the table and fold dumplings together. It was teamwork and everybody was happy about this. So they also learned how to cook. They're very good cooks.

Do you have a cooking philosophy? I am constantly planning what to cook—every day I cook something different. It's boring to always cook and eat the same, so I always try something new. I cook with love—when I cook, I imagine how happy people will be who will eat my food. And more playfully, I am fond of numerology—every day has its own number and color, so if today's number is yellow, I like to make something yellow.

What do you think is the secret to being a good cook? I think that every person can cook. Even if you are not so good in the kitchen, it's no problem. Simply get a recipe, follow the recipe, and don't forget the most important ingredient—love. Just think about the people for whom you cook with big love and the food will be really good.

If you want to make something very simple, quick, and easy for dinner, what do you make? If I have dumplings I've made in the freezer, we just boil them and eat those. If I have no dumplings, I like to fry potatoes with onion and scramble them with eggs. I put salt, and if you want, you can add ground black pepper or ground cayenne pepper. Sometimes I'll also make a quick tomato and onion salad (page 231) on the side.

If you want to have something sweet after a meal, but you don't want to make a whole dessert, what do you have? Raisins, walnuts, and dried apricots are always on the Uzbek table. You can have them before a meal and you can have them after a meal. I also usually cook jams and jellies. We can use those like dessert after a meal. You can eat it by itself on a spoon, or you can spread it on a piece of bread or cracker and add a little bit of cheese, too.

What is your favorite food to eat that's not from Uzbekistan? I love pizza very much. I've tried pizza in different places, but I think that New York pizza is the best.

What do you like about teaching for the League of Kitchens? I love to cook, I love to socialize with people, and I love to create something. And with the League of Kitchens, I get to do all those things. I love that in my classes are people from different places and with different professions. And I love when my students cook with great interest and then at the end of the class, they enjoy the food that we cooked together. This is a really, really good part of the class, my favorite part. Also, the online classes have been a very good experience for all of us. I watch how my students who have never cooked these foods, at the end of the class, they make beautiful, beautiful sambusas or dumplings, for the very first time. This is so exciting. I love it.

What do you feel like you've learned from the other instructors and being part of this team of women from all around the world? One thing I love about being part of the League of Kitchens is that I can take the classes of the other instructors—I can try new foods and learn how to cook them. I've learned so much from the other instructors, and with great pleasure. I love all the food that our instructors cook. It's very delicious, and I think that they also put love in every part when they cook—that's why it's so good.

DAMIRA INATULLAEVA
Дамира Инатуллаева

Cachumber

(INDIAN CUCUMBER AND TOMATO SALAD)

Instructor: Yamini Joshi

"I love to make cachumber because it adds extra flavor to any meal, and people love it." —Yamini

Fresh, crunchy, tart, and spicy, cachumber is a common side for almost any Indian meal. It's best when made and served within the hour, when all the vegetables are still crisp and the lime juice is bright and fragrant. Yamini prefers to use mini Persian cucumbers if she can find them—they're closer to the long thin varieties she grew up eating. But you can really use any cucumbers, including the bigger supermarket-style varieties. Just make sure to peel those first to remove the waxy skin. When you have time, you can cut everything a little smaller and more precisely—when you're in a hurry, slightly larger pieces are fine.

Yamini really likes things spicy, and she uses 2 whole green chiles in this salad. For just a tiny amount of heat, use ¼ of a chile and remove the seeds. When she's serving children (or anyone who doesn't like chiles), she'll just leave the chiles out of the salad entirely and serve them whole on the side so that the adults who want them can eat them with the meal.

This is the recipe from Yamini's maternal side—her father's family uses chopped ginger instead of the onions, which is partly why Yamini often makes a simple fresh pickle to serve alongside the cachumber by julienning fresh ginger and fresh turmeric, then squeezing lime juice on the top and sprinkling it with salt.

Serve with: the dal on page 157 or the khichari on page 146.

¾ pound (340 g) cucumbers (3 to 4 Persian or 1 medium)

¼ pound (115 grams) red onion (about ½ medium)

¼ to 2 green bird's-eye chiles, optional

1½ teaspoons Diamond Crystal kosher salt

¼ pound (115 g) fresh cilantro (about 1 bunch)

½ pound (225 g) plum tomatoes (about 2 medium)

1 tablespoon roasted cumin powder (page 23)

½ teaspoon black pepper powder

¼ cup (60 ml) fresh lime juice (from 1 to 2 limes)

1   **Prepare the cucumber, onion, and chile:** Remove the ends from ¾ pound (340 g) cucumbers (3 to 4 Persian or 1 medium). If they have waxy skins, peel them, then roughly chop them into ¾-inch (2 cm) pieces. You should have about 1½ cups. Put them in a large serving bowl.

2   Peel the ¼ pound (115 grams) red onion (about ½ medium) and roughly chop it into ⅓-inch (1 cm) pieces. You should have about 1 cup. Add this to the bowl with the cucumbers.

3   Remove the stems from the ¼ to 2 green bird's-eye chiles, if using. Cut the chiles in half lengthwise, then roughly chop them into ⅛-inch (0.3 cm) pieces. Add them to the bowl with the cucumbers, then add the 1½ teaspoons Diamond Crystal kosher salt.

4   Use your hands or a spoon to mix the cucumbers, onions, chiles, and salt together. Set the bowl aside.

5   **Prepare the cilantro and tomatoes:** Trim the ends of the ¼ pound (115 g) fresh cilantro (about 1 bunch) up to where the leaves begin, then thinly slice the leaves and tender stems. You should have about 1 packed cup chopped cilantro.

6   Before you add the cilantro to the bowl with the cucumber and onion, check to see how much

cucumber liquid has pooled at the bottom of the bowl. A few tablespoons at the bottom of the bowl is fine, but you don't want the salad to be soaking in water. If there's a lot, you can drain it off and discard it (or drink it—it's delicious). Then mix in the cilantro.

7   Slice the ½ pound (225 g) plum tomatoes (about 2 medium) in half lengthwise, remove the stem end, and use your fingers to remove and discard as much of the pulp and seeds as you can. Roughly chop the tomatoes into the same size pieces as the cucumber, about ¾-inch (2 cm) dice. You should have about 1 cup. Add them to the bowl with the rest of the vegetables. (You don't need to mix them in yet.)

8   **Finish the cachumber:** Add the 1 tablespoon roasted cumin powder and ½ teaspoon black pepper powder to the bowl.

9   Juice 1 to 2 limes to get ¼ cup (60 ml) lime juice, then add the juice to the bowl. Toss everything together gently until the salad is very well mixed.

10 **Serve and eat the cachumber:** Serve the cachumber within an hour of making it at room temperature. It's best served to each person in their own small bowl, to catch the juices, but you can also put it out on the table to serve as a family-style side with other dishes.

Yamitsuki

(JAPANESE "ADDICTIVE" CABBAGE)

Instructor: Aiko Cascio

"My grandson loves this. He can't stop eating it!" —Aiko

"Addictive" cabbage is the best-known name for this dish in Japan, where it's a very popular restaurant dish. (You'll see it in the States, too, on the menu at most Japanese yakiniku spots, which specialize in grilled meats.) It's amazing how so few ingredients make such a delicious and flavorful salad.

This is traditionally made with Taiwanese or flathead cabbage, which has looser, softer leaves than the varieties more commonly sold at most supermarkets. It softens quickly with help from salt and a little marination—it's a lot like the Korean vegetable salads called namul that I grew up eating. You can also use any other kind of cabbage to make this dish—Napa works well, as it's fairly soft. If you do end up using a green cabbage, you'll likely have to keep it salted for just a little longer to soften it.

It's tempting to make a double batch since this is so good, but don't do it—the raw garlic that gives this salad its flavor becomes just a little too strong once it sits overnight. This is best eaten right away, and you don't really want leftovers.

The restaurant version of this dish often includes a pinch of powdered kelp, MSG, or kombu in the dressing for even more savoriness, and Aiko does, too, if she has any on hand. But it really doesn't need it.

Serve with: anything grilled or barbecued. This is also one of many sides Aiko likes to serve as part of a traditional Japanese meal, where you have three or four different dishes in small bowls with your own larger bowl of rice. You could pair this with the miso soup on page 194.

1 pound (450 g) flathead or Taiwanese cabbage (about ½ cabbage)

3 tablespoons plus ⅛ teaspoon Diamond Crystal kosher salt, divided

¼ ounce (7 g) garlic (about 2 medium cloves)

2 tablespoons toasted sesame oil

¼ teaspoon ground black pepper

1 tablespoon untoasted sesame seeds

1 **Prepare the cabbage:** Peel away any damaged outer leaves from the 1 pound (450 gram) flathead or Taiwanese cabbage (about ½ cabbage). Trim any brown or oxidized bits, then remove the solid white heart of the cabbage core—you can usually do this just by cutting out a little triangle with the tip of a large knife.

2 Cut the leaves of the cabbage into rough 1¼- by 1¼-inch (3 cm by 3 cm) square pieces. If you spot any very thick pieces, like the parts of the leaves that were closer to the core, cut them not into squares but into thin slices about ¼ inch (0.6 cm) wide.

3 Wash and drain the cut pieces of the cabbage in a colander in the sink—they do not need to be totally dry. Put the cabbage pieces in a very large mixing bowl and sprinkle them with 3 tablespoons of the Diamond Crystal kosher salt, then use your hands to mix it in. Crunch and scrunch the leaves with your hands, making sure they're all separated, well mixed in with the salt, and beginning to soften. Let the salted cabbage sit for 10 minutes.

4   **Make the dressing:** While the cabbage sits, peel the ¼ ounce (7 g) garlic (about 2 medium cloves), then use a Microplane or the star holes of a box grater to shred it into a smooth paste into a small mixing bowl. You should have about ½ tablespoon. (Discard the tough end.) Whisk the 2 tablespoons toasted sesame oil, remaining ⅛ teaspoon Diamond Crystal kosher salt, and ¼ teaspoon ground black pepper into the bowl with the garlic.

5   **Check the cabbage:** After 10 minutes, the cabbage should be slightly wilted and taste slightly salty. Test a leaf by rinsing it under running water and tasting it—it should taste like the leaf absorbed some salt. (If not, let it sit for 10 more minutes and then taste again.) Put the cabbage pieces in a colander or salad spinner and wash off all of the salt under running water, then drain the cabbage as well as you can—it won't be bone dry, but it shouldn't be sopping wet. Let it sit until you are ready to dress the salad.

6   **Dress the salad:** When you're ready to serve the dish, transfer the cabbage to a serving bowl and add the dressing. Use two large spoons (or chopsticks) to make sure it's fully mixed into the cabbage. Sprinkle the salad with the 1 tablespoon untoasted sesame seeds, again making sure everything is mixed together.

7   **Serve the addictive cabbage:** You can either serve this family style in a large bowl on a table or you can give each diner a small bowl as part of a larger meal with rice. This is best eaten the day it's made, as the garlic intensifies in the dressing over time.

Achik Chuchuk

(UZBEK SPICY TOMATO AND ONION SALAD)

Instructor: Damira Inatullaeva

"'Achik' means spicy and 'chuchuk' means tender, pleasant, sweet. This salad is fresh and delicious." —Damira

For such a simple and easy salad, this is just so satisfying. Cutting the vegetables into quarters before you slice them is key to the composition of this dish—the quarter-slices of onion and tomato give the salad the ideal proportions of both in each bite and make it extra delicious. This has neither vinegar nor oil—it's really just about the acidity of the tomato and the pungency of the onion. And because you salt the onions and massage them before adding the tomatoes, they soften and release their juices, which become a kind of marinade. I also love how the onions are just a little saltier than the tomatoes—almost like they're quick pickled—and how the salad has a modest but surprising kick from the cayenne. You can use a little less if you're worried about too much heat, then add more to taste at the table.

This salad is best when made just before it's served, and when the tomatoes are very ripe and in season. It will still taste good after one day in the refrigerator, but as it sits, the tomatoes and onions will begin to get mushy and watery.

Serve with: any meal as a salad or vegetable side. This is often served as part of a spread of small plates and dishes. It's great with the meatballs on page 75 and also goes especially well with any kind of roasted or grilled meat.

¼ pound (115 g) red onion (about ½ medium)

½ teaspoon Diamond Crystal kosher salt

¾ pound (340 g) slicing tomato (about 1 large)

Scant ⅛ teaspoon ground cayenne pepper

½ tablespoon finely chopped fresh dill (leaves only)

½ tablespoon finely chopped fresh cilantro (leaves only)

1. **Make the salad:** Peel the ¼ pound (115 g) red onion (about ½ medium). Cut the onion into quarters, then slice into quarter-rings about ⅛ inch (0.3 cm) thick. You should have about 1 cup. Put the slices in a small mixing bowl.

2. Add the ½ teaspoon Diamond Crystal kosher salt to the bowl with the onions and use your hands to massage the salt into the onions until they've wilted a bit.

3. Remove the stem end from the ¾ pound (340 g) slicing tomato (about 1 large). Cut it into quarters, then cut each quarter into slices about ¼ inch (0.6 cm) thick. Put the tomatoes in a medium mixing bowl and then add the onions and the scant ⅛ teaspoon ground cayenne pepper and gently mix everything together.

4. Prepare the ½ tablespoon finely chopped fresh dill (leaves only) and ½ tablespoon finely chopped fresh cilantro (leaves only), if you haven't already. Set them aside.

5. **Serve the salad:** Put the tomatoes and onions in a serving bowl or on a plate and garnish the top with the chopped dill and cilantro. This salad should be served within an hour or so of being made.

Soba Salad

(JAPANESE NOODLE SALAD)

Instructor: Aiko Cascio

"This looks good, tastes good, and is perfect for a hot day." —Aiko

Aiko didn't grow up eating this version of cold soba noodles in Japan, but instead tasted it at a Japanese restaurant in Manhattan, then asked a friend to help her make it at home. Above all, this is a delicious and flexible recipe, and so perfect for a summer meal. The medium-cooked "jammy" eggs help make the salad more substantial. You can add more or less of each vegetable to your taste, or omit any vegetables you don't like. I love the mung bean sprouts, daikon sprouts, and shiso leaves in this, but it's still really good with just cucumbers, carrots, tomatoes, and baby salad greens—ingredients you can get anywhere. Just try to find a salad green mix that does not include baby spinach—it's a little too tough. You really want very feathery and light baby greens.

The dressing is sweet and spicy and yummy, and uses a small amount of gochujang, a Korean red chile paste that is increasingly easy to find in supermarkets. It adds a very mild and lovely touch of heat, but it also works as a thickener. You can also use Aiko's fabulous sesame dressing (on page 256) with this salad, which is a little more kid-friendly.

It's best to prepare the soba right before you begin the dressing and prepare the vegetables for the salad, as you'll need to use most of your sink to cool and wash the noodles. That also gives the soba time to fully drain.

For the salad

4 servings cooked, washed, and drained soba (see page 235)

1 tablespoon rice vinegar

⅛ teaspoon Diamond Crystal kosher salt

4 large eggs

1 medium carrot

4 mini Persian cucumbers (or 1 medium)

12 grape tomatoes

½ cup (1½ ounces/40 g) daikon radish sprouts, or any kind of microgreens

¼ pound (115 g) mixed baby salad greens (preferably without spinach)

¼ pound (115 g) mung bean sprouts

6 shiso leaves, optional

Pinch of Diamond Crystal kosher salt, optional

For the dressing

6 tablespoons rice vinegar

3 tablespoons white sugar

3 tablespoons toasted sesame oil

3 tablespoons soy sauce

3 tablespoons gochujang (Korean red chile paste)

2 tablespoons mirin

1   **Prepare the noodles:** Follow the instructions for Perfect Soba Noodles on page 235 to cook, wash, and drain 4 servings, then set them aside to cool.

2   **Prepare the eggs:** Put 5 cups (1.2 L) cold tap water in a large saucepan and stir in the 1 tablespoon rice vinegar and ⅛ teaspoon salt. Bring the seasoned water to a boil over high heat, then lower the heat to medium or medium-high so that the water stays at a low but sustained boil. Use a slotted spoon to gently but quickly lower all 4 large eggs into the water. Cook for 7 minutes. While the eggs are cooking,

Continued

prepare a bowl of ice water. When the eggs are done, transfer them to the ice water. Use the back of a spoon to crack the shells around the eggs and let them sit in the ice water for another 3 minutes. Peel them under cold running water and set them aside.

3   **Make the dressing:** In a small mixing bowl, whisk together the 6 tablespoons rice vinegar, 3 tablespoons white sugar, 3 tablespoons toasted sesame oil, 3 tablespoons soy sauce, 3 tablespoons gochujang (Korean red chile paste), and 2 tablespoons mirin. Set the dressing aside while you prepare the vegetables.

4   **Prepare the vegetables:** Peel the 1 medium carrot and trim the top and bottom ends, then cut it into long, thin strips about ⅛ inch (0.3 cm) wide and ⅛ inch (0.3 cm) thick. The easiest way to do this is to cut the carrot lengthwise into ⅛-inch (0.3 cm) slices—so the slices look like wide ribbons or mini lasagna noodles—then cut those slices into ⅛-inch (0.3 cm) strips. (You can also use a mandoline, or even one fitted with the julienne blade; wear a protective glove if you do this.)

5   Cut the 4 Persian cucumbers (or 1 medium) into long strips just a little thicker than the carrots, about ¼ inch (0.6 cm) wide.

6   Trim any especially tough or unattractive stem ends from the 12 grape tomatoes, then cut them in half.

7   If your ½ cup (1½ ounces/40 g) daikon radish sprouts (or any kind of microgreens) are still on their fiber base, cut them off at the base with a pair of scissors. (You can leave any you don't think you will use on the base—they will stay fresher longer.)

8   Make sure the ¼ pound (115 g) mixed baby salad greens are washed and dry, then pick out any wilted or browned pieces. Do the same with the ¼ pound (115 g) mung bean sprouts.

9   Gently wash only the front of the 6 shiso leaves, if you're using them—the back has the majority of the aromatic oils that enhance the herb's flavor—then slice them into ⅛-inch (0.3 cm) thick ribbons. Set all the vegetables aside while you finish the salad.

10 **Finish the salad:** Use clean kitchen scissors to cut the soba in half or thirds: Do this by picking up a few strands with your hands in the colander and cutting them with the scissors—they don't have to be perfectly even. The main goal is to cut them down a bit to make the salad easier to eat. Transfer the cut soba to a large serving bowl.

11 Give the dressing a quick stir to make sure it's blended, then add half of it and the prepared vegetables to the soba. Toss everything together using tongs, chopsticks, or two forks, then add more dressing as desired. Toss it again, then add a pinch of Diamond Crystal kosher salt to taste, if desired.

12 Slice the eggs in half lengthwise.

13 **To serve and eat the soba salad:** Serve the tossed salad in individual deep soup bowls, garnished with a hard-boiled egg. This is easiest to eat with chopsticks.

Perfect Soba Noodles

MAKES 4 PORTIONS

The main thing to remember about soba noodles is that you need to wash and swirl the noodles in cold water after they're cooked, "like laundry," says Aiko. This stops the cooking process and also removes any extra starch. It may seem like a lot of work, but the result is perfectly cooked soba. Cooked noodles can sit uncovered for an hour or two—they won't get sticky because you will have washed off all the starch.

One tricky thing about soba noodles, which are made of buckwheat flour, is that the amount of noodles per package isn't consistent across brands. The total weight of the package varies, the weight of the individual serving bundles inside the packages varies, and the width and length of the noodles can vary, too. For four servings, you can just use 4 bundles, if your soba comes pre-bundled. If not, for four people you want about ³/₄ pound (360 g) of dry, uncooked soba. If you find an 8-ounce package or have a scale, that's easy to determine. But if you don't, just guesstimate—a little more or a little less will be fine.

Here's how to prepare soba to make the soba salad on page 232:

1   Fill a large stockpot with at least 4 quarts (16 cups/3.8 L) of water and bring it to a boil over high heat. While the water heats, make sure your kitchen sink is empty and that you have a colander and another large pot (or a large mixing bowl) at the ready in or by the sink.

2   When the water is at a rolling boil, add the soba noodles, separating them as they soften in the water with a fork or chopsticks. Adjust the heat so the pot cooks at a gentle boil and doesn't boil over. Cook the noodles according to the package directions—this is usually 4 to 5 minutes, and the noodles should be al dente.

If the instructions aren't on the label, just watch the noodles and check them frequently for doneness after 4 minutes. (If you really don't like al dente noodles, that's okay—just cook them a minute or two longer, to your liking. Just be careful not to let them get too soft, as they will continue to cook as you drain them, and buckwheat noodles can get mushy when overcooked.)

3   When the noodles are done, immediately drain them in the colander in the sink. Working quickly, transfer the noodles to the clean pot (or mixing bowl) under the tap and turn on the cold water. Stir the noodles with tongs or chopsticks in the running water until they're cool—use your hands to make sure all the noodles have cooled completely.

4   Once the noodles are cool, use your hands to transfer them from the water back to the colander. Empty the starchy water from the pot, then fill it back up with cold tap water. Put the soba into the water and use your hands to swirl the noodles in the cold water back and forth for 10 to 15 seconds, the same way you might rinse rice, and then rub the noodles very gently between your hands for a second or two (the key word here is gently). Use your hands to remove the soba to the colander and repeat the process one or two more times—swirling the noodles in fresh water—until the water is fairly clear. Transfer the noodles back to the colander to drain until you're ready to use them.

Horiatiki Salata

(GREEK CUCUMBER, TOMATO, ONION, OLIVE, AND FETA SALAD)

Instructor: Despina Economou

"Food is a huge part of the Greek culture, and it has less to do with flavors and more to do with ingredients—we take them extremely seriously, and we're not prepared to use any substitutes." —Despina

"Greek salad" is ubiquitous and not just in Greece, and mediocre versions abound. But Despina's version is a different experience altogether. In fact, I didn't particularly like Greek salad until I tried Despina's. In her version, it's all about the different sizes and shapes of the vegetables—the large tomato wedges, the smaller half-moons of cucumber, the thinly shaved red onion—and the proportions of the various ingredients with just the right balance of vegetables to feta to olives. Despina likes to buy a variety of feta called Arahova—it's a Greek feta made from a mix of sheep's and goat's milk, and it's both creamy and tangy. She crumbles her feta by hand, which allows it to blend into the dressing, and the seasoning quantities of olive oil, red wine vinegar, wild Greek oregano, and salt are just perfect. Of course, this is a salad that truly shines in the summer when you can get really good tomatoes.

Serve with: the chicken and potatoes on page 48 or the whole fish on page 94.

1 pound (450 g) tomatoes on the vine
   (about 4 medium)

½ pound (225 g) cucumber, preferably English
   (about ½ large)

⅛ pound (60 g) red onion (about ¼ medium)

¼ pound (115 g) feta cheese, preferably Greek

8 Kalamata olives

¾ teaspoon dried oregano, preferably Greek
   wild oregano

1 teaspoon Diamond Crystal kosher salt

¼ cup (60 ml) extra-virgin olive oil

1 teaspoon red wine vinegar

1   **Prepare the salad:** Cut the 1 pound (450 g) tomatoes on the vine (about 4 medium) in half and then cut each half into wedges about 1 inch (2.5 cm) thick. You'll get about 3 cups of tomatoes. Put the tomato wedges in a large serving bowl.

2   Peel the ½ pound (225 g) cucumber, preferably English (about ½ large). Cut it in half lengthwise, then into ¼-inch (0.6 cm) half-moons. You should have about 1½ cups cucumbers. Add them to the bowl with the tomatoes.

3   Peel the ⅛ pound (60 g) red onion (about ¼ medium), slice it in half from root to stem, trimming the ends, and then, parallel to the equator, slice it as thinly as you can. You'll get about ½ cup onion. Add it to the bowl with the tomatoes.

4   Add the ¼ pound (115 g) feta cheese to the bowl, using your fingers to break it into bite-sized pieces as you do.

5   Add the 8 Kalamata olives, then sprinkle on the ¾ teaspoon dried oregano and 1 teaspoon Diamond Crystal kosher salt. Drizzle the ¼ cup (60 ml) extra-virgin olive oil over the top, then drizzle with the 1 teaspoon red wine vinegar.

6   Use two spoons to toss the salad together until everything is coated with the oil and vinegar.

7   **Serve and eat the salad:** Serve and eat the salad within an hour of preparing it.

Afsari Jahan

Afsari was born in the Bangladeshi city of Rajshahi, known historically for its production of silk. She spent decades working in the garment industry, first as a merchandiser in Dhaka and later in Manhattan's famous garment district. It's fitting that Afsari approaches cooking like an art form—she believes the way food looks is as important as it tastes, which becomes apparent in the careful way she plates each and every dish. Afsari grew up watching her mother cook, but she herself didn't learn to cook until she and her husband and young son moved to Singapore and she had to cook everything herself. She then taught herself how to cook through trial and error and many phone calls to her mother in Bangladesh. In 2000, she and her family moved again, this time to New York City, where she now regularly caters parties and large events. Afsari lives in Brooklyn. She has one grown son and two grandchildren.

What do you love about cooking? Making my food look beautiful is my passion. If food doesn't look good on the plate, I don't want to eat it! Making something look beautiful adds to the experience of eating and makes it a celebration.

What do you think is the secret to becoming a good cook? First thing, you have to love to cook. When you love to do anything, you're always eager to learn and improve. So, this is the secret to being a good cook. And you have to know your ingredients. Like the onion in Bangladesh is in the shallot family—it has less water and more flavor. Most of the onions here are sweeter and more watery. So, knowing that, you have to cook with them differently. And if you use frozen meat or fresh meat, frozen meat has more water, so you have to consider that. Another factor is the kinds of pots and pans you're using and the kind of stove. Those are things you have to learn to manage.

Do you have any self-care tips from the kitchen? One of my sisters never uses any soap or cleanser in the shower. She always uses only besan, or chickpea flour. For the hair, we use eggs. Just crack one egg and beat it lightly. Put it onto your hair, and after fifteen or twenty minutes you wash it. And if people have a problem with hair falling out, they make a fresh onion paste and rub it on their scalp and wait until it's dry before washing it out.

If you want something sweet and you don't want to prepare a whole dessert, what will you make?
I take plain yogurt and add fresh fruit, like mango or melon or lychee. And sometimes I add fresh shredded coconut with a little bit of molasses or jaggery (page 22) or honey.

What do you like about teaching for the League of Kitchens? I love to teach for the League of Kitchens because I love people. And the League of Kitchens gives me the opportunity to meet different groups of people from different parts of the world and different cultures. I also love learning from my students.

Afsari Jahan

আফসারী জাহান

野菜

Vegetales

सब्जियाँ

خضروات

lazavika

овощи

سبزيجات

VEGETABLES

سبزیجات

तरकारी

Vegetales

sayuran

राजियाँ

Légumes

Shakkariya ni Sukhi Bhaji

(INDIAN SPICED SWEET POTATOES)

Instructor: Yamini Joshi

"This is my all-time favorite. The taste is so good." —Yamini

This recipe is so easy, but flavorful, thanks to the curry leaves and whole cumin seeds, which are both so fragrant when you add them to the hot ghee. You can use any kind of sweet potato, or even a mix, but Yamini especially likes to use either white Asian-style sweet potatoes or purple sweet potatoes because they're a little more firm and subtly sweet. It's a good idea to use a nonstick skillet if you have one—the sugars in the sweet potatoes caramelize and they can easily stick to the pan. Another trick to keep them from sticking is to make sure the ghee and pan are both very hot before you add the potatoes.

Curry leaves are like a cross between a vegetable and an herb, because you use so many of them. You can often find fresh ones at South Asian supermarkets, or frozen or dried varieties online. Yamini uses at least three green chiles cut into large pieces, which exposes the seeds and makes this dish quite spicy. If you want some of the flavor of the chiles but only a hint of heat, you can just make a slit at the top of one chile. For more heat, chop just one or even a half of a chile, as you like. But note that even one chile chopped will still be fairly spicy.

Serve with: basmati rice and the dal on page 157.

1 pound (450 g) white, purple, or orange sweet potatoes (about 2 medium)

1 teaspoon Diamond Crystal kosher salt

1 to 3 green bird's-eye chiles

1 tablespoon ghee

1 teaspoon whole cumin seeds

10 fresh, dried, or frozen curry leaves

¼ teaspoon black pepper powder

1 **Steam the sweet potatoes:** Trim the ends from the 1 pound (450 g) white, purple, or orange sweet potatoes (about 2 medium) and cut them each into 3 or 4 chunks.

2 Put a steamer basket or a colander into a saucepan filled with a few inches of water and bring the water to a boil. Add the sweet potato pieces to the basket or colander, cover the pot, and steam them until you can easily pierce the cubes with a knife, about 15 minutes.

3 Remove the sweet potatoes from the pot and let them sit until they're cool enough to handle. Use your hands to remove the skin, then cut the chunks in half so that you end up with pieces that are about 1 inch (2.5 cm) square (they don't have to be perfectly uniform). You should have about 2½ cups. Sprinkle the sweet potato pieces with the 1 teaspoon Diamond Crystal kosher salt and set them aside.

4 **Saute the sweet potatoes:** Trim the tips of the stems of the 1 to 3 green bird's-eye chiles. Use the tip of a knife to make a small slit at the top of each chile. For more heat, cut 1 to 3 of the chiles into large pieces about 1 inch (2.5 cm) wide.

5 Heat the 1 tablespoon ghee in a 12-inch (30 cm) nonstick skillet over medium heat until 1 cumin seed sizzles immediately when you drop it in. Add 1 teaspoon whole cumin seeds on top of the pooled ghee and cook just until it begins to foam (this happens quickly), then stir in the 10 fresh, dried, or frozen curry leaves, the

green chiles, the salted sweet potatoes, and ¼ teaspoon black pepper powder.

6 Saute everything over medium heat, stirring with a wooden spoon or spatula, for 1 minute, then sprinkle 1 teaspoon of tap water over the pan, cover it, and reduce the heat to medium-low. Let everything cook for 2 to 3 minutes, until the sweet potatoes get a little browned on the bottom, then turn off the heat.

7 **To serve and eat:** Serve the sukhi bhaji hot, warm, or at room temperature, typically as a side dish.

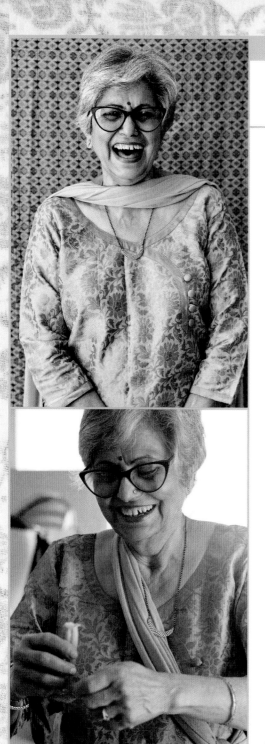

Rachana Rimal

Rachana was born in Kathmandu, the capital of Nepal, a country that shares borders and culinary traditions with China, Tibet, and India. Rachana's grandfather worked as an administrator for the king, and when Rachana was just sixteen, she married the grandson of the king's physician. (He was seventeen, and they're still married.) Throughout Rachana's years in Nepal, her father oversaw the farming of a family-owned property many miles from Kathmandu. He would send fresh food home from the farm, which her mother and sisters-in-law would cook for her, her six siblings, and thirty to forty-five members of their extended family. Rachana loved to cook even at a young age and spent many hours watching her mother in the kitchen—she especially enjoyed learning the recipes that had been passed down to her mother over many generations.

Rachana came to the US in 2006. In addition to working with the League of Kitchens, she does her own private catering. In 2018, she cooked the first-ever Nepalese dinner at the James Beard House, a huge honor for both Rachana and the League of Kitchens. She has two grown daughters, a grown son, and two grandchildren, and lives with her husband and mother-in-law in New Jersey.

What makes Nepalese cuisine special? Our food is influenced by China, Tibet, and India, so we have dumplings, biryani, pilau, and other dishes that we have taken from other cultures but make differently. We experiment with these dishes, mixing up what we like from these other cuisines, and we add our own spices to everything. The typical Nepalese meal is rice, dal, and vegetables, and we eat six or seven items at a time. For special occasions, we eat a lot of sweets and a lot of meat dishes. It is very cold in the mountainous and hilly regions of Nepal, so people always want to eat hot dishes. Our food is very healthy because we don't use much fat, and we use a lot of vegetables.

What do you love most about cooking? When people come over and they like my food, I am very happy. I love to feed people. I love to call people to come over and eat my food—that is my passion. I think food is love. When people eat my food, they feel my love. And when they love my food, I feel their love.

Do you have a cooking philosophy? Whatever I cook, it is special for me—all of my mind goes into whatever I cook, and I give it my all. Also, whatever food I cook, I try to experiment but keep the main theme intact. My inspiration is my mother. Anytime I cook, I think of her. I always remember her saying, "We are all from God, so when you feed somebody, you are engaged in a Godly act." She taught me to feel God through food.

If somebody was just learning to cook, what advice would you give them? Be patient. That is most important for the new cook. And start with very easy recipes so you are not in a panic. Also, if you want to be a good cook, you have to toast and grind your spices in your own kitchen.

If you wanted to eat something sweet after a meal, but you didn't want to make a whole dessert, what would you eat? If I have rice, I like to eat it with some cold milk and sugar. Very easy and very good—a very good dessert.

What is your favorite food that's not Nepali? Thai curry, that's my favorite. And the second is Italian: any kind of pasta.

What do you like about teaching for the League of Kitchens? The League of Kitchens has a lot of similarities with Nepali culture. I love to invite people to my home and present my food. The other thing I love about being part of the League of Kitchens is that we are like a family—we are friends and we are like sisters. We are not separate, we are not competitors or anything. Each instructor is very good at cooking their own food, so we can learn from each other.

RACHANA RIMAL

रचना रिमाल

Pou

SERVES 4 TO 6

(BURKINABÉ GREENS WITH TOMATO SAUCE)

Instructor: Yipin Benon

"I love to see the green. The tomato sauce in this dish is also so good with spaghetti or rice or fried yams." —Yipin

When I first tasted Yipin's greens, I was shocked by how soft and tender they were. She had made collards, but they almost had the texture of spinach. Then she showed me her technique—she boils the collards for about 15 minutes in water with a little baking powder mixed in. She then drains them, rinses them with cold water, and squeezes out any extra liquid with her hands. The baking powder softens the collards, but also keeps them bright green. The greens cook down a ton—so even though this recipe calls for so many pounds of greens, just know that they reduce considerably as they cook. Yipin also likes to make this with curly kale because she says it's closer to the taste of the greens she would eat in West Africa.

Yipin then mixes the cooked greens with an intensely savory sauce made from that flavor foundation of West African cooking—onions, peppers, tomatoes, and garlic, all of which are deeply caramelized at high heat. This is the vegetarian version, but sometimes she'll cook these greens with chunks of beef, lamb, or a fish like tilapia, salmon, or mackerel. (If you want to try that, you should fry the meat or fish first, and then add it and any drippings into the sauce when you add the tomato paste.) She will also put this tomato sauce (without the greens) over rice or spaghetti or use it as a dipping sauce for fried yam, sweet potatoes, or sweet plantains. Basically, you can spin this recipe in lots of directions, depending on your taste and your mood.

Serve with: white rice (either jasmine or parboiled) as a meal, or by itself as a vegetable side.

¾ ounce (20 g) garlic (about 6 medium cloves)

⅓ pound (150 g) red bell pepper (about ½ large)

⅓ pound (150 g) yellow bell pepper (about ½ large)

1 pound (450 g) red onion (about 2 medium)

1 pound (450 g) plum tomatoes (about 4 medium)

½ cup (120 ml) neutral oil

1 tablespoon Diamond Crystal kosher salt, or more to taste

½ cup (120 ml) tomato paste

1 tablespoon baking powder

3½ pounds (1.6 kg) collard greens or curly kale (3 to 4 large bunches)

1 **Prepare the ingredients for the tomato sauce:** Peel the ¾ ounce (20 g) garlic (about 6 medium cloves). Grate the ¾ ounce (20 g) garlic (about 6 medium cloves) over the fine holes of a grater into a medium bowl. You should have about 1 tablespoon.

2 Remove the membrane and seeds from the ⅓ pound (150 g) red bell pepper (about ½ large) and ⅓ pound (150 g) yellow bell pepper (about ½ large). Cut them into ⅓-inch (1 cm) dice. You should have about 2 cups. Add the bell peppers to the bowl with the garlic.

3 Peel the 1 pound (450 g) red onion (about 2 medium) and cut it into ½-inch (1.3 cm) dice. You should have about 3 cups. Add it to the bowl with the garlic and peppers.

Continued

247

VEGETABLES

4   Cut the 1 pound (450 g) plum tomatoes (about 4 medium) into ½-inch (1.3 cm) dice. You should have about 3 cups. Put them in a separate bowl.

5   **Cook the sauce:** Put the ½ cup (120 ml) neutral oil in a wide but deep pan, like a 5-quart (3.5 to 5 L) nonstick pot or saute pan. Add the onion, peppers, and garlic and stir so that they're all coated in the oil. Cover the pot, keeping the lid ajar if it doesn't have a hole for steam, and turn the heat to medium-high. Cook the vegetables for 10 minutes, stirring frequently so they don't burn on the bottom (especially if you don't have a nonstick pot).

6   Add the chopped tomatoes and 1 tablespoon Diamond Crystal kosher salt. Keep the heat on medium and cook, uncovered and stirring often so that it doesn't burn, for about 30 minutes. The mixture in the pot will reduce and turn a dark reddish brown.

7   Stir in the ½ cup (120 ml) tomato paste. Turn the heat to low and let the sauce cook, uncovered, for about 15 minutes, stirring occasionally. Keep it warm until you're ready to add it to the collard greens.

8   **Prepare the collard greens:** While the tomato sauce is simmering, fill a large soup pot with 10½ cups (2.5 L) water and add the 1 tablespoon baking powder. Bring to a boil over high heat.

9   Take the 3½ pounds (1.6 kg) collard greens (3 to 4 large bunches) and cut off the stems where they meet the bottom of the leaves and discard them. Cut the collards (leaves and tender stems) crosswise into strips about ¾-inch (2 cm) wide. Put them in a very large mixing bowl.

10   Put the bowl in the sink and wash the sliced collards under running water, lifting them up and shaking them and scrubbing them in between your hands. It's okay if they get wilty or crushed as you go. Lift the collards out into a colander or another bowl or container. Clean out any sand or grit on the bottom of the bowl, then repeat the washing process at least once more—if your collards are very sandy, you may want to do it a third or fourth time, until there is almost no sand left in the bottom of the bowl.

11   Drain the washed collards. When the water is at a boil, add them to the pot, pushing the leaves down into the boiling water with a large spoon. Once the water comes back to a boil, cook the collards for 15 minutes. The leaves will become soft and darker green. Drain the collards into a colander or bowl in the sink and rinse them under running cold tap water until the leaves are cool enough to handle. Use your hands to squeeze as much of the water as you can from the collards.

12   Return the heat under the tomato sauce to medium-low. Add the squeezed collards and stir everything together well. Taste for salt and add more if needed, then cook for about 5 minutes, stirring every once in a while. Keep warm until you're ready to serve.

13   **Serve and eat the collards:** Serve as a vegetable side with other dishes or as a main meal with rice.

Bamia

(AFGHAN OKRA WITH TOMATO SAUCE)

Instructor: Nawida Saidhosin

"We have this always—usually as a side dish for a family meal. But some people like it in bread like a sandwich. When you use very fresh okra, it's extra delicious." —Nawida

Nawida has a wonderful technique for cooking okra—she trims away just the tip of the stem and the tip of the tail, without cutting into the interior, and she keeps the pods otherwise whole. All of the sticky gel that so many people dislike stays inside as the okra is pan-fried and then simmered in tomatoes, garlic, and onions with coriander powder and turmeric.

Nawida is fastidious about picking out perfect, fresh pods—she prefers them to be between 2½ and 4 inches (6.4 cm and 10 cm) in length with absolutely no brown spots. But sometimes it's hard for me to find okra that fits those standards—I have actually used quite large okra with some brown spots, and even cut the really large ones in half because I don't mind the gel, and this dish is still great! She also looks for very good quality tomatoes—in a grocery store, those are usually the ones sold as "on the vine."

Serve with: the rice with garlic and cloves on page 179 or plain basmati rice, and the korma murg on page 39, or reheated for lunch folded into bread, ideally lavash or pita.

1½ pounds (680 g) okra

1 pound (450 g) yellow onions (about 2 medium)

¾ pound (340 g) tomatoes on the vine (about 3 medium)

¾ ounce (20 g) garlic (about 6 medium cloves)

2½ teaspoons Diamond Crystal kosher salt

1½ tablespoons roasted coriander powder (page 24)

¼ to 1 teaspoon crushed red pepper flakes

1 teaspoon ground turmeric

½ teaspoon black pepper powder

¾ cup (180 ml) neutral oil

1. **Prepare the ingredients:** Use a sharp knife to trim both ends of each pod of the 1½ pounds (680 g) okra. For the stem end, shave off just the "hat" at the very end of the pod. (The goal is to remove the stem, but not cut open the pod to expose the seeds.) For the tip end, trim off just the very tough end of the point, about 1/16 inch (0.2 cm).

2. Cut the 1 pound (450 g) yellow onions (about 2 medium) into ½-inch (1.3 cm) dice. You should end up with about 3 cups. Set them aside.

3. Cut the ¾ pound (340 g) tomatoes on the vine (about 3 medium) in half lengthwise, then trim out the small white triangle of membrane at one end. (It won't ever cook down in the sauce.) Cut the tomato into the same size pieces as the onion. You should end up with about 1½ cups. Set aside.

4. Peel the ¾ ounce (20 g) garlic (about 6 medium cloves) and finely mince it; you should have about 1 tablespoon. Set aside.

5. Put the 2½ teaspoons Diamond Crystal kosher salt, 1½ tablespoons roasted coriander powder, ¼ to 1 teaspoon crushed red pepper flakes, 1 teaspoon ground turmeric, and ½ teaspoon black pepper powder in a small bowl and set it aside.

Continued

6   **Cook the okra:** Heat the ¾ cup (180 ml) neutral oil in a 12-inch (30 cm) saute or frying pan with deep sides (2 to 3 inches/5 to 7.3 cm) over medium-high heat. When the oil begins to shimmer, add the okra. Try to lay it in the pan in just one layer, with just a little bit of overlap if necessary. Let it fry for about 45 seconds, then use a spatula to mix and toss the okra in the hot oil a few times, making sure every piece is coated, and then spread it back into one layer.

7   Again let the okra fry for about 45 seconds, then use the spatula to move the okra around in the pan a few times, to make sure it's cooking on all sides and that it doesn't brown or burn. (The pods will also begin to shrink slightly and fit more easily in the pan.) Cook, stirring very frequently, until all the okra is beginning to soften and turn brighter green—it won't yet be fully cooked through—usually another 2 to 3 minutes.

8   Turn off the heat under the pan and use a slotted spoon to remove the okra to a mixing bowl and set it aside. Drain the oil from the pan to a heatproof measuring cup. Add back ¼ cup (60 ml) of the oil to the pan.

9   **Prepare the tomato sauce:** Heat the oil over medium-high heat until it shimmers, then add the diced onions. Cook the onions, stirring frequently, until they get very browned, about 10 to 12 minutes.

10 Once the onions have browned, stir in the tomatoes until they're fully mixed together with the onions. Let them cook for about 30 seconds, then cover the pan. You might need to lower the heat slightly once the lid is on, so the onions and tomato cook at a simmer but don't burn. Cook for about 5 minutes, stirring every once in a while, until they're both very soft.

11 **Finish the dish:** Once the onion and tomatoes are soft, stir in the minced garlic and the combined spices. Then stir in the okra and any liquid that's collected in the bottom of the bowl.

12 Add 2 tablespoons of water, then mix everything so that all the okra is covered with the sauce. Cover the pan again and adjust the heat so that it cooks at a simmer for 2 minutes.

13 Check the doneness of the okra with a knife: If it's soft and easy to pierce all the way through, turn off the heat and let it sit until you're ready to serve it. If not, cook for 1 to 2 more minutes and check it again. Turn off the heat and let the okra rest until you're ready to serve it.

14 **Serve and eat the okra:** Bamia can be served hot, warm, or at room temperature, either on individual plates or in a serving bowl on the table.

Yasai no Temaki Zushi

MAKES 12 TO 16 HAND ROLLS

(JAPANESE VEGETABLE HAND ROLLS WITH SESAME DIPPING SAUCE)
Instructor: Aiko Cascio

"This is an easy and fun way to make sushi at home. My mom taught me the dipping sauce for this recipe, and my grandson loves it. Now he puts it on all his vegetables." —Aiko

These hand rolls are so festive, fresh, and satisfying, and much less frustrating than trying to make sushi rolls at home. Plus, assembling and eating them is a fun, interactive meal, kind of like a taco bar, where everyone can assemble their own hand rolls to their liking. You can also make a platter of hand rolls in advance, but try to serve them immediately, or the seaweed will get soggy. Aiko serves a sweet sesame sauce with these rolls, in addition to the more traditional soy sauce. Making it is technically optional—Aiko says you can really use any vinaigrette or dressing you have on hand—but I urge you to try it, as it makes these rolls extra-appetizing and delicious. It doesn't take long, and you can even make it ahead. She likes to put the sauce in a small squeeze bottle so that people can squirt a bit into their hand rolls, rather than dipping the whole thing and getting it soggy. If you don't have one, she recommends using a small spoon to dribble it on.

Aiko takes so much care with technique at every step, and that's another reason these are exceptional. She uses just a little less water than normal when she makes the rice, so it'll perfectly absorb the vinegar and mirin seasoning mix. (She uses a Zojirushi rice cooker, but the recipe below includes directions for either a rice cooker or the stovetop.) She makes sure the vegetables are cut to the same width and length, which makes the rolls both more beautiful and easier to eat. And in my daughter Sylvie's favorite trick, the rolls are held together with just a little hidden dab of rice so they don't fall apart as you eat them. For the best results, you really want to prepare the rice right before you make the rolls, but if you need to do it a few hours in advance, season it right away once it's finished cooking, then set it aside with a damp paper towel draped across the top of the bowl to keep it from drying out.

Beyond all the classic fillings we've listed here, you can really add any kind of vegetables you like or whatever you have on hand. But I highly recommend getting some shiso leaves, enoki mushrooms, and daikon sprouts, if you can. All three add a lot of Japanese flavor to the meal. Aiko will also sometimes pick up some sushi-grade fish, like tuna or salmon, and some ikura (salmon roe) or tobiko (flying fish roe), if she's near a fish store or Japanese market, to add to the rolls with a little wasabi and pickled ginger. (If she's using fish, she'll use soy sauce on the rolls instead of the sesame dressing.) Her miso soup with tofu is a perfect complement and adds some protein to the meal.

Serve with: The miso soup on page 194.

1½ cups (340 g) short-grain sushi rice

3 tablespoons rice vinegar (unseasoned)

½ teaspoon mirin

⅛ teaspoon Diamond Crystal kosher salt

1 to 2 tablespoons white sugar

At least four of the vegetables listed below:

    2 mini Persian cucumbers
    (about 5 inches/12.7 cm long), ends trimmed

    1 red, yellow, or orange bell pepper,
    cored and seeded

    2 medium carrots, peeled and ends trimmed

    1 large ripe (but still firm) avocado

    3 leaves Boston, butter, or red leaf lettuce

    3 scallions, green parts only

Continued

1 5.5-ounce (150 g) package enoki mushrooms

1 4-ounce (115 g) package sprouted daikon radish seeds, or any kind of sprouts or microgreens

6 shiso or perilla leaves

A handful of finely shredded purple cabbage

10 sheets sushi nori (roasted seaweed)

Sesame dressing (recipe follows) or vinaigrette, for drizzling

Soy sauce, for drizzling

1   **Make the rice:** Put the 1½ cups (340 g) short-grain sushi rice in a strainer over a bowl in the sink. Turn on the water and use your hand to swish the rice around in a circular motion, with the water running over it. Dump the water and repeat this process four times—the water may not be perfectly clear, but it will be close.

2   Measure 2 cups (275 ml) of water, then remove 3 tablespoons. If you're using the stovetop to make the rice, place the washed rice and the measured water in a medium saucepan with a tight-fitting lid. Bring the water just to a boil, then reduce the heat to a simmer and cook, covered, for 20 minutes. Let sit, covered, for 10 minutes more.

If you're using an Asian rice cooker, the measuring cup for rice that comes with it is actually ¾ cup, not 1 cup. So, to make the correct amount of rice for this amount of seasoning, you need to use 2 "rice cooker cups" of rice. You should then put in the amount of water for 2 cups of "sushi rice" as written on the rice cooker bowl. Use the "sushi rice" setting to cook.

3   While the rice cooks, prepare the sushi rice seasoning liquid: In a small mixing bowl, whisk together the 3 tablespoons rice vinegar, ½ teaspoon mirin, ⅛ teaspoon Diamond Crystal kosher salt, and 1 to 2 tablespoons sugar, to taste. Set this aside.

Aiko likes her sushi rice to have a pronounced sweetness, but you can use the lower amount if you're mindful about adding extra sugar.

4   As soon as the rice is done, season it: Turn the rice out into a clean, very large mixing bowl or wooden salad bowl (traditionally sushi rice is prepared in a wooden bowl so that the wood absorbs extra moisture). Pick out and remove any burnt or brown grains. Sprinkle on the seasoning liquid, using a rice paddle or a wooden spoon to break up the mound of rice and fully incorporate the seasoning as you do. Be gentle but thorough: Use the sides or edge of the paddle or spoon to mix it in fully, cutting with the side of the paddle or spoon, and then lifting and turning so that all of the grains are coated. Be sure to avoid mushing the rice too much with the back of the paddle. This will take several minutes of mixing. As you mix the rice, you can also use a piece of cardboard or a small paperback book to fan the rice, which will speed up the process of cooling it to room temperature. (It also makes the rice just a little shinier, which is desirable in well-made sushi rolls.)

5   When you're done, set the rice aside and leave it uncovered to cool to just barely warm or room temperature.

6   **Prepare the vegetables and nori while the rice cools:** The main goal is to make most of the vegetables about the same length. As you prep the ingredients for the rolls, set them out on a large platter or tray to make it easier for everyone to pick out their fillings as they make their hand rolls.

7   Cut the 2 mini Persian cucumbers (about 5 inches/13 cm long), ends trimmed, 1 red, yellow, or orange bell pepper, cored and seeded, and 2 medium carrots, peeled and trimmed, into rectangular strips about ⅛ inch (0.3 cm) wide. If

the carrots are a lot longer than the cucumbers, cut each strip into two pieces.

8   Peel the avocado and cut it lengthwise into strips about ¼ inch (0.6 cm) wide. (You can also use Angie's technique of cutting the avocado in half and using a knife to slice and lift out individual slices; see photo, page 198.) Cut the 3 lettuce leaves into pieces about 5 inches (13 cm) square. Cut the 3 scallion greens lengthwise into three pieces around 4 inches (10 cm) long. Trim the brown or root ends of the 1 5.5-ounce (150 g) package enoki mushrooms, rinsing the ends under running water if needed, and separate the mushrooms into small clumps.

9   If your 4-ounce (115 g) package of sprouted daikon radish seeds, or any kind of sprouts or microgreens, came on a fiber base, cut them off at the base with a pair of scissors. (You can leave any you don't think you'll use on the base; they'll stay fresher longer.)

10 Don't wash the 6 shiso or perilla leaves unless you really need to; it can reduce the flavor and aroma from the back of the leaf. Put them stacked on the tray. Prepare the handful of finely shredded purple cabbage, if you haven't already.

11 Use scissors to cut 10 sushi nori sheets in half lengthwise into two long rectangular pieces: You can stack the nori sheets and cut them all in one or two batches.

12 **Serve and eat the rolls:** Put a piece of nori in your clean palm with the shiny-side down. Use a paddle or wooden spoon to place a scant ¼ cup (about 4 tablespoons) rice, on a diagonal, on one side of a rectangle of nori. (Be careful not to use too much rice, or you won't have enough for your last few rolls.) The rice should not cover the whole side of the rectangle of nori, but instead make a diagonal base for the fillings. (See photo, page 257.)

13 Layer a few of the ingredients diagonally on the half of the nori right over the rice, being careful not to overload the roll—you can use any combination you like, but a good rule of thumb is to use just a small handful of fillings, total. (For example, one roll might have 1 shiso leaf pressed on top of the rice, then 4 or 5 sprouts, 6 stems of enoki mushrooms, 2 pieces of cucumber, and 1 piece of avocado, or you could use a smaller number of fillings but more of each one.) If the fillings have a defined top (such as the enoki mushrooms or shiso leaves), those should all face the same direction, and away from you, so they poke out from the top of the roll after you roll it, like a bouquet of flowers.

14 After you've added all the fillings, take the corner of nori closest to you on the side where you just put the rice and fillings, and then fold it over the fillings to make a triangle. The fillings should be sticking out quite a bit at the end facing away from you. Roll that triangle up into the rest of the sheet of nori to make a cone around the fillings. Then take about ½ teaspoon of rice and dab it onto the end corner of the piece of nori; use it to press the cone closed. Put the sesame dressing (recipe follows) or vinaigrette and the soy sauce in small serving bowls and serve them with a small spoon so each person can drizzle a little dressing onto their rolls with each bite. (Or put the sauces in small squeeze bottles.)

15 If you want to have a DIY hand roll party, just set all the vegetables, rice, sheets of nori, and dressing or soy sauce on the table and let everyone make their own, following the instructions above. If you're making a platter of hand rolls in advance, make sure to serve them as soon as possible so the nori doesn't get soggy.

Continued

Aiko's Sesame Dressing

MAKES ABOUT ¾ CUP (175 ML)

This salad dressing can easily be doubled and can also be made several days in advance. Store it in a tightly sealed jar in the refrigerator, but bring it to room temperature and give it a shake or stir before you serve it. To use it as a dipping sauce for vegetables like edamame or blanched green beans, Aiko often leaves out the dashi or water so it's a little bit thicker. You can also add a little gochujang, or Korean chile paste, if you want this to be spicy.

Be careful not to overprocess the sesame seeds—the goal is to have some texture from the seeds, setting it apart from the tahini paste.

3 tablespoons raw sesame seeds

3 tablespoons white sugar

3 tablespoons rice vinegar (unseasoned)

3 tablespoons dashi (see page 196) or water

2 tablespoons neutral oil

2 tablespoons tahini paste

1 tablespoon soy sauce

1 teaspoon toasted sesame oil

⅛ teaspoon Diamond Crystal kosher salt, or more to taste

1 **Toast the sesame seeds:** Put 3 tablespoons raw sesame seeds in a 9½-inch (24 cm) skillet over medium-high heat. Toast the sesame seeds, shaking the pan or stirring frequently, until they turn light brown. This will happen fast—usually anywhere from between 1 and 3 minutes—so watch the pan the entire time to make sure they don't burn, and remove them from the heat as soon as they turn brown. While the sesame seeds are still warm, transfer them to a coffee or spice grinder (or a smaller food processor) and give them just a few pulses, just until they're finely ground. Be careful not to overprocess them or they'll turn into a paste.

2 **Make the dressing:** Scrape the ground sesame seeds into a medium mixing bowl and add the 3 tablespoons white sugar, 3 tablespoons rice vinegar, 3 tablespoons dashi or water, 2 tablespoons neutral oil, 2 tablespoons tahini paste, 1 tablespoon soy sauce, 1 teaspoon toasted sesame oil, and ⅛ teaspoon Diamond Crystal kosher salt. Whisk everything together until both the tahini and the sugar are completely mixed in before using. Taste for salt before serving.

Yamini Joshi

Whether she's teaching you the proper way to handle spices or how to roll a perfectly circular roti, Yamini is committed to making everything from scratch using the freshest ingredients, always. She was born and raised in Mumbai, but her family was originally from Rajasthan. She grew up in a multi-family apartment building that she shared with around fifty family members. Yamini was interested in cooking from a young age and learned to cook from her mother, grandmothers, and aunts, taking on some of the family cooking responsibility at age ten.

Yamini's father was a lawyer who was friends with people from many different cultural backgrounds, and he took her to eat in their homes, introducing her to many different cuisines. Her father was also a good cook, and she would watch him cook for large community religious festivals. At home, her family cooked mostly Rajasthani food, but she had a lot of neighbors and friends who were from other regions, and she learned to cook food from all of them. After she married, she learned how to cook the cuisines of southern India, too. She soon became known as one of the best cooks in her entire extended family. Yamini moved to New York City with her husband and three daughters in 1999. After years of bringing lunch to share with her coworkers at a jewelry company in Manhattan, she started a small catering business in 2009. She now has four grandchildren and lives in Queens.

Why do you love to cook? I don't really love to eat—I love to cook. I love to feed and nourish people and that makes me happy. Cooking also brings me closer to the five elements—fire, water, air, earth, and space. All of these elements are like gods to me. Whenever one eats it also nourishes all five elements of the body.

What do you think it takes to be a great cook? It helps to think in a positive way when you are cooking, which then puts positive vibrations into your food, making it taste delicious. Also, you have to focus on where to use your spices and their measurements, to balance their taste. And if you put extra salt, for example, you may well ruin your dish. Or when you are adding turmeric, if the recipe says a quarter teaspoon or half teaspoon, and you add one teaspoon, then you also spoil the taste. It will taste bitter, and not the flavor you want.

Can you describe your cooking philosophy? I believe that when you cook you are worshipping God and making an offering with your food. When I cook, I focus on achieving the proper texture and flavor so that I can honor the gods. To me, God is living in every human being.

What are some of your favorite home remedies from the kitchen? When you feel a cold coming on, the first step is to start drinking hot water with fresh ginger juice and a little salt or honey. For a full cold remedy sometimes we add some black pepper—the spiciness cuts your cold and cough. For a sore throat, add turmeric powder to hot water and add a little honey, and we sometimes add ginger and fresh mint leaves. For the kids we take some jaggery (page 22) and ghee, add a bit of turmeric, and make a round ball, soft like candy. Or take some honey, put turmeric in that, add some ghee and fresh ginger, and tell them, "Lick it. It's so sweet." As soon as they lick the honey, they will feel better.

What are your favorite self-care tips from the kitchen? Generally, if you want nice, soft skin, try to avoid soap. Instead apply a little coconut oil on your skin, rub it a little bit, and just wash with warm water. For the face, take a little chickpea flour, add some milk or some yogurt, then make a thick paste. Apply it to your face, and just leave it for a few minutes, then wash your face. Before you wash your hair, apply yogurt to your scalp and let it sit for ten minutes. Sometimes while you're cooking and you're grating some coconut or grating some cucumber, you have leftover juice—you can drink the juice or apply the juice on your hair. And you can put cucumber peel on your skin—it will feel so refreshing. After you squeeze a lemon or lime, boil the peel with water and you can use that steam. It's good to inhale when you have a cough or cold, and it's good for your skin. And nothing gets wasted.

What foods or herbs do you grow? In my apartment I grow curry leaves, mint, and basil. I have lemongrass and a carom seed plant too.

What is your favorite food that's not Indian food? I love Mexican food. I like hot sauce, guacamole, tostadas, and beans. I also love Lebanese food—falafel, pita, hummus, and lots of tabbouleh salad.

What do you like about teaching for the League of Kitchens? The League of Kitchens has helped me to work independently and has given me so much happiness in my life. When the people come to my home, they're all strangers. But after cooking together and sitting at one table, we become like one family.

YAMINI JOSHI

यामिनी जोशी

Tourlou

SERVES 4 TO 6

(GREEK BAKED VEGETABLES)

Instructor: Despina Economou

"This is such an easy dish and a delicious thing to do with whatever vegetables you have in the refrigerator."
—Despina

What I love about this dish, which is reminiscent of a ratatouille, is that the vegetables basically slow-cook in their own juices with plenty of olive oil, so you really taste the concentrated flavor of the vegetables. Like ratatouille, tourlou is good right out of the oven or at room temperature—Despina often crumbles creamy feta on top before she serves it, especially if she's eating it as a main meal with some crusty bread.

This list of vegetables is Despina's ideal mix of ingredients for the very best flavor, but she says you can leave some out or use more of one or another or whatever else you have on hand, like okra, flat beans, or summer squash. She uses longer pale green sweet peppers because they have thinner skins, but any sweet peppers will do. Despina also grates the tomatoes on a box grater to crush the pulp and release the juices, leaving them without the skins—a trick I love that she uses in many of her dishes. This is the perfect recipe to make when you bring home too many vegetables from the farmers market or are faced with an overflowing CSA box. As you make this, you'll probably be thinking that this is way too many vegetables, but they shrink a ton as they cook down. Whatever vegetables you use, I suggest you follow Despina's recommendations for how to cut them—these sizes are perfect for this length of roasting time, and when they're all mixed together, they create a wonderfully pleasing eating experience. Make sure to use a large enough roasting pan (or two casserole dishes) so that the vegetables are basically in one layer.

When Despina was growing up in Greece, she would sometimes take this dish to the bakery to have

them roast it along with the chicken and potatoes on page 48—at that time, most Greek homes didn't have ovens. In fact, if you're not inclined to use your oven, she says you could even cook this in a wide pan on the stovetop, too, as they would sometimes do when she was a kid.

Serve with: the chicken and potatoes on page 48, or the fish on page 94.

1 pound (450 g) zucchini (2 to 3 medium)
1 pound (450 g) eggplant (about 1 medium)
¼ pound (115 g) carrot (about 1 medium)
½ pound (225 g) bell pepper, any color (about 1 medium)
½ pound (225 g) yellow onion (about 1 medium)
¾ ounce (20 g) garlic (about 6 medium cloves)
1 pound (450 g) russet potatoes (about 2 medium)
1 pound (450 g) plum tomatoes (about 4 medium)
½ cup (120 ml) extra-virgin olive oil
4 teaspoons Diamond Crystal kosher salt
¾ teaspoon freshly ground black pepper or black pepper powder
⅛ pound (60 g) fresh flat-leaf parsley (about ½ bunch)
Bread, for serving, optional
½ pound (225 g) feta cheese, optional

1   **Prepare the ingredients:** Preheat the oven to 375°F (190°C).

2   Remove the stem ends from the 1 pound (450 g) zucchini (2 to 3 medium). Cut them in half

Continued

The LEAGUE OF KITCHENS Cookbook   260

lengthwise and then into slices about ½-inch (1.3 cm) wide. You should have about 4 cups. Put them in your largest mixing bowl.

3   Cut the 1 pound (450 g) eggplant (about 1 medium) lengthwise into quarters, then into pieces about ½-inch (1.3 cm) wide. You should have about 5½ cups. Add them to the mixing bowl.

4   Peel the ¼ pound (115 g) carrot (about 1 medium). Trim the ends, cut the carrots lengthwise, then cut into half-moon slices about ¼ inch (0.6 cm) wide. You should have about ¾ cup. Add them to the mixing bowl.

5   Remove the stem from the ½ pound (225 g) bell pepper (about 1 medium). Cut it lengthwise and remove the seeds and membrane. Then cut the strips into 1-inch (2.5 cm) wide chunks. You should have about 2 cups. Add them to the mixing bowl.

6   Peel the ½ pound (225 g) yellow onion (about 1 medium). Cut it in half from root to stem, then into ¼-inch (0.6 cm) half-moons, parallel to the equator. Separate into rings. You should have about 1½ cups. Add them to the mixing bowl.

7   Peel the ¾ ounce (20 g) garlic (about 6 medium cloves), then roughly chop them. You should have about 2 tablespoons. Add them to the mixing bowl.

8   Peel the 1 pound (450 g) russet potatoes (about 2 medium). Cut out any black spots, then cut the potatoes in half lengthwise and then into ½-inch (1.3 cm) half-moons. You should have about 2½ cups. Add them to the mixing bowl.

9   Cut the 1 pound (450 g) plum tomatoes (about 4 medium) in half lengthwise. Grate them on the large holes of a box grater over the mixing bowl. (You may not be able to grate all of the skin and tough membrane—discard what you can't grate.) You should end up with about 1¼ cups.

10   Add the ½ cup (120 ml) extra-virgin olive oil, 4 teaspoons Diamond Crystal kosher salt, and ¾ teaspoon freshly ground black pepper or black pepper powder to the bowl with the vegetables and use your hands to mix everything together until well incorporated.

11   Trim the tough stems from the ⅛ pound (60 g) fresh flat-leaf parsley (about ½ bunch). Finely mince the parsley. You should have about ½ cup. Set this aside separate from the rest of the vegetables.

12   **Cook the vegetables:** Put the seasoned vegetables in a 13- by 16-inch (33 cm by 40 cm) or similar-sized roasting pan. The goal is to get them mostly in one layer—a little overlap is fine. (If they don't fit, you can put them in two smaller roasting pans or casserole dishes.) Add ⅓ cup (80 ml) water, cover the pan tightly with foil, and bake for 30 minutes.

13   Remove the foil and cook for about 30 minutes more, until the vegetables are almost soft. (If the pan is very dry at this point, sprinkle 2 to 3 tablespoons of water over the top.) Add the parsley and cook for 10 minutes more. Keep warm until you're ready to serve.

14   **Finish the dish:** Toast the bread, if using. Crumble the ½ pound (225 g) feta cheese, if using, on top of the vegetables.

15   **Serve and eat the tourlou:** Serve the tourlou with the toasted bread on the side.

Lubiyeh

(LEBANESE GREEN BEANS STEWED WITH TOMATOES AND GARLIC)

Instructor: Jeanette Chawki

"This is my favorite food. I remember when my momma would make lubiyeh, I would love to make a sandwich with onion. I would sit on the stairs with my friends in front of our house and eat it, and everyone always said, 'Oh, can you make one for us?' I always kept going up and making more sandwiches." —Jeanette

These stewed green beans are so savory and rich, with a very subtle kick from the Aleppo pepper. Even though they're vegan, they taste as if they're made with bone broth. It's extra rewarding given how simple this recipe is and how few ingredients it calls for.

The sweet red pepper paste, sold in Middle Eastern markets and labeled "tatli biber salcasi" by Turkish brands, adds a lot of umami and a deep, moderately sweet flavor. It's such a versatile ingredient to have in your fridge—in any recipe that calls for tomato paste, I'll just sneak in a little bit for some extra oomph. There's also a ton of garlic in this dish (which mellows as it cooks), which adds savoriness as well. Jeanette often buys her garlic pre-peeled for this recipe, and you could, too. When Jeanette sees Romano beans— flat green beans—at the store, she'll grab them and use them, as those are her favorite.

The key to these green beans is that you cook them until they're really soft and turn army green. If you're used to crisp-tender green beans, you just have to trust that this way of cooking green beans is going to be fabulously tasty, silky, and flavorful.

Jeanette always eats lubiyeh with pieces of a raw white onion that has been crushed, squeezed, and rinsed so that it's extra sweet and tender. The raw onion adds such an enlivening contrast to the luscious green beans. And something about the jagged flower-petal shape of the onion pieces makes them extra yum. Plus, it's very fun to smash a whole unpeeled onion with a heavy cutting board!

This is good hot or cold, but best when warm, says Jeanette. She will often serve this as a vegetarian dinner with the rice and vermicelli on page 167 so that you can spoon the green beans and sauce on top of the rice. But she also likes to make a sandwich in a rolled-up piece of lavash or thin pita with some of the raw onions. The other way she serves it is to toast a pita or piece of flatbread until it's very crispy and charred and then top it with the green beans and sauce. The sauce soaks into the center of the bread, and that part ends up soft and delicious.

Serve with: white rice or the rice and vermicelli on page 167, or as a side to any of the other Lebanese recipes in this book.

2 pounds (900 g) string beans or flat green beans

⅛ pound (60 g) garlic (about 18 medium cloves)

1¼ pounds (570 g) plum tomatoes (about 5)

1 tablespoon sweet red pepper paste (tatli biber salcasi)

1½ teaspoons tomato paste

½ teaspoon white sugar

½ to 1 teaspoon crushed Aleppo pepper flakes

½ cup (120 ml) extra-virgin olive oil

1 tablespoon Diamond Crystal kosher salt, or more to taste

1 large white or yellow onion, for serving

Thin pita, lavash, or another flatbread, for serving, optional

1 **Prepare the ingredients:** Trim the ends of the 2 pounds (900 g) string beans or flat green

Continued

beans if they're not already trimmed. Put the beans in a bowl. Use your hands to break the beans into two or three pieces. You want the pieces about 1½ inches (3.8 cm) long. You should have about 7 cups.

2 Peel the ⅛ pound (60 g) garlic (about 18 medium cloves). Trim off any rough or damaged root ends. If you have any large cloves, cut them in half lengthwise. (You want most of them to be no wider than ⅓ inch [1 cm]). You should have about a scant ½ cup.

3 Bring about 6 cups (1.5 ml) water to a boil in a medium saucepan. As soon as the water comes to a boil, carefully add the 1¼ pounds (570 g) plum tomatoes (about 5) and let them cook just until the skins begin to break, 4 to 5 minutes. Turn off the heat and drain them. As soon as the tomatoes are cool enough to handle, remove and discard as much of the skin as you can.

4 Cut the tomatoes into rough ½-inch (1.3 cm) chunks, removing any white or green parts near the stem. You should have about 3 cups. Put them in a bowl. Into a separate small bowl, measure out the 1 tablespoon sweet red pepper paste (tatli biber salcasi), 1½ teaspoons tomato paste, ½ teaspoon white sugar, ½ to 1 teaspoon crushed Aleppo pepper flakes, and ½ cup (120 ml) water. Stir everything together until the paste is dissolved into the liquid, and set it aside.

Jeanette uses a paring knife to roughly peel the tomatoes, and then squeezes out any juices left in the peels before discarding them.

5 **Cook the beans:** Heat the ½ cup (120 ml) extra-virgin olive oil in a large (12-inch/30 cm) wok or skillet with deep sides over high heat.

6 Add the garlic and fry, shaking the pot occasionally, until the cloves lightly brown, about 90 seconds. Add the green beans and stir with a wooden spoon. Turn the heat to medium-

low and stir in the 1 tablespoon Diamond Crystal kosher salt. Add 1 cup (240 ml) water and stir it in. Raise the heat to high to bring the water back to a simmer, then lower it again to medium-low. Cover and cook, stirring occasionally, just until the beans are cooked through, about 20 minutes.

7 Stir in the tomatoes and the pepper paste mixture, increase the heat to high, and cook until the liquid comes to a boil. Cover the pot, keeping the lid slightly ajar, reduce the heat to medium-low, and cook until the tomatoes are very soft, the sauce has thickened slightly, and the garlic is tender, about another 20 minutes. Taste for salt and add more if needed. Keep warm until you're ready to serve the beans.

8 **Prepare the onion and the bread:** Clear space on the counter. Put down a clean dish towel and place on top of it a whole unpeeled white or yellow onion. Smash the onion with a heavy cutting board 2 to 5 times, then peel it. It will be completely broken—that's what you want. Squeeze the whole onion over the sink between your hands to remove some of the juices. Wash the onion under cold running water, squeeze it between your hands again, then pull it apart into pieces, removing the roots and any stem, and put it on a small serving plate. (You could also slice it and wash it, if you're in a rush.)

9 If you're using pita, separate the circles so you have two thin pieces. Then bake or toast the thin pita, lavash, or another flatbread on a skillet or right over a burner, if you have a gas flame, until the flatbread is very crispy or blackened in a few spots. (If you're making sandwiches, just warm the bread, don't make it crispy.)

10 **Serve and eat the beans:** Serve the stewed green beans and raw onion as a vegetable side with rice, or with pita, lavash, or other flatbread, either open-faced or rolled into a sandwich.

Rayo Ko Saag

(NEPALI STIR-FRIED MUSTARD GREENS)

Instructor: Rachana Rimal

"Saag is anything green—this is an everyday, all-year saag—it's not very complicated, it's fast, and everybody loves it." —Rachana

Saag is served at nearly every Nepali meal in some form. This is Rachana's husband's family's version (which she finds fresher-tasting than the version she grew up with). Rachana typically uses a little less salt than you would expect, but that's because these greens are usually served with other things that are quite salty, like the cauliflower and potato dish on page 278. You can add more salt to taste, if you like.

The ideal greens for this dish are Chinese flat-leafed mustard greens, which are leafier, sweeter, and far less bitter than the curly versions you normally find at most supermarkets. You can usually find them at Asian supermarkets or occasionally farmers markets, especially in the summer, but you can also substitute any other leafy Asian green like choy sum or bok choy. Rachana also occasionally makes this with a mix of leaf spinach and watercress, which will give you the hint of bitterness typical of Asian greens that makes this so delicious. I've also made this with curly kale, and it tastes great.

You can find the ajwain seeds and mustard oil in many Asian or Indian supermarkets (or online). See page 20 for more information on mustard oil; even though it's widely and traditionally used in small amounts for cooking in other countries, in the United States it's always labeled as massage oil.

Rachana does several small, subtle things to coax a ton of flavor from just a handful of ingredients. Instead of cutting the greens, she tears them with her hands, because that gives you a better mouthfeel and flavor; for the same reason, she slices the ginger and pounds it in a mortar and pestle just until it becomes a rough

paste rather than a smooth puree. She also adds half the ginger in the beginning, with the slightly bitter and very aromatic ajwain seeds in the hot mustard oil, and half toward the end—so you get the complexity of cooked ginger and the freshness and flavor of nearly raw ginger.

Serve with: the fried cauliflower and potato on page 278, the Nepali yellow dal on page 141, and basmati rice.

1 pound (450 g) Asian leafy greens, such as Chinese flat-leaf mustard greens, choy sum, or bok choy (about 1 large bunch)

½ ounce (15 g) fresh ginger (about 1 inch/2.5 cm long)

1 dried red Indian chile (about 1½ inches/3.8 cm long)

½ teaspoon whole ajwain seeds

1 tablespoon mustard oil

½ teaspoon Diamond Crystal kosher salt

1 **Prepare the ingredients:** Make sure the 1 pound (450 g) Asian leafy greens (about 1 large bunch) are well-washed, and trim away the very end of the stems if they're especially dry or damaged. Use your hands to tear the leaves into pieces about 2 inches (5 cm) square. Break the stems into pieces about 2 inches (5 cm) long. Set the torn greens aside.

2 Peel the ½ ounce (15 g) fresh ginger (about 1 inch/2.5 cm long) with a spoon. Cut it into slices about ⅛ inch (0.3 cm) thick, then smash

them in a mortar and pestle until they're fully crushed but still have some texture and are not yet a fine paste. (If you don't have a mortar and pestle, you can grate the ginger on the small holes of a box grater.) You should have about 1 tablespoon. Set the crushed ginger aside.

3   Break the 1 dried red Indian chile (about 1½ inches/3.8 cm long) into a small bowl (or leave it whole, if you don't want this dish to be as hot) and add the ½ teaspoon whole ajwain seeds. Set this aside.

4   **Cook the greens:** Put the 1 tablespoon mustard oil in a 12-inch (30 cm) wok or skillet and turn the heat to high. When the oil is hot, add the chile (broken or whole) and ajwain seeds. Turn off the heat and add half of the ginger, stirring it so that it fries in the oil for about 30 seconds.

5   With the heat still off, add all of the greens to the pan. Put the heat on medium, then use your spatula, tongs, or two large spoons to flip and turn all of the greens in the pan so they all touch the heat and the hot oil, moving them up from the bottom to the top so everything begins to wilt. When they've all touched the hot oil, cover the pan and let the greens cook for 2 minutes.

6   Uncover the pan and use a spatula to stir the greens so that everything is well incorporated. Cook the greens, stirring occasionally, for about 3 more minutes, until the liquid evaporates. Then stir in the ½ teaspoon Diamond Crystal kosher salt.

7   Cook for 2 more minutes, then stir in the remaining half of the ginger.

8   Cook for about 2 minutes more, stirring occasionally, until the stems are slightly translucent and the leaves are very soft but the color is still bright green.

9   **Serve and eat the greens:** Serve the greens hot, warm, or at room temperature as a side with other dishes.

Burani Bonjon

SERVES 4 TO 6

(AFGHAN EGGPLANT, TOMATOES, AND CHILES WITH YOGURT SAUCE)

Instructor: Nawida Saidhosin

"It's very easy and fast to make this, and I love it. When I'm alone for lunch, I make it with just one eggplant."
—Nawida

This dish is a favorite when Nawida teaches it in her classes. It's fast and delicious, and the stacks of tomato and eggplant drizzled with garlic yogurt look impressive. Nawida usually serves this as a side, but it also makes a great vegetable main when served with a little bread, because it's so rich and satisfying and also has some protein from the yogurt. Nawida prefers Afghan bread, which is typically long and flat with a little puffiness, similar to focaccia.

You really want to make this dish with small Italian or Asian eggplants, rather than the giant varieties common in American supermarkets. Smaller eggplants have fewer seeds, so they're less bitter, and you don't need to salt them in advance. They also tend to take up a lot less oil. No matter which kind you're using, look for the smallest you can find and those whose stems are still green, rather than brown, though that's usually only possible if you're buying them at a farmers market or a store with a lot of turnover. If the stems are bright green, just remove any fuzzy leaves at the base, peel the stem, and leave it. Nawida says that's her favorite part.

Nawida usually uses five whole jalapeños when making this dish, but if you want less heat, use just two and remove the seeds and membrane.

Serve with: bread (like lavash or pita), or Nawida's chicken curry on page 39, for a bigger meal.

For the eggplant

1¾ pounds (795 g) small Asian or Italian eggplants (about 3)

1 pound (450 g) tomatoes on the vine (about 4 medium)

2 to 5 large jalapeño chiles

¾ ounce (20 g) garlic (about 6 medium cloves)

1 tablespoon roasted coriander powder (page 24)

1 teaspoon ground turmeric

2 teaspoons Diamond Crystal kosher salt

½ teaspoon black pepper powder

1½ tablespoons tomato paste

2 cups (475 ml) olive oil, neutral oil, or ghee, divided

Dried mint

Red chile powder, optional

For the yogurt sauce

½ ounce (15 g) garlic (about 4 medium cloves)

½ cup (120 ml) labne or plain whole milk Greek yogurt

½ teaspoon Diamond crystal kosher salt

1 **Prepare the vegetables:** Trim the stems from the 1¾ pounds (795 g) small Asian or Italian eggplants (about 3). (If you have fresh eggplants with green stems, peel away the fuzzy leaves at the base and leave the stems.)

2 Use a vegetable peeler to remove the skin of the eggplants and the stems (if using). Cut the eggplants in half across the equator, so you end up with two sections 2 to 3 inches (5 to 7.6 cm) in length. Then cut each section into ½-inch (1.3 cm) planks. Set these aside.

3 Remove the stems from the 1 pound (450 g) tomatoes on the vine (about 4 medium) and

Continued

cut them into ¼-inch (0.6 cm) thick slices. Set them aside. Remove the stems from the 2 to 5 large jalapeño chiles, cut them lengthwise into fourths, and set them aside. For less heat, remove the seeds and membranes.

4   **Make the tomato sauce:** Peel the ¾ ounce (20 g) garlic (about 6 medium cloves) and grate it over the small or star holes of a grater into a small bowl. You should have about 1 tablespoon. Add the 1 tablespoon roasted coriander powder, 1 teaspoon ground turmeric, 2 teaspoons Diamond Crystal kosher salt, ½ teaspoon black pepper powder, and 1½ tablespoons tomato paste. Add ½ cup (120 ml) of water to the bowl and whisk until smooth. Set this aside.

5   **Fry the eggplant:** Line a large plate or baking sheet with paper towels.

6   Heat 1 cup (240 ml) of the olive oil, neutral oil, or ghee in a 12-inch (30 cm) frying pan or skillet over medium-high to high heat. You want the oil to be very hot and shimmering but not smoking, or the eggplant will burn. Add a single layer of the eggplants, making sure they don't overlap. (You will have to fry them in batches.)

7   Fry the eggplants just until they begin to brown on the bottoms, 2 to 3 minutes. Flip them and fry on the other side just until they're beginning to brown, another minute or so. When they're brown on both sides, remove them to the paper towel–lined plate. They will not yet be cooked all the way through. Repeat until all the eggplants are cooked, adding ¼ to ½ cup (60 to 120 ml) olive oil, neutral oil, or ghee as necessary. Then set the plate with the fried eggplant aside.

8   **Make the yogurt sauce:** Peel the ½ ounce (15 g) garlic (about 4 medium cloves) and grate them over the small or star holes of a grater into a small bowl. You should have a scant tablespoon. Add ½ cup (120 ml) labne or plain whole milk

Greek yogurt, ½ teaspoon Diamond crystal kosher salt, and ½ cup (120 ml) of water and stir until smooth. Set this aside.

9   **Finish the dish:** Put 2 tablespoons of the olive oil, neutral oil, or ghee in a 5-quart (4.8 L) Dutch oven or saucepan. Do not turn on the heat yet. Add 2 tablespoons of the tomato sauce to the bottom of the pan, stirring it a little so it mixes with the oil. Layer about a third of the tomato slices over the sauce. Layer a third of the fried eggplant slices on top of the tomatoes. Then add a few slices of the jalapeño.

10 Repeat this process two more times, starting with 2 tablespoons of the sauce. Put any leftover sauce and jalapeños on top.

11 Cover the pot and cook over high heat for 5 minutes. As it cooks, give the pan a swirl every minute or so (or when you hear it sizzle on the bottom) to gently distribute the sauce and keep the vegetables from sticking. Do not stir.

12 Turn the heat to low and let the eggplant and tomatoes cook without stirring, covered, until everything is soft and cooked through and most of the sauce has thickened in the bottom of the pot, about 15 minutes. Turn off the heat but leave the pot covered on the stove to stay warm.

13 **Serve and eat the eggplant:** You can serve this family style or in individual bowls. Spread some of the yogurt sauce on the bottom of the serving plate or each bowl. Then use a wide spatula to lift the eggplants, tomato, and jalapeños and place them on top of the sauce. The goal is to keep the layers. Drizzle another two spoonfuls of yogurt sauce across the top.

14 Dust the top of the dish with a little crumbled dried mint and a pinch of red chile powder, if using. Then use a small spoon to scoop up some of the oil from the bottom of the pot and drizzle it over the top.

Horta

SERVES 4 TO 6

(GREEK BOILED GREENS WITH LEMON JUICE AND OLIVE OIL)

Instructor: Despina Economou

"This combination of greens is closest to the flavor I grew up eating in Greece." —Despina

Horta means "wild greens" or "weeds" in Greek, and it's a central dish of Greek cuisine. Despina grew up foraging wild greens from the fields near her home, and so the exact mixture of greens in the horta would vary from day to day but would often include wild dandelion, sow thistle, wild Swiss chard, and wild escarole. What stayed the same, however, was the cooking method—boiling the greens in salted water and then dressing them with lemon juice, olive oil, and salt. (Despina's family would always save the cooking water and drink it or use it to make soup, since it's full of flavor and nutrition.)

The first time I ate Despina's horta, I was really surprised—I had never tasted greens that were so good. You can use this approach with any greens, but I strongly recommend trying Despina's specific combination—curly kale, spinach, escarole, and dandelion—which she says is a close approximation of the flavor she grew up with. This combo and these ratios—a half-pound of each—give you a really nice balance of bitter and sweet flavors and a pleasing range of textures—juicy, silky, and a bit more bite.

Traditionally, horta is eaten with fish, says Despina, but she serves it with any meat or main dish, and often all by itself for a light meal with toasted bread and olives or feta cheese. If you don't want to buy and wash four bunches of greens (or can't find one of them), you can make this with any combination of them—just make sure you have about two pounds (900 g) of greens total—it will still be delicious.

Serve with: the whole roast fish on page 94 or the roasted chicken and potatoes on page 48.

2 tablespoons plus ½ teaspoon Diamond Crystal kosher salt, divided
½ pound (225 g) curly kale
½ pound (225 g) chicory or escarole
½ pound (225 g) dandelion greens
½ pound (225 g) fresh spinach, preferably not baby
2 large lemons
¼ cup (60 ml) extra-virgin olive oil, preferably Greek
¼ pound (115 g) feta cheese, optional
12 black or green olives, optional
Bread, for serving

1 **Bring the water to a boil:** Bring 14 cups (3.3 L) water to a boil in a large stockpot over high heat. Once it comes to a boil, add 2 tablespoons of the Diamond Crystal kosher salt.

2 **Prepare the greens:** Make sure the ½ pound (225 g) curly kale, ½ pound (225 g) chicory or escarole, ½ pound (225 g) dandelion greens, and ½ pound (225 g) fresh spinach, preferably not baby, are well-washed.

3 Remove the stems from the curly kale and discard them (they're too tough). Trim just the tough ends of the stems from the chicory or escarole, the dandelion greens, and the spinach.

4 Slice the kale, chicory or escarole, and dandelion greens into 3-inch (7.5 cm) pieces. Slice the spinach into 3-inch (7.5 cm) pieces, but keep them separate from the rest—you'll add it to the water later.

Continued

271 VEGETABLES

5   **Cook the greens:** Add the kale, chicory or escarole, and dandelion greens to the boiling water (do not add the spinach). Push the greens under the water with a spoon so they all wilt. When the pot comes back to a full rolling boil, lower the heat just slightly so that the pot cooks at a hearty simmer but doesn't boil over. Cook the greens, stirring occasionally, for 4 minutes.

6   Add the spinach, pushing it down under the water with a spoon. Cook, stirring occasionally, for 3 more minutes.

If you can only find baby spinach, wait 5 minutes to add it, and let it cook for just 2 minutes.

7   Lift the greens from the pot with a large slotted spoon or spider into a colander in the sink, pushing and pressing them down with a potato masher or large spoon to squeeze out most of the water. Move the greens around once or twice, pressing and squeezing each time to get as much water from the greens as possible.

8   Set the greens aside to cool slightly in the strainer in the sink or over a bowl. Dress them just before you're ready to serve them—you can dress them warm or at room temperature, but you don't want them to be really hot.

9   **Dress the greens:** When you're ready to serve the greens, drain any water that has collected at the bottom of the cooked greens and discard it, then transfer the greens to a serving bowl.

10 Squeeze 1 of the lemons to get 2 tablespoons of fresh lemon juice and put it in a small bowl. Add the ¼ cup (60 ml) olive oil and the remaining ½ teaspoon Diamond Crystal kosher salt. Whisk everything together, then pour it over the greens in the serving bowl. Use two forks or spoons to mix and stir everything together. Taste the greens for salt and add more if needed.

11 **Prepare the accompaniments:** If serving with feta, cut the ¼ pound (115 g) feta cheese into slices and put them on a small plate. If serving with olives (Despina tends to serve the horta with only olives or only feta, not both), put out a bowl of the 12 black or green olives. Slice the remaining lemon into wedges and put them on a small serving platter. Toast the bread, if desired.

12 **Serve and eat the greens:** Serve the horta with the sliced lemons, toasted bread, and olives or feta.

Sauce Gombo

SERVES 4 TO 6

(BURKINABÉ OKRA SAUCE WITH CHICKEN)

Instructor: Yipin Benon

"I love the green color of okra sauce. It is so beautiful." —Yipin

The flavor of this dish will be somewhat familiar to fans of Louisiana gumbo or Low-Country okra stew—both have roots in West Africa. As in those dishes, okra's slippery "gel" is a key feature—it's all about making the sauce as "wiggly" as possible, as Yipin and her family would say. As with many of Yipin's recipes (and for much of Burkinabé cuisine), she builds flavor and a ton of umami by first sauteing meat in fat, then using that fat to cook many aromatic vegetables. In this version of sauce gombo, Yipin uses only chicken. But she will often add dried, smoked mackerel or cooked shrimp, which she blanches and adds about fifteen minutes before the sauce is done.

Yipin always looks for the freshest, brightest okra and tosses it with baking powder before cooking, which keeps it a beautiful bright green. Another trick is to not cover the pot after you add the okra until after the sauce has finished cooking. This recipe calls for thick, bright orange palm oil, which is used as a primary cooking oil in many parts of Africa and has a nutty flavor and aroma. (Yipin says that many people like to start the dish by frying the peppers, garlic, and onion in palm oil, but she prefers the flavor when she adds it at the end.) For more about how she uses the Scotch bonnet chile in this recipe and how she prepares the chicken, read the headnote for sauce pâte d'arachide on page 45—it's the same in both recipes.

Cutting up this much okra into tiny pieces is definitely a labor of love, but it feels really worth it in the end, when you just can't stop eating it. As with the sauce pâte d'arachide, serve this over white rice, and try eating it with your hand—it'll be extra luscious and delicious.

2½ to 3 pounds (1.2–1.4 kg) bone-in chicken parts

1 Goya Sazón seasoning packet, any flavor, such as cilantro and tomato, optional

2 teaspoons Diamond Crystal kosher salt (plus 3½ teaspoons, if you're not using the Sazón or bouillon)

1 tablespoon garlic powder

⅓ cup (80 ml) neutral oil

⅓ pound (150 g) bell pepper, any color (about ½ large)

¾ pound (340 g) red onion (about 1 large)

¾ ounce (20 g) garlic (about 6 medium cloves)

1⅓ pounds (600 g) plum tomatoes (about 5 large)

1½ pounds (680 g) whole okra pods

½ cup (120 ml) tomato paste

1 teaspoon baking powder

1 teaspoon chicken bouillon powder, optional

½ cup (120 ml) palm oil

1 Scotch bonnet chile, optional

Cooked white rice (either parboiled or jasmine), for serving

1 **Prepare the chicken:** If you're using a whole chicken, follow the steps on page 32 to cut the chicken into 2½ to 3 pounds (1.2–1.4 kg) of parts before moving on to the next step.

2 Following the instructions on page 32, use a large, sharp knife or cleaver (or a pair of kitchen shears) to cut the breast crosswise through the bone into three pieces about the same size. Use

Continued

The LEAGUE OF KITCHENS Cookbook   274

the same method to cut the thighs into two or three pieces about the same size as the pieces of chicken breast, and then the legs and wings into two pieces.

3   Use your hands to remove any pockets of yellowish fat underneath the skin. A little leftover fat is fine—just try to remove as much as possible so the gravy ends up flavorful but not greasy. Put the chicken parts in a large mixing bowl and place them in the sink.

Like many of our instructors, Yipin likes to wash the chicken under running water in the sink after she cleans it. The USDA recommends against this, as it can spread bacteria around your sink or your kitchen. If you choose to do the same, just make sure to clean your sink carefully when you're done.

4   Put the pieces skin-side down in a wide, deep nonstick pan, like a 5-quart (4.8 L) saute pan or pot. (You want the chicken in as close to one layer as possible.)

5   Sprinkle the chicken pieces with the 1 Goya Sazón seasoning packet, if using. If not, sprinkle on 1 teaspoon of Diamond Crystal kosher salt. Cover the pan with the lid slightly ajar, unless it has a hole for the steam. Turn the heat to medium and let the chicken cook, covered, for 10 minutes.

6   Stir in the 1 tablespoon garlic powder until it coats the chicken. Cook, uncovered, for about 10 minutes, stirring frequently, then add the ⅓ cup (80 ml) neutral oil to the pot. Cover the pan with the lid slightly ajar, unless it has a hole for the steam, and fry the chicken pieces until they're golden brown all over, stirring occasionally to prevent sticking, about 10 minutes. Remove the chicken pieces to a bowl, cover it with a plate or foil, and set it aside.

7   **Prepare the rest of the ingredients:** While the chicken is frying, prepare the rest of the ingredients.

8   Remove the membrane and seeds from the ⅓ pound (150 g) bell pepper (about ½ large). Cut it into ⅓-inch (1 cm) dice. You should have about 1 cup. Put it in a bowl.

9   Peel the ¾ pound (340 g) red onion (about 1 large) and cut it into ½-inch (1.3 cm) dice. You should have about 2 cups. Add it to the bowl with the peppers.

10 Peel the ¾ ounce (20 g) garlic (about 6 medium cloves). Grate the garlic over the fine holes of a grater. You should have about 1 tablespoon. Set it aside.

11 Cut the 1⅓ pounds (600 g) plum tomatoes (about 5 large) into ½-inch (1.3 cm) dice. You should have about 3½ cups. Set aside.

12 Trim the top and tail of the 1½ pounds (680 g) whole okra pods. Cut the okra lengthwise into fourths and then into slices about ⅛ inch (0.3 cm) thick. You will have about 6 cups. Set the okra aside in a large mixing bowl.

13 Measure out the ½ cup (120 ml) tomato paste, if you haven't already.

14 **Make the sauce:** To the pot in which you cooked the chicken, add the chopped peppers and onions and fry them over medium heat, uncovered and stirring frequently, for 5 minutes. Add the grated garlic. Cook, stirring frequently, for 5 minutes, then add the chopped tomatoes. Continue to cook, stirring frequently, for 5 minutes, then add the ½ cup (120 ml) tomato paste, stirring until it's well incorporated.

15 Sprinkle the 1 teaspoon baking powder on top of the okra, mix with your hands, then add the okra to the pot. Add the 1 teaspoon

chicken bouillon powder, if using. If not, add 2½ more teaspoons Diamond Crystal kosher salt. The heat should still be on medium. Cook, stirring frequently, for 5 minutes, then add the ½ cup (120 ml) palm oil and stir until it's well-incorporated. Cook for 3 minutes, stirring frequently.

16 Add the chicken pieces back to the pot along with any juices that have accumulated in the bowl, 1½ cups (350 ml) water, and 2 teaspoons Diamond Crystal kosher salt. Add the 1 whole Scotch bonnet chile, if using, right in the center of the pot, letting it float on top (don't stir it in).

17 Lower the heat to medium-low and simmer until the okra is soft, not crunchy, and the sauce is thick, about 15 more minutes. Keep warm while you prepare the cooked white rice, either parboiled or jasmine, or until you're ready to eat.

18 **Serve and eat the okra sauce:** Serve the sauce on top of cooked white rice, with a little of the Scotch bonnet chile, if desired. Make sure each person gets at least one piece of chicken.

Cauli Aalu Tareko

SERVES 4 TO 6

(NEPALI FRIED CAULIFLOWER AND POTATO)

Instructor: Rachana Rimal

"The spice aroma of this recipe is out of this world. Try this, and you will love it." —Rachana

As with many South Asian recipes, you may be looking at this and saying I'll never make that, there are twenty items on the ingredients list! Way too complicated. But that first glance is deceptive. Really, this recipe has four ingredients: cauliflower, potatoes, oil, and a seasonings blend. Yes, there are a lot of spices. But measuring out spices takes very little effort (especially if you use a masala dabba—a South Asian spice box made specifically for keeping multiple spices at the ready—to store them).

I also know that buying so many spices, if you don't already have them in your pantry, can feel like a hurdle. But if you go to a South Asian grocery store (or online), you can find them all in one place, often very affordably priced. And it's a worthy investment! South Asian food cooked at home is vastly different from, and better than, most South Asian food at restaurants, because home cooks can use spices in greater quantity.

This everyday cauliflower and potato dish, which Rachana learned from her mother, is the perfect example of South Asian home cooking that's full of well-balanced, delicious, complex flavors. It's also the perfect tutorial for how to use spices in a variety of ways—in this recipe you make a spice paste and temper additional spices in oil.

Like many Nepali recipes, this dish calls for jimbu, a dried herb with a garlicky-onion flavor. Jimbu can be hard to find, but this recipe is still fantastic without it. The chiles are optional—use the lesser amount if you don't want too much heat, or none at all. If you can't find dried red Indian chiles, just look for another hot dried red chile about the same size, such as arbol or cayenne.

Serve with: the greens on page 266, the Nepali dal on page 141, and white basmati rice.

For the spice paste

½ ounce (15 g) fresh ginger root
    (about 1 inch/2.5 cm square)

0.4 ounce (10 g) fresh turmeric
    (about 1½ inches/3.8 cm long), or
    1 tablespoon ground turmeric

½ to 2 dried red Indian chiles
    (about 1½ inches/3.8 cm long), optional

4 green cardamom pods

1 black cardamom pod (see page 21)

1 tablespoon whole coriander seeds

1 teaspoon whole cumin seeds

1 2-inch (5 cm) cinnamon stick (about 2 g), or
    1 3-inch (7.5 cm) piece Indian flat cinnamon

4 whole cloves

1 large Indian bay leaf (page 21), or
    2 bay laurel leaves

For the cauliflower

3 pounds (1.4 kg) cauliflower
    (about 1 large head or 1½ small heads)

1 pound (450 g) red potatoes (3 to 4 large)

1 dried red Indian chile
    (about 1½ inches/3.8 cm long), optional

½ teaspoon whole cumin seeds

¼ teaspoon whole ajwain seeds

1 teaspoon jimbu, optional

⅛ teaspoon asafetida

2 tablespoons chopped fresh cilantro

½ teaspoon whole fenugreek seeds

1 teaspoon ground turmeric

1 tablespoon Diamond Crystal kosher salt

1 cup (240 ml) neutral oil

Continued

The LEAGUE OF KITCHENS Cookbook   278

1   **Prepare the spice paste:** Peel the ½ ounce (15 g) fresh ginger root (about 1 inch/2.5 cm square) and 0.4 ounce (10 g) fresh turmeric (about 1½ inches/3.8 cm long), if using. Cut the ginger root and turmeric into thick slices and put them in a small blender or food processor. If you're using ground turmeric, add 1 tablespoon to the blender or food processor.

2   To the blender, add the ½ to 2 dried red Indian chiles (about 1½ inches/3.8 cm long), if using, 4 green cardamom pods, 1 black cardamom pod, 1 tablespoon whole coriander seeds, 1 teaspoon whole cumin seeds, 1 2-inch (5 cm) cinnamon stick (about 2 g) or 1 3-inch (7.5 cm) piece Indian flat cinnamon, 4 whole cloves, and 1 large Indian bay leaf or 2 bay laurel leaves.

3   If you're using fresh turmeric, add 2 tablespoons of water to the blender or food processor. If you're using ground turmeric, add ¼ cup (60 ml) of water. Process everything until it's a fine paste, shaking the blender or food processor to make sure everything is well incorporated. Set the spice paste aside.

4   **Prepare the rest of the ingredients:** Remove and discard the stems and leaves from the 3 pounds (1.4 kg) cauliflower (about 1 large head or 1½ small heads), trim off any brown spots, and cut it into florets about 3 inches (7.6 cm) wide. You should have 11 to 14 large florets. Then cut the florets in half lengthwise. Set them aside.

5   Peel the 1 pound (450 g) red potatoes (3 to 4 large). Cut the potatoes in half lengthwise, then lengthwise again into ½-inch (1.3 cm) wide strips. You should have about 3½ cups. Put the potatoes in a bowl of water and set them aside.

6   Put the 1 dried red Indian chile (about 1½ inches/3.8 cm long), if using, ½ teaspoon whole cumin seeds, ¼ teaspoon whole ajwain seeds, 1 teaspoon jimbu, if using, and ⅛ teaspoon asafetida in a small bowl and set it aside.

7   Prepare the 2 tablespoons chopped fresh cilantro, if you haven't already, and set it aside.

8   Measure out into separate bowls the ½ teaspoon whole fenugreek seeds, 1 teaspoon ground turmeric, and 1 tablespoon Diamond Crystal kosher salt. Measure 2 tablespoons water into a separate small bowl.

9   **Cook the cauliflower and potatoes:** Pour out the water from your bowl of potatoes. Place all your measured-out spices, the spice paste, and the small bowl of water near the stove. Heat the 1 cup (240 ml) neutral oil in a 12-inch (30 cm) nonstick wok or skillet over medium-high heat until it begins to shimmer.

10 Add 1 fenugreek seed—if it immediately bubbles, add the ½ teaspoon whole fenugreek seeds and, stirring constantly so they don't burn, cook just until they begin to pop and turn dark brown, about 10 seconds. Stir in the combined spices (the chile, cumin, ajwain seeds, jimbu, and asafetida) and cook just until they darken, about 10 seconds.

11 Stir in the potato slices—be careful, as they will splatter—then lower the heat to medium. Sprinkle on the 1 teaspoon ground turmeric and gently mix it into the potatoes. Add the cauliflower florets and 1 tablespoon Diamond Crystal kosher salt, mix everything together, and cook for about 30 seconds.

12 Stir in the spice paste and mix gently just until it's well incorporated. Add 2 tablespoons of water and cover the pan, leaving the lid slightly ajar. Lower the heat to medium-low and cook until the cauliflower is tender, stirring every 5 to 10 minutes or so, for 35 to 45 minutes. Keep the cauliflower warm until you're ready to serve it.

13 **Serve and eat the cauliflower:** Sprinkle the 2 tablespoons chopped fresh cilantro over the top of the cauliflower just before you serve it, either family style or in individual bowls.

Kateh Estamboli

(PERSIAN GREEN BEANS WITH TOMATO SAUCE AND RICE)

Instructor: Mahboubeh Abbasgholizadeh

"Cinnamon is one of the secrets of our food, actually—cinnamon, saffron, and rose water, together." —Mab

This is a wonderful vegetarian one-pot meal and perfect comfort food. It's a dish Mab's father loved to cook, and the seasoning is so classically Persian: saffron, cinnamon, and just a hint of rose water, with quick-pickled red onions and whole milk yogurt on the side. The green beans get pan-fried, stewed with tomatoes and onions, then cooked with the rice until that wonderful crusty tahdig forms. It has a delicious savoriness and an intense caramelized tomato flavor—Mab always uses the Bionaturae organic brand of unsalted tomato paste, which comes in a jar and is the closest in taste she can find in regular supermarkets to the homemade pastes found in Iran.

While this recipe is Mab's father's, adding the oil to the rice at the end by pouring it through a few small holes is Mab's mother's technique—it results in a perfectly crispy tahdig. There are six holes, the center representing God's light and the other five representing Mohammmed and members of his family. Mab likes to name her family and friends as she makes the holes, and traditionally, she says, cooks also pray, as they make the holes, that the rice will turn out well. They also offer a prayer of gratitude for the rice itself. "Harvesting the grain is a difficult process," says Mab, "and so many people give their lives as part of that."

Mab also says that this is a great potluck dish—you can make it a few hours in advance, cool it in the pot with the top off, then take the whole pot to the picnic. You really need aged extra-long-grain basmati rice for this dish (see Nawida's challow on page 179)—it has better flavor and it's very hard to overcook or mess up through all these steps, as it rarely gets mushy. If you plan to serve the rice right away, you can also prepare the accompaniments while you cook the beans—that's what I usually do.

Serve with: the accompaniments listed here, or with the Persian chicken kabobs on page 29 for a bigger meal.

For the kateh estamboli

1½ cups (300 g) aged extra-long-grain basmati rice

1 pound (450 g) green beans

⅓ pound (150 g) red onion (about ½ medium)

3 tablespoons extra-virgin olive oil, divided

2 tablespoons unsalted butter

¼ teaspoon ground cinnamon

⅛ teaspoon crushed red pepper flakes

2 tablespoons unsalted tomato paste

¼ teaspoon (0.25 g) saffron threads (about 1 large pinch)

1½ teaspoons Diamond Crystal kosher salt

½ teaspoon rose water

For serving

½ pound (225 g) red onion (about 1 medium)

½ cup (120 ml) apple cider vinegar

1 teaspoon dried mint

2 cups (475 ml) whole milk yogurt, optional

1 **Prepare the rice:** Bring 3 cups (700 ml) of water to a boil. (Once it boils, leave it covered to keep it warm.) You will also need a large, clean kitchen towel for wrapping the lid of the pot as the rice cooks.

2 Put the 1½ cups (300 g) aged extra-long-grain basmati rice in a 5-quart (4.8 L) Dutch oven or

Continued

saucepan, preferably nonstick. Put the pan in the sink and wash the rice under cool running water, moving it around with your fingers, until it runs clear. Drain off as much of the water as you can and set the pot aside.

3   **Prepare the beans and tomato sauce:** Trim the ends of the 1 pound (450 g) green beans and cut them into pieces about 1 inch (2.5 cm) wide.

4   Peel the ⅓ pound (150 g) red onion (about ½ medium) and cut it into ⅓-inch (1 cm) dice. You should have about 1 cup.

5   Heat a 12-inch (30 cm) skillet with deep sides over medium heat, then add 2 tablespoons of the extra-virgin olive oil.

6   When the oil is hot (a green bean placed in the pan should begin to sizzle immediately), spread out the trimmed and cut beans evenly in the pan. Fry the green beans, stirring every once in a while but making sure to always spread them back into one layer after you do. The beans are done when the color changes and some of them are beginning to brown, after about 5 minutes. If you taste one, it will be al dente, with just a little crunch.

7   Turn off the heat and transfer the beans to a bowl with a slotted spoon, leaving as much of the oil in the pan as you can.

8   Add the onion to the pan and put the 2 tablespoons unsalted butter on top. Turn the heat back to medium and stir constantly until the butter is fully melted into the onions. Cook the onions, stirring every once in a while, until their color fades, 2 to 3 minutes.

You add the butter on top of the onions so the onions release a little water as the butter melts, preventing the butter from burning.

9   Stir in the ¼ teaspoon ground cinnamon and let it cook for about 45 seconds. Stir in the

⅛ teaspoon crushed red pepper flakes and cook for about 45 seconds. (By now, the onions may be a little darker brown—that's fine.) Stir in the 2 tablespoons unsalted tomato paste and lower the heat to medium-low. Cook for about 1 minute, stirring frequently, until the color changes. (It may look clumpy.)

10   Stir in the fried green beans, coating them with the onion and tomato paste mixture. Then slowly pour in 1 cup (240 ml) of the water you brought to a boil, moving the measuring cup around the pot as you pour in the water. Raise the heat to medium so that the pot cooks at a simmer, with plenty of small bubbles, but not at a rolling boil.

11   Let the pot simmer uncovered for about 3 minutes, then stir in the ¼ teaspoon (0.25 g) saffron threads (about 1 large pinch) and 1½ teaspoons Diamond Crystal kosher salt. Cover the pot, lowering the heat as necessary so that it continues to cook at a simmer. Cook, stirring occasionally, until the beans are very soft and you can cut them with the side of a spoon, about 20 minutes. Turn off the heat.

12   Spoon the green beans and tomato over the washed and drained rice in the Dutch oven. Pour 1½ cups (350 ml) of the hot water gently over the green beans and rice, and then drizzle on the ½ teaspoon rose water. Do not stir it yet.

13   Put the pot over medium-high heat, and just when it comes to boil, give the pot a little swirl to make sure the liquid is mixed throughout the rice (If you mix it with the spoon, the rice will get sticky and clumpy.) Lower the heat to medium-low so that you still see small bubbles.

14   Cook, uncovered, until nearly all the water has been absorbed by the rice, usually about 4 to 5 minutes. (It will be wet, but you won't see any standing liquid.) Use the end of a wooden spoon to make one small (½-inch/1.3 cm) hole in the center of the pot and 5 more holes around

the edge, like spokes on a wheel. Take the remaining 1 tablespoon of extra-virgin olive oil and pour it gently into the 6 holes.

15 Take the clean kitchen cloth and wrap it around the lid of the pot, tying the corners into a knot so the edges of the towel don't droop down and accidentally catch on fire. Then place the wrapped lid back on the pot and press to make sure it's tightly sealed. Put the heat on low and cook for about 20 minutes, until the bottom of the rice is browned and crispy (you won't really be able to check—you just have to trust!). When the rice is done, keep it on the stovetop to stay warm until you're ready to serve it.

16 **Prepare the accompaniments:** When you're ready to serve the rice, peel the ½ pound (225 g) red onion (about 1 medium). Cut the onion into ⅓-inch (1 cm) dice and transfer it to a small serving bowl. Mix in the ½ cup (120 ml) apple cider vinegar, then sprinkle the top of the bowl with the 1 teaspoon dried mint, crumbling it with your fingers as you do.

17 If you're serving the yogurt, put the 2 cups (475 ml) whole milk yogurt in a serving bowl and whisk it until smooth.

18 **Serve and eat the rice:** Remove the lid from the pot of rice. Use a large plate (slightly larger than your pot) to cover the top of your pot, then, holding the plate on tightly, flip the pot onto the plate so that the rice and tahdig fall out. The bottom may not be evenly golden brown—it may be light or even very dark in some spots—but it should be crunchy and crispy.

19 Put the vinegared onions and the yogurt on the table. Use a spatula or large serving spoon to give everyone both a piece of the tahdig and the fluffy rice and green beans inside. Encourage everyone to add onions and yogurt to their plates to eat in between bites of rice and green beans.

Larisa Frumkin

Larisa was born in 1934 in the bustling Black Sea port of Odesa in Ukraine but moved to Moscow while very young. Her father was a high-ranking naval intelligence chief who'd interrogated Hermann Goering at the Nuremberg Trials; her mother was an architect and a painter. Cooking was a huge challenge in the former USSR, where long lines and chronic shortages were a daily reality, but like so many busy women, Larisa could conjure up small feasts out of a few root vegetables and a couple of eggs. Her Moscow kitchen was always full of guests.

Always at odds with the repressive Soviet regime, in 1974 Larisa and her young daughter found themselves stateless refugees to the US with no right of return, though after Gorbachev opened the border in the late 1980s, she was able to reunite with her family. In Philadelphia, and then in New York, Larisa taught ESL in elementary schools while her daughter, Anya von Bremzen, became a professional food writer—many of Larisa's recipes are included in Anya's James Beard Award–winning cookbook, *Please to the Table*. After retiring from teaching, Larisa worked as a volunteer guide at the Metropolitan Museum of Art and became obsessed with reconstructing historic feasts. After *Saveur* magazine published a story on her nineteenth-century Russian meal, Larisa and Anya began to cook their way through the twentieth century, which became the basis of Anya's acclaimed memoir, *Mastering the Art of Soviet Cooking*—Larisa is the protagonist.

What makes Russian cuisine special? What are some iconic Russian dishes? Russia in my day was part of the Soviet Union, which was a huge empire with many ethnicities and very diverse cuisines. Politically it was so repressive, but the cultural mix was incredibly rich. My own heritage is Jewish-Ukrainian, but all my life I lived in Moscow, the capital, where one could try Georgian, Uzbek, or Armenian food. Then there were typical Soviet dishes eaten all over, especially cooked vegetable salads like vinegret (page 215) or salad Olivier, dressed with mayonnaise. Russia is also known for soups and baked goods. They make wonderful pirozhki, or savory pastries, and large filled savory pies calls piroghi. Blini are another popular dish. They are served with sour cream, smoked salmon, red or black caviar, and jam. My favorite Russian food is boiled potatoes and herring. This dish is always part of a Russian dinner and is usually served as an appetizer.

What do you love about cooking? I started to be interested in cooking in Russia during gloomy times. We often didn't have enough food. Cooking was a way to escape. I was dreaming about different periods of history, different cooking, different ways of serving. It started when I was thirteen or fourteen years old. I looked up recipes in different cookbooks. At first I was very clumsy in the kitchen, but little by little I really started doing something different, especially later when I invited my friends and people came to my dinners. We really felt like it was a different world. I love parties, and I love to cook for friends and family.

How did you learn how to cook? I learned how to cook from everyone around me. My mother was a good cook, but she wasn't interested in it. She was an architect, and she did her duty in the kitchen, but it was not inspiring. Some of her recipes were really good, and I definitely followed and kept them. I personally read cookbooks, especially when I started learning English. It was very good for my repertoire.

What do you like to cook for yourself if you want to make something quick and easy but still tasty? Actually, I hate cooking for myself. When I'm alone, I eat something like bread and butter with some sausage and cheese. But when I want some warm food, I boil eggs or make omelets. If I really want something homemade, I fry potatoes. Fried potatoes are my favorite, favorite dish. Also, I love boiled potatoes and herring—that's my favorite.

And what is your favorite food to eat that's not from your culture? I like Chinese, French, or Italian. And I especially like the cuisines of Iran and Turkey—that's great, great, great food.

What do you like about teaching for the League of Kitchens? I love teaching people about some of the dishes I have mastered in my life. I love to teach people how to cook, and I like to share my experiences.

Larisa Frumkin

Лариса Фрумкин

デザート と ドリンク
菓子 と 飲み物

Dulces Y Bebidas

मिठाई 3 पातीय़

حلويات ومشروب

Γλυκά και ποτά

Сладости и напитки

SWEETS AND DRINKS

شیرینی جات و نوشیدنیها

شیرین و نوشیدنی .

मिठाई र पिय पर्दाब

Dulces y Bebides

मिठाई - चाय और
शरबत

Manisan dan Minuman

Kesar Shrikhand

(INDIAN SAFFRON YOGURT PARFAIT WITH MANGO)

Instructor: Yamini Joshi

"This dish is a favorite of my family. When I eat it, it makes me think of many happy occasions." —Yamini

Featuring saffron, sugar, and rose water, this dish is refreshing and satisfying even though it's also so easy to make. The key is whisking the yogurt until it's very smooth—it really changes the texture. Ideally you want a thick, strained whole milk yogurt like Greek yogurt for this dish. You can also make your own "hung yogurt," as Yamini does, by hanging regular yogurt (hers is homemade) in cheesecloth from the faucet in the sink for a few hours until most of the whey has drained away. (She also collects the whey, which is very nutritious, to use in drinks or other dishes.) Yamini uses several very small Indian Alphonso mangoes, which are famously sweet and floral, when she can find them. If you're using larger mangoes, you will likely need only one or two.

Serve with: any meal as dessert, or as a snack.

4 cups (946 ml) plain whole milk Greek or strained yogurt

½ teaspoon (0.5 g) saffron threads (about 2 large pinches)

1½ tablespoons rose water

2 tablespoons white sugar, or more to taste

1½ pounds (680 g) mango (about 2 small or 1 large)

Red grapes or pomegranate seeds, optional

1 **Season the yogurt:** Put the 4 cups (946 ml) plain whole milk Greek or strained yogurt in a medium mixing bowl. Add the ½ teaspoon (0.5 g) saffron threads (about 2 large pinches), 1½ tablespoons rose water, and 2 tablespoons white sugar. Whisk everything together until the yogurt is completely creamy and smooth. Set the yogurt aside to let the flavors meld while you cut up the mango. (You can keep the seasoned yogurt in the fridge for several hours before you add the mango and serve it.)

2 **Finish the parfait:** Remove the peel from the 1½ pounds (680 g) mango (about 2 small or 1 large). Then cut the flesh into ½-inch (1.3 cm) cubes. You should have about 2 cups.

3 Taste the yogurt for sweetness. If you think it needs more sugar, gently mix in 1 tablespoon at a time, tasting after each addition.

4 **Serve and eat the parfait:** Divide the yogurt into individual bowls and then divide the cubed mango on top. Sprinkle with a few red grapes or pomegranate seeds, if using.

Sharlotka s Yablokami

SERVES 4 TO 6

(RUSSIAN "GUEST-AT-THE-DOORSTEP" APPLE CHARLOTTE)

Instructor: Larisa Frumkin

"Warm or cold or the next day, or for tea or for dessert—it's very, very good." —Larisa

This is not the French or English version of a charlotte, made with ladyfingers, but more like a fruit-topped pound cake (it's actually very similar to Marian Burros's famous plum torte from the *New York Times*, and Larisa does sometimes make it with plums). It's also the rare cake recipe that isn't finicky. It looks very impressive and tastes so good, but it's really a forgiving recipe and genuinely so simple. It seems like you won't have enough batter, as it's only about an inch thick, but it will double as it bakes, and it surrounds the fruit beautifully. The batter will feel hard to spread—but don't worry, it'll eventually even out. You can use any kind of fruit or berry with this batter, but Larisa prefers the combination of tart green apple (with just a hint of lemon) and raspberries or blackberries.

Serve with: any meal as dessert, or as a snack.

1 stick (8 tablespoons/115 g) plus 1 tablespoon unsalted butter, divided

1 cup (120 g) all-purpose flour

1 teaspoon baking powder

⅔ cup (133 g) white sugar

1 teaspoon vanilla extract

1 small pinch Diamond Crystal kosher salt

2 tablespoons sour cream or plain whole milk yogurt

2 large eggs

½ pound (225 g) Granny Smith apple (about 1 medium)

2 tablespoons fresh lemon juice (from about ½ lemon)

6 ounces (170 g) blackberries or raspberries (about 1 small box)

1 teaspoon powdered sugar

1 **Bring the butter to room temperature:** At least an hour before you want to bake the cake, take the 1 stick (8 tablespoons/115 g) plus 1 tablespoon unsalted butter out of the refrigerator to let it come to room temperature. (You can also microwave it on the lowest heat setting just until it's soft.)

2 **Preheat the oven and prepare the pan:** Line the bottom of a 9-inch (23 cm) cake pan with a circle of parchment paper. (The easiest way to do this is by tracing the bottom of the pan on the parchment with a pencil, then cutting out the traced circle.)

3 Use a paper towel to spread 1 tablespoon of the butter over the parchment and about 1 inch (2.5 cm) up the sides of the pan using your fingers or a spatula.

4 Preheat the oven to 350°F (175°C) and make sure the rack is in the center of the oven.

5 **Make the batter:** Put the 1 cup (4¼ ounces/120 g) all-purpose flour in a large mixing bowl, add the 1 teaspoon baking powder, and set aside.

6 Put the ⅔ cup (133 g) white sugar, the 1 stick (8 tablespoons/115 g) very soft room temperature butter, 1 teaspoon vanilla extract, and 1 small pinch of salt in another large mixing bowl, then use a hand mixer to beat on high

Continued

speed just until everything is mixed together, usually less than a minute.

7   Add the 2 tablespoons sour cream or plain whole milk yogurt and one of the eggs to the bowl with the butter and sugar. Use the hand mixer to beat at a high speed just until the yogurt and egg are incorporated, less than a minute. Add the second egg and mix again just until everything comes together.

8   Add half of the flour to the bowl and mix it with the hand mixer just until the flour is fully incorporated. Add the rest of the flour and mix it until it's fully incorporated. Use a spatula to scrape down the sides of the bowl and stir until everything is smooth.

9   **Compose the cake:** Use the spatula to dollop the batter evenly over the buttered parchment paper in the pan, then spread it into an even layer about 1 inch (2.5 cm) thick. The batter will be thick, almost like frosting, and will feel a little hard to place and spread, and the parchment may wrinkle or buckle around the sides. That's normal—just do your best to get it as even as possible. Set the pan aside.

10   Peel and quarter the ½ pound (225 g) Granny Smith apple (about 1 medium), removing the core with a sharp knife. Slice each quarter as thinly as possible, about ⅛ inch (0.3 cm) thick, and put the slices in a small mixing bowl. Squeeze the 2 tablespoons of fresh lemon juice (about ½ lemon) over the sliced apples and toss gently until they're all coated.

The lemon keeps the slices from browning, but Larisa also loves the lemony taste.

11   Place the apples evenly across the batter—they can overlap slightly. Then use your fingers to press them into the batter so that the slices are still visible on top of the batter but sunken in.

12   Sprinkle the 6 ounces (170 g) blackberries or raspberries (about 1 small box) evenly over the top of the batter. Use your fingers to gently press them into the batter. It's okay if they're still resting on the top—the batter rises and engulfs them.

13   **Bake the cake:** Bake the cake on the center rack for 50 to 55 minutes, until it's lightly browned. Let it cool on a wire rack for 20 minutes. Remove the cake on the parchment paper to a serving plate (running a knife or spatula around the edge of the cake to loosen it, if necessary), then pull out the parchment paper.

14   **Serve and eat the cake:** You can serve the cake warm or at room temperature (it's very good the next day, as well), with tea or for dessert. When you're ready to serve it, dust the top with the 1 teaspoon powdered sugar (you can sprinkle it on directly or you can sift it through a strainer for a more even application) and then cut it into wedges.

Kagati Ko Sarbat

(NEPALI SPICED LEMONADE)

Instructor: Rachana Rimal

"We drink this in late spring, when it's very refreshing and good for your health." —Rachana

This fantastic lemonade—made with black pepper, cinnamon, cardamom, and lots of sugar—is meant to be very sweet. You're not supposed to drink a whole tall glass, the way you do with American lemonade, but rather a small amount, and the sugar really balances out the spices. (If you want to drink a lot of it, try reducing the sugar by half or diluting the lemonade with more water.) When Rachana was growing up, her mother traditionally made this for a late spring festival called Akshaya Tritiya. But Rachana's family really loves it, so she makes it all the time—in fact, she'll often have a small glass for breakfast, with sweet things like halva or even the Nepali version of pancakes. Sometimes she serves it at her classes as the welcome drink when students first arrive.

It also makes a great mixer: Rachana was the first person to ever cook Nepali food at the famous James Beard House in New York City, and when she did, we turned this lemonade into a cocktail with the addition of a little vodka.

Serve with: snacks or other sweet dishes for breakfast.

2 cups (400 g) turbinado cane sugar, Sucanat, or jaggery

¼ cup (60 ml) fresh or bottled lemon juice (from about 2 to 3 lemons)

1 tablespoon black pepper powder

1 tablespoon cardamom powder (see page 305)

1 tablespoon ground cinnamon

1 lime, optional, for serving

Ice, for serving

1 **Make the lemonade:** Put the 2 cups (400 g) turbinado cane sugar, Sucanat, or jaggery in a mixing bowl. Add the ¼ cup (60 ml) fresh or bottled lemon juice (from about 2 to 3 lemons). Stir in the 1 tablespoon black pepper powder, 1 tablespoon cardamom powder, and 1 tablespoon ground cinnamon.

2 Add 5½ cups (1.3 L) water to the bowl and whisk everything together until the sugar is dissolved and the cinnamon is mixed in—this usually takes at least 3 to 4 minutes.

3 Pour the lemonade through a fine-mesh strainer into a pitcher. Wash the lime, if using, and cut it into round slices about ⅛ inch (0.3 cm) thick.

4 **Serve and drink the lemonade:** Serve the lemonade over ice in small glasses, garnished with slices of the lime tucked into the glass, if using.

Firni

(AFGHAN MILK PUDDING)

Instructor: Nawida Saidhosin

"This is the dessert people always make at home, because they always have all these ingredients. And everyone loves it." —Nawida

Firni is almost like a panna cotta, or a very light milk pudding, and just as Nawida says, it's the classic, fast, easy, everyday dessert Afghan families make at home because they always have milk, sugar, cornstarch, ground cardamom, and rose water. It feels just perfectly sweet and it's cooling after having a spicy meal. The only bit of labor it requires is a few minutes of continuous stirring on the stove until the firni gets to the right consistency.

Nawida prefers to make her firni in a very thin layer, usually between ½ and ¾ inch (1.3 and 2 cm) tall. This amount should fit in one large 9- by 13-inch (23 by 33 cm) casserole dish, but you can use two smaller dishes, too. On a weeknight, Nawida will serve it straight from the pan, still a little soft and wobbly. For special occasions, she'll make it in a cut-glass dish and serve it from that. It's very special with the ground nuts on top, but it's great without them, too, in which case it needs very few ingredients.

Though you can buy cardamom pre-ground, I strongly recommend you grind it yourself. You don't have to roast it first, so it only takes a few seconds. The results are so much fresher tasting, and so much more aromatic than buying it pre-ground. In addition, the cardamom for this dish should not be too finely ground—just make sure there are no chunks or pieces. It's the same with the nuts for the top, if you use them—you want them roughly ground, with a little bit of texture.

Serve with: any meal as dessert, or as a snack.

½ cup (45 g) shelled pistachios, walnuts, or almonds, optional

1 tablespoon whole green cardamom pods or ½ tablespoon ground cardamom

3½ cups (820 ml) whole milk, divided

¼ cup (30 g) cornstarch

1 teaspoon rose water

7 tablespoons white sugar

1 **Prepare the serving mold:** Get the serving dish you will use to chill and serve the firni and have it ready near the stove.

2 **Prepare the nuts and the cardamom:** Grind the ½ cup (45 g) shelled pistachios, walnuts, or almonds, if using, in a small food mill, spice grinder, or food processor until they become a coarse powder, and make sure there are no large pieces or chunks (you can pick them out, if need be). Set them aside.

3 Put the 1 tablespoon whole green cardamom pods in a spice grinder or small food processor and grind until they're a coarse powder, shaking the bowl once or twice to make sure you process all the pieces. Set aside ½ tablespoon of ground cardamom for the firni. (If you have any left over, it will keep in a tightly sealed jar for several weeks.)

Continued

4   **Prepare the milk and cornstarch:** Pour 3 cups (700 ml) of the milk into a 5-quart (4.8 L) Dutch oven or stockpot. Set this aside.

5   In a small bowl, mix the remaining ½ cup (120 ml) milk with the ¼ cup (30 g) cornstarch. Stir it together, set the bowl aside for about a minute so that the cornstarch absorbs the milk, then stir it again with a spoon until the mixture is completely soft and smooth—make sure there are no lumps. Set it aside.

6   **Make the custard:** Put the Dutch oven with the milk over high heat. Stir in the 1 teaspoon rose water, ½ tablespoon ground cardamom, and 7 tablespoons white sugar. Use a whisk to mix in the sugar and cardamom powder just until the milk begins to bubble, usually 2 to 4 minutes.

7   Lower the heat to medium, then slowly pour in the milk and cornstarch mixture, whisking constantly to make sure it doesn't stick to the bottom and is fully incorporated.

8   Adjust the heat to medium-high or high so that the milk comes back to a simmer. Whisking constantly so that it doesn't stick or burn, cook until the custard thickens to the texture of glue, usually about 5 to 6 minutes. Then turn off the heat.

9   **Put the firni in the mold:** Carefully pour the firni into the serving dish in a shallow layer around ¾ inch (2 cm) high. (If you have any extra, just pour it into another vessel, or even a clean bowl.)

10 Let the firni sit for 10 minutes to cool slightly. Then use your hands to gently sprinkle the ground nuts, if using, on the top of the firni while it's still warm—it will be thicker in spots, and you don't have to cover every inch completely. You can also use the nuts to make a decorative pattern on the top.

11 Let the firni sit out at room temperature for 30 more minutes before putting it in the refrigerator—otherwise it will weep water as it cools.

12 **Chill the firni:** Refrigerate the firni, uncovered, until it's fully cold but still soft, scoopable, and jiggly, 1½ to 2 hours.

13 **Serve the firni:** Serve the firni cold or at room temperature. You can prepare individual bowls or place the whole dish on the table with a serving spoon and let everyone serve themselves.

Masala Chai

(INDIAN TEA WITH GINGER, LEMONGRASS, AND MINT)
Instructor: Yamini Joshi

"It's the best chai to drink because of all the herbs—they soothe your body. It's good for your health!" —Yamini

Many people are familiar with a chai made with milk, sugar, and warm spices like clove, cinnamon, and cardamom. But this herb-forward version is also traditional in India. Chai is the Hindi word for tea, and there are endless variations with different spices and aromatics steeped with tea in hot milk.

This chai is equally soothing and flavorful but has a bright floral freshness from the mint and lemongrass and a spicy kick from the fresh ginger. This recipe was her father's favorite, Yamini says, and they learned it from the family's Ayurvedic doctor.

Yamini's version is always extra aromatic because she uses the fresh green leaves of lemongrass, which have a more floral scent than the stalks. In India, she grew it outside (so does my mother-in-law in Connecticut); here, in New York City, Yamini keeps a bunch of fresh lemongrass stalks growing in a jar with about an inch of water, the same way many people grow green onion bulbs or radish tops. The green leaves begin to sprout after about two weeks, and then they get huge—you just cut off what you need to make your tea. If you don't have time to grow any or can't find lemongrass that still has some leaves attached, the best substitute is not the white stalk but dried or frozen leaves, which are usually sold at South Asian markets. If you don't have fresh mint, you can swap in dried mint.

Yamini likes to use a tea brand called Wagh Bakri Premium International Blend, which is an Assam tea named after the northeastern region of India where it's grown. Assam teas are strong and sometimes said to be malty in flavor—Irish breakfast tea is also an Assam tea. If you can't find it or don't like to consume caffeine, you can skip it. Growing up, Yamini's family would often make this without the tea as a delicious herbal drink—one that helps keep away colds and viruses.

This recipe is easily doubled, tripled, or multiplied into whatever quantity you need. When Yamini is teaching classes, she will make a large batch of chai and put it in an insulated coffee dispenser so that students can help themselves to hot chai whenever they like.

Serve with: sweets, as a snack between meals, with breakfast, or even after dinner, with or without the black tea.

2 tablespoons dried chopped lemongrass leaves, or 3 tablespoons (6 g) fresh or frozen green leaves

½ cup (8 g) picked fresh mint leaves (from about ¼ bunch), or 1 tablespoon dried mint

½ ounce (15 g) fresh ginger root (about 1 inch/2.5 cm square)

¼ teaspoon ground cardamom

4 teaspoons white sugar, or more to taste

2 teaspoons loose black Assam tea leaves, optional

⅔ cup (160 ml) whole milk

1   **Prepare the ingredients:** If you're using fresh or frozen lemongrass, cut the 3 tablespoons (6 g) fresh or frozen leaves into ½-inch (1.3 cm) pieces. If using dried, measure out the 2 tablespoons. Set the lemongrass aside.

Continued

301   SWEETS AND DRINKS

2   Pick the leaves for the ½ cup (8 g) fresh mint leaves (from about ¼ bunch) if you haven't already. Set them aside.

3   Use the edge of a spoon to remove any damaged or tough peel from the ½ ounce (15 g) fresh ginger root (about 1 inch/2.5 cm square).

4   Gather all the remaining ingredients and have them at the ready: ¼ teaspoon ground cardamom, 4 teaspoons white sugar, 2 teaspoons loose black Assam tea leaves, if using, and ⅔ cup (160 ml) whole milk.

Freshly ground cardamom is always much better than pre-ground. You can make a bunch and store it for up to a month. Just follow Nawida's instructions from her yellow cake recipe on page 305.

5   You will also need a grater you can easily hold over a saucepan (do not use a rasp-style grater or one with star-shaped holes, or the mint and ginger will get stuck in the teeth) and a small strainer.

6   **Make the tea:** Heat 1⅓ cups (315 ml) water in a medium saucepan over medium-high heat. Once the water begins to simmer, lower the heat to medium-low and add the lemongrass leaves.

7   Using the small holes of a handheld grater, grate the ginger directly into the water.

8   Bunch a handful of the mint leaves and grate them over the water in the same way. Some of it will partially grate, some of it will partially shred, and some will be crushed or whole or mangled—that's okay, just let everything drop into the water. The point is to release some of the aromatic oils of the mint into the tea, not to have it perfectly grated. If you're using dried mint, add 1 tablespoon into the water.

9   Increase the heat to medium-high, then stir in the ground cardamom, sugar, and tea, if using.

10 When everything begins to simmer again, pour in the milk, gently stirring or swirling the pan as you do. Lower the heat to medium-low and let it simmer, stirring frequently, just until the color darkens slightly, about 3 minutes. Turn off the heat.

11 **Serve and drink the tea:** Pour the tea through a small fine-mesh strainer directly into a cup or mug (or serving pitcher) and serve immediately, adding more sugar to taste, if desired.

Cake Jawari

(AFGHAN YELLOW CAKE WITH ROSE WATER, CARDAMOM, AND TWO TOPPINGS)

Instructor: Nawida Saidhosin

"This is not considered a special-occasion cake, but everyone loves it. It's an everyday cake to serve with tea."
—Nawida

Flavored with freshly ground cardamom and a little rose water, this cake is made with both all-purpose flour and corn flour (which is milled more finely than cornmeal). It has an ideal ratio of cake, topping, and just a little crunch, which you get from the coarse yellow semolina flour, or sooji in Hindi, that's dusted on the bottom of the pan before you add the batter. The result is both familiar and exciting—it's like the best and most interesting corn muffin ever. It's also the perfect complement to any kind of tea.

Nawida usually tops one side of the cake with mild white poppy seeds and nigella seeds, which have just a touch of bitterness, and the other side with black raisins and large pieces of walnut. You can choose just one topping, but both together on one plate make this very easy dessert so much more appealing—and this approach allows everyone to try both.

Ideally this should be baked in a rectangular metal pan about 9 by 13 inches (23 by 33 cm) so that you can easily cut the cake into diamond shapes. I use a square metal brownie pan, so the pieces come out a little thicker, but in a pinch you could also use two round cake pans or even muffin tins. Nawida sometimes uses muffin tins shaped like hearts and stars so that it's easy and fun for her kids to take a piece of cake to school. Just pay attention as it bakes, as the bake time will vary slightly with a different shape of pan.

As with the firni on page 299, though you can buy cardamom pre-ground, for this dish I strongly recommend you grind it yourself. It doesn't take very long!

Serve with: the green cardamom tea on page 109, or any tea you prefer.

4 large eggs

½ cup (120 ml) whole milk

1 tablespoon unsalted butter

2 tablespoons whole green cardamom pods or 1½ teaspoons ground cardamom

½ tablespoon rose water

1 cup (120 g) all-purpose flour

1 cup (125 g) corn flour (not cornmeal)

1 tablespoon baking powder

1 cup (200 g) white sugar

1 cup (240 ml) neutral oil or olive oil

¼ cup (60 g) fine semolina (also called sooji, or durum wheat flour)

⅓ cup (50 g) small black raisins

⅓ cup (40 g) walnut halves

1 teaspoon white poppy seeds

1 teaspoon nigella seeds

1 **Bring the eggs and milk to room temperature:** About an hour before you plan to make the cake, take the 4 large eggs, ½ cup (120 ml) whole milk, and 1 tablespoon unsalted butter out of the refrigerator so they can come to room temperature.

If you're nervous about leaving the milk out on your counter, you can wait and then gently warm it in a microwave or on the stove—it doesn't need to be warm, just no longer very cold.

2 **Prepare the ground cardamom:** Put the 2 tablespoons whole green cardamom pods in a

Continued

spice grinder or small food processor and grind them until they're a fine powder, shaking the bowl once or twice to make sure you process all the pieces. Set aside 1½ teaspoons of ground cardamom for the cake. (If you have any left over, it will keep in a tightly sealed jar for several weeks.)

3 **Preheat the oven and prepare the pan:** When you're ready to make the cake, preheat the oven to 350°F (175°C). Use a pastry brush or your hands to spread the softened butter on the bottom and sides of a 9- by 13-inch (23 by 33 cm) or 9- by 9-inch (23 by 23 cm) metal pan. Set this aside while you make the cake.

4 **Make the batter:** Add the ½ tablespoon rose water to the ½ cup (120 ml) room-temperature milk and set it aside.

5 Sift together the 1 cup (120 g) all-purpose flour, 1 cup (125 g) corn flour (not cornmeal), and 1 tablespoon baking powder into a medium mixing bowl, whisk them together, then set the bowl aside. (If you don't have a sifter, pour the flours and the baking powder one at a time through a sieve over the bowl, and then shake them into the bowl.)

6 Break the 4 room temperature eggs into a large mixing bowl. Add the 1 cup (200 g) white sugar to the bowl and beat them together with a whisk, stand mixer, or hand mixer on the medium-low setting. Do not go back and forth when you beat—keep the whisk or beaters moving in one direction, either clockwise or counterclockwise, whichever is easier for you. Beat the eggs and sugar, tilting the bowl slightly, until the mixture begins to thicken and lighten in color and then begins to look almost creamy. This will take 3 to 6 minutes of consistent beating with a hand mixer or stand mixer, and more with a whisk.

7 As soon as the eggs and sugar are ready, add the milk and rose water, the 1 cup (240 ml) neutral oil or olive oil, and the 1½ teaspoons ground cardamom. Then use the whisk, stand mixer, or hand mixer to mix them in well on the lowest setting for about 1 minute.

8 With the whisk moving or the mixer running, add the flour and baking powder mixture to the mixing bowl with the eggs and beat on low just until it's no longer fully dry, usually a few seconds. Then use your spatula to gently scrape the sides of the bowl and fold everything in for 1 full minute—if there are still a few small lumps, that's fine, but you don't want any large ones.

9 **Finish the cake:** Sprinkle the ¼ cup (60 g) fine semolina (also called sooji, or durum wheat flour) over the butter in the greased pan and shake and tap the pan so that it fully covers the buttered bottom. Shake off any extra semolina into the trash. Gently pour the batter into the pan and then shake the pan very, very gently so it's even.

10 Sprinkle ⅓ cup (50 g) raisins evenly across one side of the cake. Use your hands to break ⅓ cup (40 g) walnut halves into raisin-size pieces and sprinkle them evenly over the top of the raisins. (You don't need to press them in.) Sprinkle the other side of the cake with the 1 teaspoon white poppy seeds and then the 1 teaspoon nigella seeds.

If you only want to make one topping, you can double it and sprinkle it across the entire cake. When Nawida was still living with her mother-in-law's family in Pakistan, she had to cook daily for a household of thirty-five family members. She often ingeniously adapted recipes so she could please multiple tastes with less labor—like making a cake with two toppings at the same time.

11   **Bake the cake:** Bake the cake in the center of the middle rack for 25 to 35 minutes, until it's golden brown on the top and a skewer or toothpick comes out clean. Then remove it to a metal trivet or wire rack on the counter to cool completely.

12   **Serve and eat the cake:** Cut the cake once it's cooled to room temperature. Cut the cake into squares or diamonds about the size of brownies or dessert bars. (For smaller pans, you might want to cut them on the smaller side, as the slices will be thicker.) Pile the slices on a serving plate, alternating the toppings if you like.

Nawida sometimes bakes this cake in a clean broiler pan (without the grilling insert) that is 16 inches (40 cm) by 12¾ inches (32 cm). A broiler pan dips slightly in the middle, so the edges come out a little thinner. (It nearly always takes Nawida exactly 27 minutes in the broiler pan!) Nawida trims off these slightly crisper ends and eats them as a snack once the cake has cooled or turns them into maleeda—a snack made from crumbled corn cake mixed with oil, ground cardamom, and sugar.

Aiko Cascio

Aiko was born in Kagawa, a Japanese prefecture near Osaka known for its udon. The only girl in her large family, she learned to cook from her mother and grandmother. She moved to the US in 1979 and worked as a travel agent, until retiring. Now she finally has time for her main passion: sharing her food. No matter what she's cooking, she always follows Japanese principles like mottainai, or avoiding waste, and cooking seasonally. She is also a passionate watercolorist and gardener. She lives in Manhattan with her husband, and has two community garden plots on the Upper West Side. She has one grown son and two grandchildren.

What makes Japanese cuisine special? We just try to make the food taste like itself. We eat a lot of vegetables, and most importantly, we eat seasonally. Omotenashi is very important to Japanese cuisine—it's about hospitality. It's all about attuning to the needs and tastes of the guests—in the flowers, the dishes I serve food on, and the food. After the Second World War, we didn't have anything to eat. My mother's generation had no food at all. So we really believed in mottainai, or no waste. If you use natural material, you shouldn't waste anything, which is very unlike Western food.

Do you have a cooking philosophy? I'm always concerned with the balance of every dish and every meal—all food needs balance. Western food has salad first, then main course, then dessert. We serve everything at the same time with rice so that we can taste the balance. In one meal, I try to include tastes that are all different but work together. I also always consider nutrition— ichiju sansai, or Japanese meals that consist of one soup and three dishes, are very healthy and good for balancing the body.

What do you love most about cooking? I love to discover new flavors and ingredients and experiment with them. Whenever I eat something new and interesting, I try to re-create that flavor. I love to try new things, and I love the challenge of re-creating them. And I don't just cook Japanese food. My husband is Italian American, and I cook a lot of Italian food. I also like to cook Chinese food.

What do you grow in your garden? I actually have two garden plots at two different community gardens. I grow Japanese cucumbers, Japanese eggplants, Japanese ginger, which is called myoga, and then also shiso. Japanese cucumbers have a really good smell, much stronger than what you can get in the supermarket. The eggplant is a little softer and smaller with not many seeds. Japanese ginger is very expensive when you buy it—one piece comes to $4.50—but I have one hundred of them growing in my garden; I like to give them to friends. I get my plants from a plant exchange we do every year in the Japanese community.

What is your favorite food to eat that's not Japanese? I like pasta. Seafood pasta is my favorite.

What do you like about teaching for the League of Kitchens? At the end of each class, everyone becomes friends—there's a party kind of feeling, and people exchange emails. And I love to see people learning and succeeding at making things they've never made before. I'm kind of a shy person, and the first time I met everyone, the instructors welcomed me, and that felt really good.

Aiko Cascio
アイコ カシオ
愛子 カシオ

Acknowledgments

From the beginning, this book has been a deeply collaborative project.

To the fourteen instructors of LoK: It is such a pleasure and privilege to work with all of you. It's been an honor to be invited into your homes, your families, and your lives. Thank you for your kindness, your love, your generosity, your patience, and all your hard work. My kids are so lucky to have fourteen incredible aunties from all over the world, many of whom have known them since they were born. Eating in your homes over the last ten years has meant that I have definitely eaten better than probably anyone else on earth!

To our LoK staff—Rebecca, Sarah, Glenda, Liz, Julia, Paula, Justine, Karsyn, Arielle, and Sonya: You make work so fun! Thank you for everything you do to support me, our instructors, and our students, and for all you do to make our company run so smoothly and successfully! Thank you to all our past staff—you guys laid the foundation for all we've accomplished.

To all the students of LoK: We would not be here without you! Thank you for your continuous support all these years.

To my cowriter, Rachel Wharton: Writing this book with you has been so much fun! I could not imagine a more perfect collaborator for this project. It's been such a pleasure geeking out together on all the tiny details that make a cookbook work.

To our photographer, Kristin Teig, and our food and prop stylist, Monica Pierini: The photos are both exactly what I had hoped for and also more beautiful than I could have imagined. From the beginning, you understood the importance of shooting in the instructors' homes and having them cook and plate their food. And then you made magic. And it all felt so fun, easy, and effortless.

To my agent, Kari Stuart: Thank you for being such a calm, helpful, and supportive guide throughout this entire process. And thank you for your patience! Our first phone call was in 2018!

To the team at Harvest/HarperCollins—Deb Brody, Stephanie Fletcher, Jacqueline Quirk, Leah Carlson-Stanisic, Mumtaz Mustafa, Shelby Peak, Jennifer Eck, Katie Tull, and Hannah Dirgins: Thank you for your enthusiasm, your patience, your skill, and your support. The book is incredible in every way!

To my family and friends: I love you so much. I could not have done this (or anything!) without your continuing love, support, and encouragement.

To my daughters, Sylvie and Vivian: You are the best taste-testers and the best daughters in the world. Thank you for being open to trying every single recipe in this book! (Sometimes multiple times . . .) I love you so much, and I promise to teach you how to cook (if you're interested!).

To my husband, Dan: You have been my biggest supporter, best friend, love, and partner in life for more than twenty years. I am so grateful to you for everything!

Index

HarperCollins books may be purchased for educational, business, or sales promotional use. For information, please email the Special Markets Department at SPsales@harpercollins.com.

FIRST EDITION

Designed by Leah Carlson-Stanisic
Photography © 2024 by Kristin Teig
Food and Prop Styling by Monica Pierini

Library of Congress Cataloging-in-Publication Data has been applied for.

ISBN 978-0-06-329057-0

24 25 26 27 28 TC 10 9 8 7 6 5 4 3 2 1